MULTICULTURAL EDUCATION SERIES

JAMES A. BANKS, *Series Editor*

(continued)

MULTICULTURAL EDUCATION SERIES, *continued*

DIVERSITY & EDUCATION

A CRITICAL MULTICULTURAL APPROACH

MICHAEL VAVRUS

FOREWORD BY WAYNE AU

TEACHERS COLLEGE PRESS

Teachers College, Columbia University
New York and London

Published by Teachers College Press, 1234 Amsterdam Avenue, New York, NY 10027

The author wishes to thank the publishers below for permission to adapt the following material:

"Sexuality, Schooling, and Teacher Identity Formation: A Critical Pedagogy for Teacher Education," by M. Vavrus, 2009, *Teaching and Teacher Education: An International Journal of Research and Studies*, 25(3), 383–390. © 2009 Elsevier. Used with permission.

"Critical Multiculturalism and Higher Education: Resistance and Possibilities Within Teacher Education," by M. Vavrus, 2010, in S. May & C. E. Sleeter (Eds.), *Critical multiculturalism: Theory and praxis* (pp. 19–31), New York, NY: Routledge. © 2010 Taylor and Francis Group. Used with permission.

"Diversity: A Contested Concept," by M. Vavrus, 2012, in J. Banks (Ed.), *Encyclopedia of Diversity in Education* (Vol. 2, pp. 667–676), Thousand Oaks, CA: Sage. © 2012 Sage Publications. Used with permission.

The epigraph for Chapter 6 excerpts "Immigrant's Voice" from *Wild Animals on the Moon & Other Poems*, by N. Ayala, 1997, Willimantic, CT: Curbstone Press. Used with permission from Northwestern Univerisity Press.

The author also wishes to thank The Evergreen State College for its support with a 2013 summer Sponsored Research Grant.

Library of Congress Cataloging-in-Publication Data

Vavrus, Michael J.
    Diversity and education : a critical multicultural approach / Michael Vavrus ; foreword by Wayne Au.
        pages cm
    Includes bibliographical references and index.
    ISBN 978-0-8077-5605-8 (pbk. : alk. paper) – ISBN 978-0-8077-5606-5 (hardcover : alk. paper) – ISBN 978-0-8077-7343-7 (ebook)
       1. Multicultural education–United States. 2. Educational equalization–United States.
    I. Title.
    LC1099.3.V38 2015
    370.117–dc23   2014029632

ISBN 978-0-8077-5605-8 (paper)
ISBN 978-0-8077-5606-5 (hardcover)
ISBN 978-0-8077-7343-7 (ebook)

Printed on acid-free paper
Manufactured in the United States of America

22   21   20   19   18   17   16   15   8   7   6   5   4   3   2   1

Contents

Series Foreword

The racial, class, gender, and religious divisions within U. S. society are extensive, persistent, and intractable. Within the last decade, a number of informative and widely publicized books have documented the vast divides within the United States. Developments such as Occupy Wall Street and the contentious public debates about increasing the minimum wage have illuminated the class divisions within U. S. society. In 2007, the wealthiest one percent of the U. S. population owned more than a third of the nation's wealth (Stiglitz, 2012). In his controversial book on the state of White America, Murray (2012) contends that because of the class divides within the United States, it is "coming apart."

The steep racial, class, and religious divides within U. S. society create polarization, which makes it difficult to have productive dialogue and conversations across borders and boundaries, especially in racially, culturally, and religiously diverse classrooms. Civic education theorists such as Parker (2003), Gutmann (2004), and Hess (2009) view deliberation and productive dialogue among diverse groups as essential for the viability of a democratic and just society. This adept, informative, and engaging book will help educators to facilitate discussions and dialogue across cultural, class, racial, and religious borders because Vavrus incisively examines three ideological approaches to diversity: (1) social conservatism (2) liberal multiculturalism; and (3) critical multiculturalism. This helpful pedagogical conceptualization is a Weberian ideal-type typology. Consequently—as Vavrus perceptively points out— the categories in the typology are interactive and contextual rather than distinct and static, which make it a powerful, sophisticated, and nuanced conceptual tool. Resistance, power, and knowledge reconstruction are distinguishing characteristic of critical multiculturalism. Over time, however, the lines between liberal multiculturalism and critical multiculturalism have become blurred because some versions of liberal multiculturalism have incorporated important elements of critical multiculturalism. Vavrus describes how his analysis of the three conceptualizations is not neutral but is "compatible with standpoint theory" and "originates from critical theory." He not only makes his own positionality explicit but also describes how all knowledge reflects the positionality of its creators. Vavrus identifies Howard Zinn (2002) as an

early and influential progenitor of this important and influential idea. Sandra
Harding (1991), Patricia Hill Collins (2000), and Lorraine Code 1991) are
feminist scholars who also articulate and provide deep and incisive analyses of the relationship between positionality and knowledge construction.
Vavrus's construction of a typology of a spectrum of worldviews is consistent
with the pioneering philosophical and sociological work of Harding, Collins,
and Code.

This timely and informative book can help schoolteachers and teacher
educators engage students from diverse racial, ethnic, cultural, class, linguistic, and religious groups in productive classroom dialogues and deliberations.
The vivid ways in which Vavrus describes the spectrum of three worldviews
will enable students to identify their own positionalities as well as those of
their classmates and to understand how perspectives and ideologies are consequences of the social, cultural, and political communities into which individuals are socialized. A better understanding of myriad perspectives and points
of view can help to reduce polarization and facilitate discussion and deliberation—which is needed in the increasingly diverse classrooms and schools in
the United States.

American classrooms are experiencing the largest influx of immigrant
students since the beginning of the 20th century. Almost 14 million new immigrants—documented and undocumented—settled in the United States in
the years from 2000 to 2010. Less than 10% came from nations in Europe.
Most came from Mexico, nations in Asia, and nations in Latin America, the
Caribbean, and Central America (Camarota, 2011). A large but undetermined
number of undocumented immigrants enter the United States each year. The
U.S. Department of Homeland Security (2010) estimated that in January 2010,
10.8 million undocumented immigrants were living in the United States, which
was a decrease from the estimated 11.8 million that resided in the United States
in January 2007. In 2007, approximately 3.2 million children and young adults
were among the 11.8 million undocumented immigrants in the United States,
most of whom grew up in this country (Perez, 2011). The influence of an increasingly ethnically diverse population on U.S. schools, colleges, and universities is and will continue to be enormous.

Schools in the United States are more diverse today than they have been
since the early 1900s when a multitude of immigrants entered the United States
from Southern, Central, and Eastern Europe. In the 20-year period between
1989 and 2009, the percentage of students of color in U.S. public schools increased from 32% to 45% (Aud et al., 2011). If current trends continue, students
of color will equal or exceed the percentage of White students in U.S. public
schools within one or two decades. In 2010–2011, students of color exceeded
the number of Whites students in the District of Columbia and in 13 states (listed in descending order of the percentage of ethnic minority students therein):

Hawaii, California, New Mexico, Texas, Nevada, Arizona, Florida, Maryland, Mississippi, Georgia, Louisiana, Delaware, and New York. (Aud et al., 2012). In 2009, children of undocumented immigrants made up 6.8% of students in grades kindergarten through 12 (Perez, 2011).

Language and religious diversity is also increasing in the U.S. student population. The 2012 American Community Survey estimated that 21% of Americans aged 5 and above (61.9 million) spoke a language other than English at home (U. S. Census Bureau, 2012). Harvard professor Diana L. Eck (2001) calls the United States the "most religiously diverse nation on earth" (p. 4). Islam is now the fastest-growing religion in the United States, as well as in several European nations such as France, the United Kingdom, and The Netherlands (Banks, 2009; Cesari, 2004). Most teachers now in the classroom and in teacher education programs are likely to have students from diverse ethnic, racial, linguistic, and religious groups in their classrooms during their careers. This is true for both inner city and suburban teachers in the United States, as well as in many other Western nations such as Canada, Australia, and the United Kingdom (Banks, 2009).

The major purpose of the Multicultural Education Series is to provide pre-service educators, practicing educators, graduate students, scholars, and policy-makers with an interrelated and comprehensive set of books that summarizes and analyzes important research, theory, and practice related to the education of ethnic, racial, cultural, and linguistic groups in the United States and the education of mainstream students about diversity. The dimensions of multicultural education, developed by Banks (2004) and described in the *Handbook of Research on Multicultural Education* and in the *Encyclopedia of Diversity in Education* (Banks, 2012), provide the conceptual framework for the development of the publications in the Series. The dimensions are content integration, the knowledge construction process, prejudice reduction, equity pedagogy, and an empowering institutional culture and social structure.

The books in the Series provide research, theoretical, and practical knowledge about the behaviors and learning characteristics of students of color, language minority students, low-income students, and other minoritized population groups, such as LGBT youth (Mayo, 2014). They also provide knowledge about ways to improve academic achievement (Au, 2011; Gay, 2010; Lee, 2007) and race relations in educational settings (Howard, 2006; Stephan & Vogt, 2004). Multicultural education is consequently as important for middle class White suburban students as it is for students of color who live in the inner city. Multicultural education fosters the public good and the overarching goals of the commonwealth.

In addition to the spectrum of worldviews that is a touchstone of this readable and compelling book, Vavrus's insightful analyses of issues such as color consciousness and color blindness, the color of criminalization and school discipline, and diversity and teacher education make this book essential reading in the challenging, contentious, and polarized times in which we live and work. I hope that it will attain the wide readership that it deserves.

–James A. Banks

REFERENCES

Aud, S., Hussar, W., Johnson, F., Kena, G., Roth, E., Manning, E., Wang, X., & Zhang, J. (2012). *The condition of education 2012* (NCES 2012-045). Washington, DC: U.S. Department of Education, National Center for Education Statistics. Retrieved from nces.ed.gov/pubsearch.

Aud, S., Hussar, W., Kena, G., Bianco, K., Frohlich, L., Kemp, J., & Tahan, K. (2011). *The condition of education 2011* (NCES 2011-033). U.S. Department of Education, National Center for Education Statistics. Washington, DC: U.S. Department of Education, National Center for Education Statistics. Retrieved from nces.ed.gov /programs/coe/pdf/coe_1er.pdf

Banks, J. A. (2004). Multicultural education: Historical development, dimensions, and practice. In J. A. Banks & C. A. M. Banks (Eds.), *Handbook of research on multicultural education* (2nd ed., pp. 3–29). San Francisco, CA: Jossey-Bass.

Banks, J. A. (Ed.). (2009). *The Routledge international companion to multicultural education.* New York, NY: Routledge.

Banks, J. A. (2012). Multicultural education: Dimensions of. In J. A. Banks (Ed). *Encyclopedia of diversity in education* (vol. 3, pp. 1538–1547). Thousand Oaks, CA: Sage.

Camarota, S. A. (2011, October). A *record-setting decade of immigration: 2000 to 2010.* Washington, DC: Center for Immigration Studies. Retrieved from cis.org/2000-2010 -record-setting-decade-of-immigration

Cesari, J. (2004). *When Islam and democracy meet: Muslims in Europe and the United States.* New York, NY: Palgrave Macmillan.

Collins, P. H. (2000). *Black feminist thought: Knowledge, consciousness, and the politics of empowerment* (2nd ed.). New York, NY: Routledge.

Code, L. (1991). *What can she know? Feminist theory and the construction of knowledge.* Ithaca, NY: Cornell University Press.

Eck, D. L. (2001). *A new religious America: How a "Christian country" has become the world's most religiously diverse nation.* New York, NY: HarperSanFrancisco.

Gay, G. (2010). *Culturally responsive teaching: Theory, research, and practice* (2nd ed.). New York, NY: Teachers College Press.

Gutmann, A. (2004). Unity and diversity in democratic multicultural education: Creative and destructive tensions. In J. A. Banks (Ed.), *Diversity and citizenship education: Global perspectives* (pp. 71–96). San Francisco, CA: Jossey-Bass.

Harding, S. (1991). *Whose knowledge? Whose science? Thinking from women's lives.* Ithaca, NY: Cornell University Press.

Hess, D. E. (2009). *Controversy in the classroom: The democratic power of discussion.* New York, NY: Routledge.

Howard, G. R. (2006). *We can't teach what we don't know: White teachers, multiracial schools* (2nd ed.). New York, NY: Teachers College Press.

Lee, C. D. (2007). *Culture, literacy, and learning: Taking bloom in the midst of the whirlwind.* New York, NY: Teachers College Press.

Mayo, C. (2014). *LGBTQ youth and education: Policies and practices.* New York, NY: Teachers College Press.

Murray, C. (2012). *Coming apart: The state of White America 1960–2010.* New York, NY: Crown Forum (Random House).

Parker, W. C. (2003). *Teaching democracy: Unity and diversity in public life.* New York, NY: Teachers College Press.

Perez, W. (2011). *Americans by heart: Undocumented Latino students and the promise of higher education.* New York, NY: Teachers College Press.

Stephan, W. G. & Vogt, W. P. (Eds.). (2004). *Education programs for improving intergroup Relations: Theory, research, and practice.* New York, NY: Teachers College Press.

Stiglitz, J. E. (2012). *The price of inequality: How today's divided society endangers our future.* New York, NY: Norton.

U. S. Census Bureau (2012). Selected social characteristics in the United States: 2012 American Community Survey 1-year estimates. Retrieved from factfinder2. census.gov/faces/tableservices/jsf/pages/productview.xhtml?pid=ACS_12_1YR _DP02&prodType=table

U.S. Department of Homeland Security. (2010, February). *Estimates of the unauthorized immigrant population residing in the United States: January 2010.* Retrieved from www.dhs .gov/files/statistics/immigration.shtm

Zinn, H. (2002). *You can't be neutral on a moving train: A personal history of our time.* Boston, MA: Beacon Press.

Foreword

I write this foreword to *Diversity Education: A Critical Multicultural Approach* during a moment of national turmoil in the United States, where less than a week ago Michael Brown, an unarmed African American young man, was shot and killed by police in Ferguson, Missouri. Locally in Ferguson there has since been a powerful uprising by people there against the abuse and violence of state power that they have felt and witnessed through the killing of Michael Brown—abuse of violence they've likely experienced most of their lives. Their feelings were only reinforced when the predominantly White local police force responded to these uprisings with a fully militarized response, including shooting rubber bullets into crowds of peaceful protestors and arresting prominent members of the media reporting what had been happening there.

Nationally, the killing of Michael Brown by the police and the subsequent militarized police response have heightened conversations not just around the killing of unarmed Black men and woman by police (another incident occurred in Los Angeles just days after Brown was killed) but around the violent responses to the "threat" of Black bodies more generally, particularly by Whites in the United States. Whether it is Michael Brown, Trayvon Martin, Oscar Grant, Darius Simmons, Ezell Ford, Renisha McBride, John Crawford, or Jordan Davis —all unarmed African Americans who were killed in the last two years—it seems that Blackness itself is enough to invoke levels of fear and suspicion leading to murderous violence from state authorities and non-Blacks alike.

This reality is only made clearer if we compare these shootings to the treatment of armed White Americans. White gun rights advocates have been gathering in several U.S. states, openly carrying semiautomatic weapons and other guns, menacing bystanders and provoking fear in the process. The response from state authorities has been minimal. Or take the example of when conservative, White rancher Cliven Bundy refused to pay the federal government and resisted authorities with an armed militia. The authorities treated Bundy with kid gloves, and there was no militant or violent response from the government to quell Bundy's gun-backed rebellion.

There is a stark contrast here: If you're Black and unarmed, you are still seen as a threat—and you can be killed with little forethought. If you're a White conservative and armed, while some civilians may be in fear, the state will think

long and hard about how to respond to you, if at all. What this tells me is
that, despite any victorious claims to having landed in a post-racial, Obama-
is-president utopia, there is still a very deep and strong current of racism and
White supremacy in the United States, and it is one that is getting sharper as
race and class inequality sharpen as well.

So it is in this context that I find Vavrus's book *Diversity and Education: A
Critical Multicultural Approach* to be so important, not because I think this one
book will immediately fix the Fergusons of the world (no one book has that
power), but because *Diversity and Education* enters into such important conversations about inequality and change in such powerful ways. *Diversity and Education*
can not only help us have these conversations about racism, institutionalized
oppression, and cultural fear; it can also offer an intervention that can move
readers toward a deeper critical consciousness about diversity and multicultural
education in their own lives.

Diversity and Education is a critically important book because of the work it
does. By drawing on a wide range of fields, disciplines, and scholarly sources;
by building arguments about the realities of lived experiences of people today
based on contemporary statistics; and by starting with the root of how we make
sense of the world (the politics of our varying worldviews), Vavrus is making a
fundamental argument here that our consciousness about our experiences and
the experiences of others can grow and change through our own understanding
of the positionalities of ourselves and others. And most importantly, Vavrus
is also arguing that this growth in consciousness is critical to helping us make
better decisions and take concerted action in our daily lives, both inside the
classroom and out.

So, as I watch the Ferguson police assault protestors with military force and
fear deeply for the lives of children there and elsewhere (especially children of
color who too often fall to violence of one kind or another), I am consoled by
Vavrus's *Diversity and Education: A Critical Multicultural Approach* because it lays a
clear path for students and teachers to critically consider issues of power and
inequality so that they may move into the world not burdened with fear but
empowered with strength of understanding.

—Wayne Au

Acknowledgments

An important impetus for the ideas and information in this book came from the undergraduate and graduate students I teach, many of whom I observed in student-teaching internships in public school classrooms. Students' desire to overcome a miseducation on diversity and multiculturalism fueled my writing, and I admire the courage they showed when they moved beyond a master narrative to a critical discourse and transformative actions. Paul Gallegos and The Evergreen State College's President's Diversity Fund for Equity and Social Justice Committee gave helpful advice in the early stages of my writing. Over the past few years, John Hopkins and the Faculty Diversity Institute at Saint Martin's University provided useful feedback on workshops I conducted on diversity topics, many of which appear in this book. My liberal arts colleagues at The Evergreen State College influenced the interdisciplinary approach of this book. In particular I wish to acknowledge Peter Bohmer, Savvina Chowdhury, Angela Gilliam, the late José Gomez, Jeannie Hahn, Donald Morisato, Larry Mosqueda, Therese Saliba, and Artee Young. Jon Davies's careful reading provided thoughtful and invaluable critiques of early drafts of the manuscript for which I am extremely appreciative. The constructive comments of Teachers College Press's Brian Ellerbeck, John Bylander, and Regina Gregory were quite helpful. Olivia Archibald was instrumental in her consistent and supportive sounding-board role. This book's commentary on aspects of the human condition has been influenced by lively campfire conversations over the years about the social psychology of human existence with hiking companions Phil Chard, Todd Hines, and Cynthia Hines. I further wish to thank my family and friends for their patience and understanding during what must have seemed to them to be a never-ending process. Ultimately, James Banks's friendship, steadfast support of a critical orientation, and belief in the importance of the topic of this book made it possible for this publication to see the light of day.

DIVERSITY & EDUCATION

Developing a Standpoint on Diversity

> "You can't be neutral on a moving train." . . . Events are already moving in certain deadly directions, and to be neutral means to accept that.
>
> —Howard Zinn, *You Can't Be Neutral on a Moving Train*

Howard Zinn's (2002) metaphor of a moving train describes the impossibility of a neutral political point of view from one's social location. He avoided feigning neutrality to his history students: "I would always begin a course by making it clear to my students that they would be getting *my* point of view, but that I would try to be fair to other points of view" (pp. 7–8). Zinn acknowledged that conscious and unconscious worldviews explain how people observe the same situation yet come away with different explanations for that particular condition. He was not a relativist in the sense that all views have equal value or validity. Instead, Zinn was clear that his standpoint was informed by the lived experiences of people who suffered under and struggled against oppressive practices and institutions supported by governing elites.

In the spirit of Howard Zinn, a goal of this book is to present a spectrum of points of view on diversity topics. Political and economic ideologies influence each socially located viewpoint. Such worldviews reflect a subjectivity that includes my own point of view, which is not neutral. The primary purpose, though, is to add to our understanding of the political, economic, and social forces that differentially affect material conditions and well-being of various identity groups. More specifically, this book explores the effects of debates over diversity on people of color, the poor, women, and sexual and religious minorities. Ultimately, this book addresses education and how the norms of the larger society hold consequences for school-age youth.

The writing of this book took place during "a new Gilded Age" when 10% of income earners acquired more than 50% of the United States' total income and the top 1% alone held over 20% of the total income (Lowrey, 2013, p. B1). In contrast, 45% of all children in the United States lived in economically poor families (Addy, Engelhardt, & Skinner, 2013) and disproportionately attended schools "with concentrated poverty" (U.S. Department of Education, 2013, p. 18). In my home state of Washington alone, education officials identified more than 30,000 homeless school-age children (Office of Superintendent, 2014). At the same time the U.S. Congress reduced by $5 billion a food program that served 47 million Americans who experience food insecurity (Nixon, 2014).

Meanwhile, as a majority of Americans held negative attitudes toward African Americans and Latinos, the United States maintained the highest incarceration rates in the world, a 300% increase since 1980 (Pasek, Krosnick, & Tompson, 2012; Pew Charitable Trusts, 2010; Ross & Agiesta, 2012). The incarceration rate for Whites is 450 per 100,000 residents in that racial group. This figure compares to 831 per 100,000 Latinos and 2,306 for every 100,000 Blacks, reflecting a disparity partially enabled by school disciplinary practices that disproportionly single out young people of color (Koon, 2013; Sakala, 2014). While youth migration globally was at its highest rates in recorded history, schools in receiving nations such as the United States reacted by placing restrictions on language diversity and ethnic studies (Biggers, 2012; Romaine, 2011). Women and sexual minorities faced workplace discrimination in earnings and treatment alongside a political discourse aimed at controlling female sexual and reproductive rights (Hidden Barriers, 2014; International Conference on Population and Development, 2014). While dominant religious groups weighed in against the rights of women and sexual minorities, they also encouraged discrimination against diverse religions (Hedges, 2006; Rau, 2014).

Under a long shadow cast by the 50th anniversary of the War on Poverty and the 60th anniversary of the school desegregation decision, *Brown v. Board of Education*, these contemporary events affect the point of view I take. Hence, I use *standpoint theory* as a way to situate this book's approach. Curriculum studies scholar Wayne Au (2012) explains that standpoint theory originated with an examination of "how different ways of understanding the world are implicated by different class locations within capitalism" (p. 7). As a methodological approach, Au provides five fundamental guiding themes of standpoint theory:

1.   Our experiences with material reality—which also constitute our social relations—structure our epistemology of the world in ways that both limit and enable certain ways of understanding. (p. 8)

Like Zinn's image of a moving train changing locations and perspectives of the passing landscape, standpoint theory acknowledges how our own social positions affect constructions and perceptions of our knowledge of the world.

2.   Our experience and material life is embedded in and structured by systems of domination and rule that are organized hierarchically

around power relations of race, class, gender, sexuality, nationality, and other forms of socially determined difference. (p. 9)

For issues of social difference that diversity raises and as found in Zinn's (1997, 2003) work, the application of standpoint theory deconstructs claims of neutrality and highlights how structural conditions are necessary to consider methodologically.

3. The perspectives of those in power are made functional in the lives of everyone regardless of position. (p. 9)

As a methodology, standpoint theory deconstructs what happens when dominant groups who control mainstream discourse on diversity contend that there is only one view out of Zinn's train windows, a distortion of an uneven and complex social, political, and economic terrain.

4. Standpoint is always born of struggle against common-sense, hegemonic epistemologies of those in power. (p. 9)

Because status quo orientations strive for unquestioned normalization through dominant narratives, including those embedded in public school curriculum, nondominant group members do not automatically recognize the political possibility of change to their material situation.

5. The taking up of a standpoint by the marginalized and less powerful carries with it the potential for liberation. (p. 10)

Au's final theme is the flip side of his previous theme related to hegemonic power. As Zinn (2003) documented, social movements against dominant points of view of diversity have historically been necessary to expand opportunities for political freedom and economic justice.

A CONTESTED CONCEPT

This book grew from a chapter I was invited to write for the *Encyclopedia of Diversity in Education*. The title, "Diversity: A Contested Concept" (Vavrus, 2012), caused me to ponder why this is so. What is it about diversity that elicits such strong emotions, so much so that diversity as a concept can have such varying effects on the social and economic well-being and life opportunities of young people? How does diversity per se create social divisions within a society? What diversity topics in particular create passionate opinions across the political spectrum? Finally, how can we explain these varying worldviews so that we come away with a deeper and fuller understanding of why these debates endure?

Too often viewpoints on diversity reduce to absolutist finger-pointing as to what is True and Right. Arguments over diversity can devolve into expressions of disbelief such as "How can *they* believe *that*?" In the eyes of their opponents, *they* lose their humanity and any sense of reasonableness about whatever *that* diversity issue may be. When debaters reach this level of discourse, the loudest voice in the room tries to "win." When deliberations have significant impact on the lives of children, the din in the room makes it challenging to figure out why different positions on the same issue exist. For such reasons Pang and Park (2011) argue, "Given the present-day conservative political climate, it is more important than ever that teacher educators address the criticisms of a multicultural approach to diversity in education" (p. 65).

This book builds on earlier scholarship initiated with a critical stance that examined various worldviews on diversity and multiculturalism (e.g., Chicago Cultural Studies Group, 1992; May, 1999; McCarthy, 1994; McLaren, 1994; Sleeter & Grant, 1999). Christine Sleeter's (2001) comprehensive literature review analyzed differing multicultural education ideological orientations. From a critical perspective, Sleeter explained that the political left "would have the field develop a much more explicit critique of White racism, capitalism, and patriarchy" (2001, p. 92), all topics analyzed in the following chapters. Hence, a major purpose of this book is to examine critically a spectrum of ideological approaches to diversity.

CRITICAL PEDAGOGY

The subtitle of this book, *A Critical Multicultural Approach*, signals an orientation that is compatible with standpoint theory. More specifically, this approach uses a critical pedagogical methodology. Critical multiculturalism and its application of critical pedagogy originate from critical theory. Critical theory critiques dominant narratives about society and culture. In critical theory the concept of *transformation* makes problematic the structures of history that embody who we are and have become. This theoretical framework continually interrogates the relations among knowledge, power, and social change.

As an example of an application of critical theory, consider the well-known claim in the Declaration of Independence that "all men are created equal." The knowledge construction of equality was "self-evident" to the Declaration's signatories, who lived at the top of a socioeconomic hierarchy. Besides limiting equality and political decisionmaking to property owners, the White male founders assumed racial and gender subordination as a natural exclusion to a political organization no longer ruled by a monarch. Moreover, the founders, through the Declaration, characterized indigenous populations struggling against further imperialistic dispossession from their ancestral lands as "merciless Indian Savages." In this brief example, critical theory provided a lens to consider whose knowledge defined equality; the power relations of race, class, gender, and imperialism embedded in the claim of equality; and which group of people were the intended beneficiaries of this revolutionary social change for independence.

Critical pedagogy is a *process*. Initially critical pedagogy identifies and clarifies mainstream ideological concepts in their commonsense expressions. Where dominant ideologies assert universal principles, critical pedagogy scrutinizes and exposes existing contradictions in this discourse. Critical pedagogy examines mainstream narratives in relation to actual lived experiences affected structurally by the relative power of social relations. In our example, which used "all men are created equal," a critical perspective offered a political economy context for marginal groups' exclusion from the founders' concept of freedom. This transformative vantage point produces a more complex interpretation of mainstream ideologies.

Through the application of critical pedagogy, actions taken in the name of *social justice* become more grounded in material reality. Decisions by oppressed groups such as the poor, people of color, and women, along with their allies in the context of local conditions, serve as a basis for actions that entail "a sense of hope that solidarity across differences is possible" (Sleeter, 2012a, p. 207). In summary, critical pedagogy continually tests assumptions and assertions for accuracy as part of an ongoing interrogation of political and historical claims and subsequent social justice actions.

Well-intentioned advocates for marginalized populations often skip the process of critical pedagogy. For example, liberal educators cling to a belief that evidence-based knowledge alone is sufficient to transform educational opportunities and outcomes for low-income students of color, a perspective that excludes origins and continuing manifestations of power relations. When liberal educators avoid historical and political economy struggles over educational practices, they fall short in making lasting structural changes that can best serve diverse student populations. As the critical educator Paulo Freire (1998) pointed out in *Teachers as Cultural Workers*, when "trying to escape conflict, we preserve the status quo" (p. 45).

Critical pedagogy offers an alternative to the conventional view that knowledge of isolated best practices can win the day for social justice. Critical pedagogy instead frames justice "within social relations and material conditions that are specific and concrete" (Lauderdale, 2008, p. 242), with particular attention given to the effects on equality through a political economy's distribution of opportunities and wealth. Law and sociology scholar Pat Lauderdale (2008) explains, "The study of justice should include an analysis of the fair distribution of benefits and burdens, including rights, obligations, deserts, and needs" (p. 242). For social justice to be operational, it must be grounded in concrete, lived experiences that can lead to a reduction or elimination of oppressive conditions. Mere assertions of social justice can neglect actual sources of material inequality and the role that dominant groups play in defining what is justice.

The application of standpoint theory and critical pedagogy is a more deliberative process that takes time to tease out mainstream meanings and actions surrounding diversity. This book's intent in using standpoint theory in combination with critical pedagogy is to contribute to a "liberatory educational praxis" (De Lissouvoy, 2008, p. 51) through which critical knowledge construction informs educational practices that can serve the interests of marginalized children, families, and communities.

OVERVIEW OF CHAPTERS

Chapter 1 provides a survey of contemporary diversity issues that manifest themselves contentiously in countless settings around the world. This overview emphasizes the importance of *history* to contextualize and find patterns and connections from the past to the present. Along the way we find that *multiculturalism* has its roots in contested diversity and, therefore, requires inquiry into worldviews or ideologies. Naming and using the concept of ideology is a critical strand of multicultural scholarship. The descriptors *ideology* and *ideological* carry their own connotations, depending on how they are used and by whom. Rather than using those terms to deny the importance of an opposing opinion on diversity, explanations of modern origins of ideology suggest that all of us respond from various ideological positions. Conscious and unconscious responses to arguments over diversity spring from ideologies. This thesis differs from some critical orientations that conceptualize ideology as only applicable to positions that result in dominance and oppression of others (cf. Bartolemé, 2008). The chapter further describes the value of a *political economy* perspective to demystify commonsense notions about diversity. Also included in Chapter 1 is a critical examination of the interdisciplinary field of political psychology merged with biology in its attempt to explain why people have different political ideologies.

One goal of this book is to allow us to take a step back to better understand the range of political orientations and life experiences that inform such wide opinions about diversity. Chapter 2 provides a typology of three ideological categories: *social conservatism, liberal multiculturalism,* and *critical multiculturalism.* This approach falls within a critical theoretical continuum of multicultural scholarship (cf. Ladson-Billings, 2004). Initially, each perspective might appear independent of the topic of this book, but the ideologies that create the worldviews of each category serve as bedrock explanations as to why people debate diversity so fiercely rather than simply accept it as a natural part of human existence.

Before the book wades into specific diversity topics, detailed in Chapter 2 is the value to first gain a clearer grasp of the three orientations in this typology. To clarify, a *typology* is a "way of describing groups of respondents displaying different clusters of behaviours, attitudes or views of the world" (Association of Qualitative Research, 2013, para. 1). Categories in a typology represent *ideal types*, and as such this approach assumes people in actual practice may shift their orientations across different ideologies based on their own material and cultural interests in relation to a particular diversity issue. Therefore, Chapter 2 is divided into three major sections in accordance with the book's typology of ideologies that influence thinking about diversity.

The most contentious diversity topic originates from interpretations as to the social, political, and economic impact of *racial* and *ethnic identification* in modern liberal nation-states. Chapters 3 and 4 delve into this topic with a focus on the history, political economy, and contemporary consequences of ideological orientations toward race and ethnicity. Chapter 3 examines the modern creation of the concept of *race* and its historical and contemporary effects on citizenship rights and school desegregation efforts and concludes with a discussion of the value of racial diversity in schools and neighborhoods. The shifting discourse of skin *color consciousness* and racial *color blindness* provides the larger context for Chapter 3.

Chapter 4 explores historical patterns and ideological orientations as to what appropriately constitutes a *crime* and a *just punishment*. Within this discourse a neo-Confederate narrative continues to influence public perceptions to this day. The chapter compares the political economy of expenditures for public schools in relation to funding for jails and prisons. The chapter draws attention to a "school-to-prison pipeline" and the effects of incarceration on juveniles and young adults and concludes with recommendations for alternative approaches to school suspensions and juvenile incarceration.

Class analysis in interaction with the indeterminate concept of *culture* forms the foundation of Chapter 5. Following the pattern of the previous chapters, we examine how a spectrum of ideologies perceives wealth accumulation and inequality. This inquiry includes the origins of social Darwinism and its contemporary ideological interpretations of diversity and poverty. This leads to an analysis of a reoccurring "culture-of-poverty" hypothesis and outcomes of the 1960s War on Poverty in comparison to contemporary conditions as they affect children of diverse economic and racial backgrounds. The chapter concludes with a look back at the objectives of the Civil Rights Movement's "Freedom Budget" in comparison to contemporary conditions that affect children and their families.

Chapter 6 contextualizes the conditions of immigrant and indigenous groups by a colonial monocultural and monolingual policy legacy. Highlighted is the impact of this history and current trends on immigrant and indigenous youth, including the special case of indigenous cultures and education. The chapter analyzes how differing ideological positions value incorporation of non-dominant cultures and languages into the school curriculum, especially through *ethnic studies* and *multicultural education*. The example of educational standards and practices in Texas and Arizona provides a lens through which to consider the ramifications of contested diversity. The chapter ends with a summary of what an alternative orientation based in critical multiculturalism can provide.

Chapter 7 focuses on the *ideology of patriarchy* and its intersections with gender, sexuality, and religion. The chapter considers the influence of patriarchal religious and secular values as they affect moral interpretations about appropriate social and political expressions of gender and sexuality. The chapter examines the ideological roots of a particular strand of Christian political perspectives toward gender and sexuality and how this has structured public discourse in the 21st century. The institutional responses by public school officials to curricular and student manifestations of expressions of gender, sexuality, and religion—including psychological and physical bullying of school-age children—ground these social issues in contemporary educational practices. The chapter addresses the implications of debates over religious diversity with a focus on portrayals of Muslims in patriotic discourse, especially after the events of September 11, 2001, and the implications for educational practices that affect children's understanding of and tolerance toward diverse religious orientations.

Chapter 8 revisits various topics presented in earlier chapters and makes comparisons to national *educator preparation standards*. This concluding chapter considers expectations for teachers, administrators, and teacher educators in learning about and mediating diversity debates. The chapter examines how normative diversity discourse affects preservice and inservice teacher education. The chapter critiques national teacher education standards in relation to how they respond to diversity. The chapter closes with considerations of opportunities for and constraints on critical multicultural actions through which colleges and public schools can serve as beneficial social justice sites for young people.

In summary, the book's organization and intention is to provide insights into why diversity is a contested concept and, ultimately, to weigh the effects of arguments over diversity on the future of young people. That is why this book includes representative examples of historical and ideological links to help explain contemporary arguments over diversity. Moreover, I often find my college students are unaware of the historical patterns detailed in the following chapters. Upon learning these histories and their lingering effects on schooling practices, education students in particular express dismay over the miseducation they had previously received—but then take an important step toward critically informed action. I am reminded of William Faulkner's (1951) oft-cited quote: "The past is never dead. It's not even past" (p. 93). In other words, to look at present conditions ahistorically ignores that we cannot escape the continuum of history.

Clearly each chapter could be the subject of a separate book based on the merits and validity of the topics and issues raised—and books do exist that explore discrete aspects of these subjects and themes, from many of which I have borrowed in the course of this writing. The aim of this book, though, is to provide readers access to a wide range of diversity topics and an examination of the ideological orientations and struggles that lie behind them. The hope is that this book will serve to stimulate critical reflection and dialog among education students, teachers, administrators, policymakers, concerned citizens, and scholars of multiculturalism and diversity in ways that will have a positive impact on the future of our children.

CHAPTER 1

Tensions

We particularly ask you—
When a thing continually occurs—
Not on that account to find it natural
In an age of bloody confusion
Ordered disorder, planned caprice,
And dehumanized humanity, lest all things
Be held unalterable!

—Bertolt Brecht, *The Exception and the Rule*

During the early rise of Nazism, Bertolt Brecht wrote this passage from his play *The Exception and the Rule* in 1930 (Brecht, 1930/1954). In the same spirit as Brecht, we ask ourselves throughout this book whether we should perceive dominant viewpoints on diversity as natural with outcomes that seem unalterable. Or, as Brecht implores, we can look beyond distracting explanations for causes of dehumanizing conditions and instead reconceive degrading treatment of humans as alterable and amenable to change. As we will continually discover, however, to understand causes for inequality and oppression is not necessarily a straightforward task. For now, though, beginning with a presidential address, we look to examples of tensions over diversity, societal issues that filter into the socialization of children and youth in our schools.

In 2010, U.S., President Barack Hussein Obama used the occasion of his annual "Back to School" speech to public school students to praise diversity and difference as positive features that make life beautiful:

Because it's the things that make us different that make us who we are. And the strength and character of this country have always come from our ability to recognize ourselves in one another, no matter who we are, or where we come from, what we look like, or what abilities or disabilities we have. (Obama, 2010a, para. 22)

While President Obama used the opportunity to celebrate difference, he also recognized that opposition to difference exists and can result in harassment or something "more serious" (2010a, para. 21). Emblematic of this opposition were mainstream reactions to the first publicly identified Black individual elected as a U.S. president. Declarations about both his 2008 election and 2012 reelection ranged from claims that the world had entered a color-blind, postracial era to a White populist outrage over the erosion of their historic homeland identity. Within 2 months after Obama's speech to schoolchildren, significant numbers of conservatives made successful electoral bids with calls to return America to an idealized homogeneous and unified past.

What, then, is this difference and diversity that finds both advocates and opponents? In its dictionary definition the adjective *diverse* means "of a different kind, form, character, etc.; unlike" ("Diverse," 2001, p. 574). The term *diversity* originally had a neutral connotation as simply a unique feature of some kind of difference. By the time of the American and French revolutions and the rise of the modern nation-state, a new class of political leaders evoked diversity as a positive quality to balance factions competing for political power. By the 1990s, diversity had more widely acquired the meaning we more commonly attribute it today in referencing differences of racial and ethnic identification, gender and sexuality, and class (Harper, 2013). From this contemporary use comes such expressions as *diverse students* and *cultural diversity*, both of which imply that, for individuals identified as minorities, diversity is also a lived experience.

Diversity as a lived experience places arguments over concepts of *liberty*, *freedom*, and *equality* as foundational in accounting for tensions over diversity. Balibar (2002) finds an inherent tension between the universalist demands for freedom and equality. For example, one person's equality may be an infringement or restriction on another person's freedom. Moreover, the demand for liberty and equality "is never something that can be bestowed or distributed; it has to be won" (p. 166). In practice, the concepts of freedom and equality imply "latent *insurrection*" against some aspect of societal practices (p. 164). In other words, a change of the status quo through an expansion of freedom and equality is implicit when diverse groups call for recognition of their identities and redistribution of societal opportunities and material outcomes.

Hence, President Obama's (2010a) assertion that a nation can find strength and unity through its diversity is highly debated across the political spectrum for its various interpretations of freedom and equality. This is especially the case in response to advocates who argue for an expansion of political rights. Although citizenship rights are materially embedded in the nation-state, diverse groups seeking recognition can experience an unequal access to the exercise of their political rights (Banks, 2013). Canadian-based Civility Institute director Benet Davetian (2009) contends, however, that "devolution" from a national unity can create a condition wherein "an epidemic of special interests overwhelms communalism" (p. 509). When interpreted as a pathology of special interests, diversity within liberal democracies remains for many a cause for alarm for nation-states conceived as representing a homogeneity of race, ethnicity, language, and religion.

CRISES OF NATIONAL IDENTITY

Just as there has been a conservative reaction in the United States against what the Obama presidency apparently represented, there has been a backlash against diversity in Europe. Angela Merkel, Germany's popular conservative chancellor and de facto leader of the European Union, reacted to increased immigration by declaring that "the multicultural concept . . . has failed, and failed utterly" (Connolly, 2010, para. 3). In response to France's decision to expel Roma people, the European commissioner for justice and fundamental rights condemned the actions and made comparisons to Nazi practices during World War II (Waterfield & Samuel, 2010). Sweden joined Norway and Denmark with successful, anti-immigrant political parties (Castle, 2010). The fast-growing Northern League in Italy professed an allegiance to "local culture" that approved the actions of one of its representatives who "provocatively threw a pig's head on the ground where a mosque was planned" (Donadio, 2010, p. A6). To limit free movement across its borders as envisioned by the European Union, the liberally open society of Switzerland responded to right-wing pressures and passed legislation to set immigration quotas by 2017 (Erlanger, 2014).

Indicative of the boldness of the rise of antidemocratic parties were actions of Greek citizens associated with the neo-Nazi political party Golden Dawn who were responsible for the murder of a popular musician who publicly supported antifascist actions (Baboulias, 2013). Moreover, analysts concluded that Central European racist populists have effectively "diluted the quality of democracy in Europe" (Hockenos, 2010, p. 18). In the context of the growth of a political party in Hungary that expressed homophobic and anti-Semitic sentiments, municipalities erected statues to honor a World War II Hungarian leader who deported 400,000 Jews to Auschwitz (Donadio, 2013; Kirchick, 2013). Meanwhile, European Jews, Muslims, and Christians believed that the growth of secular societies threatened their religious practices and faith (Ewing, 2012). In Russia a wide array of political and religious groups supported discrimination against homosexuals and detention of gay activists, all a legacy of intolerance that has left the nations of the former Soviet Union with widespread ethnic tensions (Barry, 2013; Levy, 2010; "Russia," 2010). Taken together, "Europe's New Fascists," as a headline in the *New York Times* put it, represents a significant challenge to diversity and liberal nation-state universal Enlightenment values of liberty and equality (Wheeler, 2012).

Outside of Europe, neo-Nazi groups that support the concept of ethnic purity and oppose foreign influences were on the rise in Israel, Chile, Taiwan, India, and Mongolia (Branigan, 2010; "Global Reach of Neo-Nazis," 2010). With 10% of native South Koreans marrying immigrants, graduates of the nation's public schools were left wondering how to interpret school textbooks that urged them to take pride in their national composition as "one blood" (Sang-Hun, 2012, p.

A10). The Dominican Republic revoked citizenship for an estimated 200,000 ethnic Haitians, in essence making them a stateless population without political rights (Archibold, 2013). In China, despite the existence of 56 recognized ethnic groups that collectively represent millions of people, the majority of Chinese contend that they are of one race and look despairingly on other ethnicities, especially those represented by darker skin (Jacques, 2012; Postiglione, 2009).

Within this contested multicultural environment, gender discrimination also exists, affecting the lives of many women around the world. Women lack access to a full range of educational and vocational opportunities and political participation. Women disproportionately carry the burden of poverty, while violence against women remains a "universal phenomenon" (United Nations [UN], 2010, p. x). Despite the presence of a female prime minister, for example, women in Germany continue to earn 22% less than men with similar occupations, and of the 58% of German women who report sexual harassment, 42% experience it at their workplaces (Eddy & Cottrell, 2013). When the European Commission proposed that women compose at least 40% of the directors on business boards, the British government reacted negatively and stated that the best way to proceed was with a "business-led, self-regulatory model" (Kanter, 2012, p. B9).

Even if she is a citizen of the United States, Miss America may be perceived as un-American and ineligible for civic participation. Take the case of Miss America 2013, who had ethnic roots in India. A host of a widely watched news program declared, "The liberal Miss America judges won't say this but Miss Kansas lost because she actually represented American values" (T. Starnes, as cited in Kim, 2013, para. 11). In 2010 similar accusations followed Miss USA, who publicly identified as an Arab American Muslim and whose family had migrated from Lebanon (Frisch, 2010).

Fiercely contested political disputes continue within nations as to which population groups legitimately represent the nation. Furthermore, a global economic boon for the wealthy and a corresponding downturn for the lower and middle classes has fueled further anxieties over diversity. The next section provides a brief overview of tensions related to economic conditions.

ECONOMIC TENSIONS

Tensions among groups accelerated during the global recession in 2007 and subsequent economic crises that continued into the 2010s. With widespread job losses and high unemployment and underemployment rates, coupled with government austerity policies designed to reduce funding for social services, including public education, affected populations have desperately looked for answers to their reduced standards of living and threatened national identities and citizenship rights. Often recipients of the blame represent a diversity of newcomers to Europe and the United States who are part of the record number of migrants globally who have left their homes in search of secure living conditions and stable employment. While business interests quietly welcome immigrants who are willing to work for low wages, the diversity of immigrants represents a social psychological dissonance as mainstream populations try to explain the erosion of their formerly held job rights and citizenship privileges. Moreover, the public expression of ethnic cultural diversity and gender and sexuality diversity within the nation-state and associated backlashes make visible the global tensions of multiculturalism.

The continuing economic crisis also contributed to economic class disparities. Most representative of the negative popular sentiment toward the class of financial investors who received governmental shielding from the economic downturn was the Occupy Wall Street movement during 2011–2012. Across the world, thousands of people in hundreds of communities used the slogan "We are the 99%" to point out that the top 1% of income earners were relatively immune from the economic crisis while the vast majority of the public experienced material suffering with little or no assistance from their governments or private businesses. Besides job losses, significant numbers of financially vulnerable families lost their homes as a result of questionable home loans—all of which added fuel to a fire of growing dissatisfaction with the preferential treatment the wealthy received. The global Occupy movement expressed a desire to reclaim public space and to create participatory democracy beyond the limits imposed nationally by dominant governing groups and their financial backers. State and local liberal democracies responded by turning to police to break up Occupy encampments and attack journalists (A. Goodman & Moynihan, 2012).

Further heightening tensions is the rise of national security nation-states. Contrary to UN protocols, the United States eavesdropped on closed committee meetings of governmental representatives from around the world as well as leaders of sovereign nations such as Germany, France, and Brazil. The major English-speaking nations who created settler colonies across much of the world by the end of the 19th century—Britain, Canada, New Zealand, Australia, and the United States—coordinated an international surveillance program through a "Five Eyes" security alliance (Romero & Austen, 2013, p. A10). With considerable resources, a national security apparatus monitored and suppressed efforts by groups who promoted an expansion of civil, political, and economic rights. The widespread exposure of national security operations in the mid-2010s revealed an unprecedented surveillance of private and civic actions of citizens and a broadening of the definition as to who is an enemy of the state (G. Greenwald, 2014). Illegal surveillance of U.S. citizens accused of no crime is apparently not a new practice as it has existed throughout most of the 20th century to the present (A. Goodman, 2014; Price, 2013; Staples, 2014).

While public resources monitor human activity, average workers look vainly to corporations and their governments to improve wages that have remained relatively stagnant despite substantial rises in the cost of living, a trend that has been building since the 1970s. In Chapter 5 we further examine the effects of economic discourse on the politics of public education and the life opportunities of young people, especially the growing number whose families are poor.

UNDERSTANDING DIVERSITY:
AN INTERDISCIPLINARY APPROACH

An interdisciplinary approach can help to understand viewpoints on diversity. Pang and Park (2011) argue,

> The multicultural teacher educator of the future must be able to marshal in-depth content from a variety of pertinent disciplines and must be able to integrate this knowledge appropriately in the training of future educators. By using data from multiple disciplines, future teacher educators and their students will gain a comprehensive understanding of the complexity of contemporary social issues. (p. 65)

The remainder of this chapter provides an overview of various interdisciplinary ways to analyze the tensions around diversity debates. These approaches include the use of *history* and the historical emergence of various social movements. Rather than viewing contemporary debates as isolated and unique, history gives us a broader lens and context to understand origins of contested diversity. Following a look at historical roots of contestations, we briefly examine the value of a *political economy* analysis. Also introduced is a definition and the roots of modern *ideologies* and their usefulness for identifying differing worldviews toward diversity. The chapter concludes with a critical examination of the interdisciplinary field of *political psychology as merged with biology* in its attempt to explain why people have diverse political ideologies.

Next, we turn to an overview of the importance of placing diversity in historical contexts. The study of history is a useful place to begin in developing an understanding of the tensions that abound around the very existence of diversity in the modern nation-state. With this purpose in mind, the chapter highlights the 20th-century self-determination independence movements from colonial rule and the U.S. civil rights movements. Within this history we consider policies designed to reduce human diversity and the development of late-20th-century movements for gender and sexuality rights.

WHY HISTORY?

Given how media report contemporary news events, people could easily conclude that each freshly reported dispute over diversity is a recent phenomenon. Or people may express surprise that certain contested diversity issues apparently resolved long ago continue to show new life. Since most news accounts fail to provide historical perspectives on current social and political divisive events, large majorities are confused and literally uninformed about the roots of contested diversity and the rise of multicultural discourse. History, however, can provide a context to better understand the roots of today's contestations over diversity.

History, the educational psychologist Sam Wineburg (2001) explains, "offers a storehouse of complex and rich problems, not unlike those that confront us daily in the social world" (p. 51). The American Historical Association adds, "Learning how to identify and evaluate *conflicting interpretations* is an essential citizenship skill" (Stearns, 1998, para. 13, emphasis added). Furthermore, history "pivots on a tension . . . between the familiar and unfamiliar, between feelings of proximity and feelings of distance in relation to the people we seek to understand" (Wineburg, 2001, p. 5). Conflicts over diversity most certainly embed this notable tension.

For now we take a brief look at history that informs our current era. The importance of a historical perspective is vital because throughout the latter quarter of the 20th century, political and social interpretations of multiculturalism changed and by the 21st century had "intensified [and were] taking centre-stage in the field of political contestation" (S. Hall, 2000, p. 212). A major topic of this book is how diversity became a prominent political topic.

MOVEMENTS FOR SELF-DETERMINATION AND CIVIL RIGHTS

Throughout the 19th century and continuing into the latter half of the 20th century, Europe and the United States held imperial control over major regions of Asia, Africa, and Latin America. The narration of mainstream history during this period represented European civilization and its ally, the United States, as the only regions with a recognizable history and culture. As part of this narrative, colonization of foreign lands and people benevolently brought "civilization" to people who lacked a culture and a history. This story left out the devastating effects of colonialism on the well-being of subjected populations and their natural resources. Independent-minded Asians, Africans, and Latin Americans, however, challenged the trumpeted generosity of the imperial reach of Europe and the United States.

Out of these challenges came self-determination movements for independence. As a result of this desire to determine their own future, numerous

European-created nations in Asia and Africa gained their independence from the late 1940s through the 1970s. The rise of self-determination movements brought international attention to the skewed nature of formerly undisputed universalist European Enlightenment values of reason, progress, individualism, and human rights. Marginalized ethnic groups forcefully pointed out how White Europeans and Americans apparently reserved these values only for themselves.

Efforts to Eliminate Diversity

In their quest to reduce human diversity and create a particular vision of a perfected human race, European fascists borrowed arguments from the pseudo-science of eugenics developed in the United States under generous private foundation grants during the first half of the 20th century. Mainstream conservatives and liberals promoted eugenics as an attempt to improve the human race by reducing the number of individuals associated with alleged defective genes traits. Those identified as defective were primarily individuals who were not White, Christian, heterosexual, or psychologically or physically "normal." In 1924, Nazi leader Adolph Hitler began his study of American eugenics and eventually went on to justify Germany's ethnic cleansing on the basis of U.S. laws and practices. By the 1930s, individual U.S. states collectively had conducted thousands of involuntary sterilizations on women under racialized eugenics laws (E. Black, 2003). In 2013, with a $10 million settlement, North Carolina, whose involuntary sterilization laws existed until 1974, became the first state to compensate surviving victims of eugenic policies (E. Cohen, 2013).

For new immigrants from Eastern and Southern Europe and existing populations of people of African, Asian, and Latin American descent, U.S. eugenics reinforced a political and social environment that was hostile to immigrant entreaties for freedom and material improvement. By 1924, U.S. immigration laws restricted the migration of people who would have expanded the nation's racial, ethnic, and religious diversity. In the aftermath of World War II and the rise of self-determination movements for independence from colonial rule, African Americans launched a concerted effort to overturn centuries of racial discrimination and violence against the full exercise of their citizenship rights. As a young man in the late 1950s, Martin Luther King Jr. began to make connections between U.S. domestic and foreign policy and the revolt of people of color against Western colonialism (Fairclough, 1984). The modern Civil Rights Movement exploded into the national psyche as White nationalists and reluctant political leaders used extralegal means against nonviolent citizens demonstrating for basic human rights. Out of this violent history, Congress in 1965 eventually revised its immigration laws by dropping its racialized national origins quotas, an action that opened border gates to the creation of today's multicultural America.

Survival of Diversity

The roots of diversity as a political issue reside in earlier international and national social movements. Led by groups that mainstream European and U.S. populations identified as not racially White and considered to be unworthy representatives of the nation-state, the modern movements for self-determination and civil rights ushered in a new discourse of multiculturalism. This historical view of social movements enables us to see how diverse identities emerged from the shadows of society and into the public spotlight to radically disrupt world-views of a mainstream White populace and the implications of diversity.

Movements for self-determination and civil rights created an identity crisis for the modern nation-state. This crisis stems from historical nation-state claims of a peoplehood of common ancestry in contrast to contemporary realities of diverse ethnic groups contending for recognition. Under ensuing challenges from diverse populations, majority populations in nation-states vigorously claim an inherent and essential identity for their home countries that they believe is beyond dispute. Some activist groups within the majority population make stringent calls to restrict citizenship rights of populations deemed threatening to notions of a unified national identity. Contemporary calls for recognition and redistribution of rights by minority groups show no sign of abating, especially given the historically unprecedented rates of global migration of populations from territories that were formerly under colonial control.

Political leaders understand that schools are sites for building support for a particular vision of a nation-state (W. C. Parker, 2012). In these chapters we explore this historical legacy of contestation over the legitimacy of a multitude of ethnic and racial identities and the consequences they have for a nation's children and their lived experiences in and out of schools. We examine how and why these diverse identities are intensely argued across the entire political spectrum and affect the life opportunities of young people. For now we turn to a summary of how gender and sexuality identities became a contested diversity issue.

MOVEMENTS FOR GENDER AND SEXUALITY RIGHTS

Despite women earning the right to vote in liberal democracies during the 20th century, women still faced gender discrimination over property and other rights, both within the home and in employment and politics. The second-wave feminism that emerged during the 1960s and 1970s found women en masse questioning why Enlightenment values were exclusively for males. Movements for civil rights and self-determination provided a language and awareness to create new diversity movements aimed at the elimination of gender and sexuality discrimination.

Legally considered the property of their fathers and husbands, daughters and wives during second-wave feminism initiated social, political, and economic challenges to male-only access to liberty and equality, which remains a contemporary diversity issue. As females of all ages expressed their desire to embrace their individuality and experience the full range of citizenship rights, no longer would women be the private property of males and ineligible for full participation in the public sphere. Yet, a strand of mainstream 21st-century discourse would continue to assert that those who advocated for the rights of women were anti-men and the cause of a perceived decline of the family and society.

Social movements initiated under second-wave feminism and the rise of the gay rights movement in the 1970s led to questioning the normalcy of strict gender and sexuality identity binaries of male–female and heterosexual–homosexual. By the 2010s, the public expressions of diverse gender and sexuality identities took form in a way nearly unimaginable by mainstream populations just 40 years earlier. As these diverse expressions expanded and struggled to gain recognition in the face of discrimination that could result in bodily violence, the public debate over the value of these "new" identities intensified rapidly in the 21st century. These contestations over recognition and expression of gender and sexuality diversity filtered down to public schools, with the question of what identities are permissible becoming a schoolhouse cultural issue. This topic is addressed in Chapter 7.

Historical background alone, however, can miss certain political and economic explanations that are necessary in order to understand contested diversity. The following section provides a brief introduction to the field of political economy.

DIVERSITY AND POLITICAL ECONOMY

Throughout these chapters, a political economy framework interprets tensions we find around the existence of diversity. The phrase *political economy* captures the interactive nature between politics and economics. The *Oxford Dictionary of Economics* explains that political economy as the original label for the field of economics "is actually a better name for the subject, as it draws attention to the political motivation of economic policies" (J. Black, 2003, p. 358). As a field of study, the focus of political economy is on the interaction between political institutions and economic systems in comparison to actual material conditions or the economic well-being of individuals and societies. How wealth and income distribution affects public schools and school-age children falls within the discipline of political economy (Watkins, 2012). As an interdisciplinary subject, political economy draws on economics and political philosophy as well as history, law, and sociology. Political economy specifically employs history to investigate how economic interests influence politics. Therefore, this book examines political economy reasoning about diversity.

DIVERSITY, WORLDVIEWS, AND IDEOLOGIES

Global tensions that surround expressions of diversity filter down to public school classrooms. Children are not immune to tensions elicited over diversity. This book incorporates a spectrum of worldviews or ideologies to understand how the same diversity issue contains multiple interpretations. Viewpoints that emanate from a particular orientation contain "both ideological and substantial premises for how we think and act . . . are deeply rooted in our subconscious" (Engen, 2009, p. 257). Hence, *worldviews are a function of ideologies* that embody cognitive and social psychological roots.

Ideologies are more than mere belief systems. Ideologies serve as precursors to the expression of worldviews and give people a lens to interpret the world around them. Ideologies are not simply rational systems of thought but contain an important emotive component: "Emotional tenor is part of what an ideology is and traditions of political thinking can be characterized by their particular emotional tones and their combination in specific contexts" (Finlayson, 2012, p. 761). Across the ideological spectrum, diversity as a contested topic elicits emotional reactions. Ideologies—consciously or unconsciously—serve as political and social justifications for how to organize the world.

Emergence of Ideologies

Significant political change during the 18th and 19th centuries away from medieval feudalism and divine rule and toward modernity set the stage for the development of ideologies among competing interests. Most telling was the rise of democracy. In the name of "We the People," the new nation of the United States famously proclaimed, "All men are created equal." A few years later, in 1789, the French populace overthrew its monarchy and declared a citizenship doctrine based on liberty and equality. A new worldview, ideologically liberal in its opposition to an absolutism of divine monarchical rule, emerged and reconceived the meaning of political participation in the United States and France—and eventually the entire world.

In practice, however, there was little agreement as to who actually constituted "the people." Conservative counterchallenges evoked a return to an authoritarian tradition and social order where rank and family lineage determined those fit for political participation. By the mid-1800s, small farmers and a rising U.S. working class offered their own ideological challenges to liberal and conservative worldviews. This generally voiceless political class advocated for a social model that envisioned an expanded polity and a common school curriculum that recognized and accounted for the material interests of those struggling to live at a subsistence level (Spring, 2010).

The lived experiences of historically marginalized groups highlight a disparity between a national ideology that proclaims "liberty and justice for all" in its Pledge of Allegiance and actual practices. To this point, W. C. Parker (2012) states,

> That liberal democracies fall short of their aspirations is a plain fact and the chief motive behind social movements that aim to close the gap between the real and the ideal. In this way, liberal democracies have a sort of built-in progressive impulse to live up to their own proclaimed principles. (p. 614)

In this ongoing ideological struggle inside and outside of schools, the political right seeks to restrict democratic participation whereas the political left wishes to expand democratic political involvement for historically marginalized populations.

Ideologies as Political Strategies

The modern era of social and political change fostered such ideologies as liberalism, conservatism, socialism, nationalism, communism, and fascism. These ideologies are "political metastrategies" that exist "in a world where political change is considered normal and not aberrant" (Wallerstein, 2011, p. 1). An ideological position alone does not make political change. Instead, an ideology contributes to a larger strategy to create a worldview in the interests of a particular governing order with specific social, political, and economic practices. Hence, ideologies are "located in opposition to something else" (Wallerstein, 2011, p. 11). An understanding of the strategic importance of ideologies helps to make sense of Song's (2010) contention that the "greatest challenge to multiculturalism may not be philosophical but political" ("Political Backlash," para. 1).

Within a climate ripe with possibilities for political change is where the concept of diversity, along with multiculturalism, finds itself with differing worldviews expressed through various ideological orientations. Despite the unifying hopes of Horace Mann in the 19th century that the common school as a public good could ameliorate ethnic, religious, and class conflicts, tensions among ideological orientations play out daily in schools. Children become the subjects of these ideological tensions over how to express diversity. Nothing is neutral in this process as teachers, administrators, parents, school boards, legislators, and the general public weigh in with various ideologically informed strategies to socialize children about the value of diversity.

Thus far, we reviewed various interdisciplinary approaches to study viewpoints on diversity. These include the value of using the multiple lens of historical contexts, political economy analyses, and ideological orientations. Multicultural studies of diversity use the interdisciplinary field of social psychology to gain insights into how people think about, influence, and relate to one another, especially in regard to group attitudes and behaviors toward diversity. Applications of elements of social psychology in its broadest sense are invaluable, for example, to understand attitudes toward interactions of group identities with schooling (Aboud, 2009; Gay, 2010; Pettigrew, 2004; Stephan & Stephan, 2004). However, when scholars cross variables gleaned from social psychology with human biology, we can find ourselves distracted by a disturbing reoccurring pattern of biological reductionism to explain differing orientations toward diversity. The following section provides an overview and critique of the current direction of the interdisciplinary field of political psychology, which overlaps with evolutionary psychology.

POLITICAL PSYCHOLOGY AND BIOLOGICAL REDUCTIONISM

During the decade of the 2010s, a growing chorus of scholars crossed normal disciplinary categories to produce research studies that examined political and ideological orientations. Generally under the academic umbrella of political psychology, these disciplines included political science, social psychology, cognitive psychology, neuroscience, and evolutionary biology/genetics. Jost and Amodio (2012) suggested labeling this interdisciplinary aspect of political psychology as "political neuroscience" (p. 59). This research generally attempts to add innate biological dimensions to what social psychologists and others previously identified in studies of social and political attitudes.

Political psychology emphasizes biological forces to account for why people have differing ideological viewpoints. Research findings are tentative, correlational, and in no cases do researchers claim cause and effect—that is, that a physiological response causes a certain belief or action. Researchers examine physiological responses, including studying brain activity and other biological indicators, in association with social and political attitudinal variables. This research does suggest linkages and associations.

Natural scientists and psychologists relate certain variables or constructs to dispositions that are of interest in studies of diversity and multiculturalism. Among the variables identified are authoritarianism, threatening situations, fear, sense of certainty and control, social system justification, conformity, closed-/open-mindedness, skepticism, conflict monitoring, stability and order, habitual responses, and disgust sensitivity. Researchers use these constructed variables to make biological associations or correlations with political ideologies and behaviors (Hennes, Nam, Stern, & Jost, 2012; Jost & Amodio, 2012; Kanai, Feilden, Firth, & Rees, 2011; Ledgerwood, Mandisodza, Jost, & Pohl, 2011; Taber & Lodge, 2006; Thórisdóttir & Jost, 2011; University of South Carolina, 2012; Wakslak, Jost, & Bauer, 2011).

In the end, this research is reductionist because it privileges and simplifies biology over social forces, ignores the complexities of human biology, and can be "poorly aligned to the realities of multicultural societies, especially under conditions of rapid diversification" (Tienda, 2013, p. 471). In contrast, H. Sebastian Seung, a leading neuroscientist in brain research, acknowledges that understanding how the brain makes decisions is complex. Seung predicts that it will take at least another 20 to 30 years to map the brain; this mapping will involve 85 *billion* brain cells with up to 10,000 connections *per cell* (Gorman, 2014). Ignoring the individual human variability in such a brain mapping endeavor, the tentativeness and enormity of Seung's brain-mapping task stands in stark contrast to political psychology's rush to politically and ideologically map human biology.

Political Psychology and Popular Culture

Political psychology in popular culture misleadingly suggests that people are born with certain ideological beliefs in their genes that inform political thinking and behavior about diversity. Both preservice and inservice teachers need to keep abreast of contemporary interpretations of political psychology to respond knowledgeably to reductionist and deterministic neurological and genetic explanations for attitudes toward diversity, especially when circulated in the imagination of popular culture. Without this awareness, political psychology research appearing as objectively "scientific" and beyond question can distract teachers in their treatment of diverse students. Marshall and Sensoy (2011) wonder, "How can teachers resist the pedagogies and corporate interests of popular culture and media in which the social world is simplified in ways that limit our understandings of complex social histories, identities, and structural inequities" (p. 6)? In this regard, biologically oriented political psychology in popular culture promotes "an unwarranted faith in the power of science to answer questions about the meaning of human existence . . . [with] a mania for genetic explanations" (Lancaster, 2006, para. 1).

Political psychology's unstated implication is that people are innately hardwired and incapable of altering their stance on political issues except through evolutionary processes. Anthropologist Roger Lancaster (2006) argues, "Genetic reductionism was never really about science; it was about ideology" ("Genomania After the Bust," para. 3). According to Evelynn Hammond (2006), Harvard professor of the history of science and of African and African American studies, "We are in the middle of a debate about the power and authority of genetic information" in which "it is the power of biology as a naturalizing discourse that has to be challenged" (paras. 9, 14). This is most evident in how the *New York Times* provided prominent opinion-page space to a biologist who reintroduced the discredited assertion that biological race exists and explains human diversity (Leroi, 2005), a topic we explore in Chapter 3. Ultimately, political psychology in popular culture can cause some to question the validity of efforts to bring about a more equitable distribution of material opportunities.

For example, the extent to which a person politically recognizes diverse identities and supports an equity-based redistribution of material resources incorrectly is framed as a function of an individual's biology rather than as social and political ideological responses. Based on an implicit assumption of fixed personality traits, political neuroscience minimizes social learning. In an analysis of the relationship of culture and cognition, Henrich and Boyd (2002) cautioned, "It will never be enough to focus on the mind and ignore the interactions between different minds" (p. 110). In a broader context, political psychology clearly weighs in on the side of nature in the long-standing "nature versus nurture" debate.

Nature Versus Nurture

Political psychology inevitably raises the issue as to whether ideological orientations toward diversity are a result of some basic physiological, internal operation—*nature*—or learned attitudes from experiences of socialization such as schooling—*nurture*. The short answer is that worldviews about multiculturalism are some combination of nature and nurture, that is, the biological and the social environment.

The first genome study to examine a range of ideological orientations involved 13,000 individuals identified as White. Researchers hypothesized that a very small number of the known 21,000 genes* appear correlated to cognitive–behavioral performance and political perspectives. The research team contended that hypothesized sites in humans for certain genes are worthy regions for further research on their potential relationship to political attitudes. In particular, this group of 14 researchers identified genetic locations that they say may account for political attitudes that stem from fear, stress, anxiety, and disgust sensitivity. In turn, they claimed that this research agenda is a legitimate direction to pursue for potential explanations of political beliefs (Hatemi et al., 2011).

These genome researchers cautioned that traits identified in specific genetic regions are not at the strength of such a heritable trait as height. When they use the phrase "genome-wide linkage," researchers made clear, "It does not indicate a gene by gene scan of the entire genome in search of individual loci that vary in ways predictive of a behavioral variation of interest" (Hatemi et al., 2011, p. 3). Instead, they search for genetic locations that *might* contain genes related to specific behaviors. Political scientist Peter Hatemi (2011) and his colleagues concluded with an interdisciplinary caution: "We contend the pursuit of such knowledge is best approached using a variety of neurobiological, cultural, and environmental methods" (p. 11), or a combination of nature and nurture. Nevertheless, overstated claims of genetic research can sound disturbingly similar to eugenic goals (cf. Specter, 2014).

McDermott and Hatemi (2014) used the term "political ecology" to conceptually describe models that make hypotheses on the relationships between biology and culture. Their descriptive models looked for causal pathways that can explain political behavior. The goal of their modeling reflects a current trend to merge political psychology with biology:

> Political outcomes which can be carefully delineated to result from a small set of decisions by a relatively few actors are unlikely to be illuminated by evolutionary approaches. However, those processes which helped regulate the social relations between individuals before political institutions existed are therefore likely to have become instantiated into human psychological architecture. The cumulative action of many actors making many decisions over time and space can lead to ingrained patterns of reaction in response to particular environmental contingencies. (p. 117)

First, McDermott and Hatemi (2014) acknowledged that a small number of people can affect political outcomes for a population, an action separate from evolutionary or biological explanations. Yet, they imply that a hardwiring into our biological "architecture" during this early evolutionary period explained the creation of political institutions. Hence, while they appear to give a nod to social forces—"particular environmental contingencies"—McDermott and Hatemi preface their remark by arguing that such political responses become biologically "ingrained patterns of reaction."

McDermott and Hatemi (2014) urged researchers "to take small differences in temperament seriously on a larger scale" to account for "*left–right differences across an ideological spectrum* (p. 124, emphasis added). They claim that knowledge of innate temperament explains political ideologies. They muddy their explanations in an assumption that "dispositional differences in political preferences and behavior across societies" originate primarily from biological interactions with a particular environment (p. 124). This interaction, they contended, then "can produce systematic and predictable cross cultural differences in political outcomes of interest" (p. 124). Finally, they concluded,

> If genetic drift occurs in biological realms, it becomes possible to build a model to explain differences across the liberal–conservative spectrum in much the same manner as we can examine differences in lactose intolerance across populations where climate affects access to fresh milk. (p. 125)

Therefore, McDermott and Hatemi mistakenly believe that how and why our biological bodies have adapted to the intake of certain foods is likely equivalent to cultural–biological interaction as to why people hold differing ideological perspectives (D. Morisato, personal communication, July 28, 2014). To further extrapolate from their theorizing, one could mistakenly conclude that how a society distributes wealth and opportunities and the extent to which a society politically recognizes diverse identities is a function of innate biological forces that culture merely enhances.

A central purpose of this book is an evaluation of political thoughts and arguments that are basic to a study of worldviews and their respective effects on the origin of various interpretations of the validity of diversity. History and political economy ground descriptions and conditions in the material world where ideologies become manifest. In the popular imagination, the constructs and speculative results of political psychology can appear to justify a reductionist appeal to account for political divisions over diversity with supposedly innate beliefs incapable of being changed. This is the case, for example, when a prominent *New York Times* opinion writer openly supports a military coup of a democratically elected party and chooses to critique the group he ideologically opposes with overt biological metaphors such as that they "lack the *mental equipment* to govern" or their "incompetence is built into the *intellectual DNA* (Brooks, 2013, paras. 7, 10, emphasis added).

To avoid going down the rabbit hole of biological reductionism to explain away ideological differences, the weight of the material presented in this book looks to the social environment—*nurture*—to identify patterns and data from history and political economy to help understand why diversity remains contested. Nature does not simply nor exclusively determine people. Otherwise, research documenting how diverse cultures nurture and socialize young people for the adult world would have to be ignored (cf. Rogoff, 2003). The observations of the sociologist C. Wright Mills (1958/2009) over a half century ago reflect a standpoint of this book on the importance of focusing on vested interests and lived experiences in order to understand diversity rather than explaining away differences on the basis of an asserted inherent and unalterable aspect of human nature. To skew analyses to biological explanations, Mills noted, is to "confine human history itself in some arid little cage of concepts about 'human nature'" (p. 52).

Political Bias in Political Psychology

Finally, political psychology researchers are not neutral. They bring their own unacknowledged political biases to explanations of differences among political ideologies. Political psychologists limit their range of analyses to a dichotomy of political ideologies: conservatism and liberalism. Researchers reflect socialization that directs them away from constructing more expansive and nuanced attitudinal measures inclusive of political values and attitudes to the left of liberalism.

Ultimately, political psychology minimizes the place of human agency for social change. For example, researchers make the across-the-board assertion that *all* political orientations respond similarly to threatened or criticized social systems, including defense of an existing system and its ideology of meritocracy (cf. Hennes et al., 2012). Such an assertion reflects historical amnesia about the Civil Rights Movement and the system challenger Dr. Martin Luther King, Jr. In his 1963 "Letter from Birmingham City Jail," King emphatically criticized liberal inactions and "the white moderate who is more devoted to 'order' than justice; who prefers a negative peace which is the absence of tension to a positive peace which is the presence of justice" (1963/1991b, p. 295). The response of King and hundreds of other civil rights advocates obviously was not to retreat in a defense of the status quo as biological political psychology would have predicted.

Political psychologists are not immune to socialization that limits politically left expressions. This is evident in how liberal democracies have continued rather successfully since Dr. King's era to minimize or silence the political left by alleging sedition rather than allowing First Amendment expressions of free speech and the right of association. Framed in evolutionary biology, political psychology in the second decade of the 21st century reifies and naturalizes conservative and liberal ideological variables present only a couple hundred years, a miniscule lapse of time in evolutionary terms. Deemphasized or absent in this contemporary strand of political psychology is a history of vested interests of those who pursue visions of a political economy to benefit the privileges of the few and those diverse populations who have resisted oppressive and inequitable situations through social movements and offered democratic alternatives.

Using the lens of history and political economy instead of political psychology, three distinct ideological orientations help us grasp the embedded values that underpin diversity and their effects on the education of children: *social conservatism, liberal multiculturalism,* and *critical multiculturalism.* Next, we analyze these three perspectives in relation to views on diversity.

NOTES

*According to the National Human Genome Research Institute, at least 21,000 genes have been identified, depending on how you define a gene, which remains indeterminate (Bodine, 2012, para. 1). Lancaster (2006) notes, "Previous widely-circulated estimates of the number of genes in the human genome had run as high as the perplexingly precise figure of 142,634" ("Genomania After the Bust," para. 1).

CHAPTER 2

A Spectrum of Worldviews

Democratic practices—dialogue and debate in public discourse—are always messy and impure.

—Cornel West, *Democracy Matters*

Diversity is an intensely debated concept across the entire political spectrum. Diversity per se does not cause social conflicts but is a lens through which narratives of assertion and denial of diversity claims become causes of social conflicts across a spectrum of worldviews. As observed in Chapter 1, President Obama (2010a) praised the value of diversity for schoolchildren. On the other hand, a prominent political commentator ridiculed the notion, placed blame on higher education as the source for how "diversity and sensitivity nonsense trickles down" to public elementary and secondary schools, and recommended "abolishing" any administrative references to "the words 'diversity,' 'equity,' 'race,' 'ethnicity,' . . . 'gender,' 'inclusion,' 'identity,' . . . 'globalization,' 'cross-cultural,' or 'multiculturalism'" (Will, 2013, p. 7). Since the word *diversity* and other associated terms reflect widely varying attitudes and actions, we conduct this examination along an ideological spectrum of social conservatism, liberal multiculturalism, and critical multiculturalism.

Multiculturalism is also a deeply contested concept as an ideological expression of diversity. For instance, while members of the Council of Europe acknowledged the existence of diversity in multicultural societies, they found the term "multiculturalism" confusing. One member suggested that multiculturalism "should be consigned to the conceptual dustbin of history" and proposed "combining freedom and diversity" as a way "not to use complicated terms" (Ash, 2012, p. 33). This echoes an earlier observation of a U.S. foreign policy observer who negatively referred to multiculturalism as a rising "cult" that could potentially have the United States "join the Soviet Union on the ash heap of history" (Huntington, 1997, pp. 32–33). Meanwhile, nearly 70% of the U.S. population believe that the nation is split on important values while a "deep philosophical divide" permeates state and federal politics (Harwood, 2013, p. A10; Saad, 2012). In this contentious environment, the purpose here is to take a step back to more broadly consider a spectrum of worldviews that result in competing arguments for what is the common good.

Before sampling in more detail how three competing conceptualizations of diversity filter into education in the following chapters, we will first consider the underlying beliefs that frame attitudes about diversity and difference. These key ideological orientations are political frames prominent in modern liberal democracies and influence how people understand diversity in relation to the individual and the group, the private and the public, and identities.

Social conservatism on the political right is the most dominant opponent of diversity and contains two elements, neoclassical liberalism—which in contemporary terms is referred to as neoliberalism—and religious fundamentalism. The second dominant orientation is *liberal multiculturalism* that supports a form of governing based on individual rights. This orientation contains elements of social conservatism but seeks to manage and accommodate diversity within existing structures of a liberal nation-state. Politically to the left of both of these positions is *critical multiculturalism*. Drawing from critical theory, this orientation rejects certain underlying assumptions of liberalism and focuses on how power relations within a stratified society affect diversity.

Although these three strands represent a typology, people in actual practice may shift their orientations among these categories, depending on their own material and cultural interests in relation to a particular diversity issue. The competing ideologies in this typology are in fundamental conflict over interpretations about human nature, society, justice, fairness, and the common good. The design of the typology provides a conceptual framework for explaining why some individuals who appear wedded to a particular worldview may in practice change their orientation.

Categorizations of diversity orientations exist in research on multicultural education. Ladson-Billings (2004) summarized how a critical perspective developed to "argue against the ways dominant ideologies are able to appropriate multicultural discourse" and to "interrupt the diversity discourse that emerged to supplant and subvert the original intentions of theorists who set out to create a pedagogy of liberation and social justice" (p. 52). Hence, this chapter and book are an extension of this approach in its examination of a spectrum of ideological approaches to diversity from a critical standpoint.

The remainder of this chapter is divided into three sections based on the typology of social conservatism, liberal multiculturalism, and critical multiculturalism. Highlighted within each section are the respective value and meanings attached to the private and public spheres, equality and equity, and a common culture, as well as how each of these conceptualizations can affect one's overall orientation toward diversity and difference.

SOCIAL CONSERVATISM

Social conservatism prioritizes the private sphere and guards private interests and identities against encroachment from the public sphere. This orientation holds a belief in a homogeneous common culture for a nation-state and argues that a specter of demographic heterogeneity and state regulation of capitalism can undermine social cohesiveness and the foundations of Western civilization. Social conservatism stands in opposition to demands from diverse groups for public recognition and redistributive rights. Consequently, social conservatism views the symbolic and material discourse of cultural diversity as an antisocial "nuisance" that obstructs social progress (Cooper, 2004, p. 120). Instead, this orientation uses diversity and multiculturalism as an instrumental means for economic exchange by adapting consumer marketing to various cultural preferences and languages.

Since its inception as an ideology in the late 1700s, social conservatism has viewed social change as problematic and potentially dangerous to an orderly society. Conservatism emerged as a reaction against the rise of popular expressions for democracy with a belief that "a strict social order was necessary to save man from himself" (Bell, 2002, p. 456). Russell Kirk (1960/2003), a leading voice of conservatism in the post–World War II era, captured this wariness with respect to change coupled with a need to maintain tradition. He highlighted the importance of the ideological values of "religious veneration, proper leadership, continuity of life, and material stability" (p. 120). Furthermore, Kirk believed that social problems cannot be reasonably solved by "a people vexed by incessant change [and] carping radicalism" (p. 120). Programs of social reform under liberal multiculturalism or deeper structural changes under critical multiculturalism are contrary to social conservatism and, therefore, ideologically troubling for this orientation.

The Private Sphere, Negative Liberty, and the Individual

Social conservatism privileges both the individual and the private sphere of life. This ideology of individualism perceives people as being sovereign in their own right. When one is free to follow one's self-interest, society benefits because self-interest contributes to the greater well-being of the family. Milton Friedman (1962/2003), recipient of the 1976 Nobel Prize for economics, articulated this perspective of social conservatism when he stated that "we take freedom of the individual, or perhaps of the family, as our ultimate goal in judging social arrangements" (p. 76). Because the individual and the family are the only social units of relevance, conservatives believe that diverse group identities, perspectives, and claims are misguided and harmful.

The worldview of social conservatism subscribes to Berlin's (1958/1969) description of "negative" freedom or liberty. Under a philosophy of negative liberty, individuals act independently, "without interference by other persons" (p. 121). In other words, a feature of the common good is that people have "liberty *from*" or "absence of interference" (p. 127). Individuals are free to pursue their own interests to attain personal goals based on their effort. For example, the logic of conservatism explains differentials in standards of living or educational attainment on the basis of individual merit and "freedom" rather than using such "catchwords" as "welfare and equality" (Friedman, 1962/2003, p. 71). In the context of negative liberty, Berlin (1958/1969) observed that "there is *no necessary connexion between individual liberty and democratic rule*" (p. 130, emphasis added).

Political Economy Origins

In economics, "liberal" means something different from its use in politics and everyday language—different from popular culture labels such as those applied to "liberal politicians" or "liberal media." At a basic level *liberal* for a political economist refers to *an absence of government interference.*

The contemporary principles of the liberalism of social conservatism harken back to Adam Smith's (1776/2001) *The Wealth of Nations.* In his famous treatise, Smith hypothesized a theory of individualism and economic freedom that contributes to the common good. He included a well-known claim that an "invisible hand" of the market would best serve the well-being of a society in the pursuit of individual self-interest without public or governmental regulations (pp. 553–554). Although Smith was living primarily in a precapitalistic era, social conservatives appropriated the invisible hand and applied it to modern capitalism.

Smith's conservative individualism can be found in U.S. constitutional law and its connection to the political economy of capitalism. By the end of the 19th century, the doctrine of individualism extended to the legal rights of corporations to operate with the freedom and security of an individual human being. In an 1886 U.S. Supreme Court decision, the chief justice stated on behalf of the other judges, "We are all of the opinion" that the 14th Amendment "which forbids a State to deny to *any person* . . . the equal protection of the laws, *applies to these corporations*" (Waite, as cited in Goldstone, 2011, p. 145, emphasis added). The extension of individual rights to the "inanimate objects" of capitalism (p. 145) continued into the 2010s with another Supreme Court ruling in which the identity of personhood was further equated with the identity of a corporation with respect to its ability to make unlimited financial donations to political campaigns. The organization that brought suit against the government,

Citizens United, illustrates an ideology of social conservatism through a mission statement that emphasizes the values of "limited government, individual responsibility, [and] free market economy," or capitalism without governmental regulations (Citizens United, 2012, para. 1).

Social conservatism identifies with capitalism because it is an economic system based on private ownership with the goal of accruing profit for individuals or an organization. Social conservatism honors capitalists, who, by definition, are the social class actively involved in owning and investing capital for profit and who derive their wealth and income from owning property. Capitalism employs *exchange value*–that is, the creation of goods and financial instruments that are exchangeable for a profit. This economic model is not designed specifically for *use value*–that is, the creation of useful goods and services to fulfill human needs. This is not to say that capitalist goods will inherently lack a social use, but rather the priority is on an exchange for a profit and capital accumulation.

Under a system of capitalism, according to the *Oxford Dictionary of Economics,* capitalists politically take "an important role in decision-making" for a society's allocation of resources (J. Black, 2003, p. 46). In practical terms, this translates to the wealthiest top 10% of the United States population exerting 15 times more influence on political decision than the remaining 90% (Bartels, 2014). Or, as Paris School of Economics professor Thomas Piketty (2014) puts it, the wealthiest segment of society wields "a significant influence on both the social landscape and the political and economic order" (p. 254).

As an example of capitalist participation in politics, corporate lawyer and future Supreme Court justice Lewis Powell articulated what would become a dominant orientation of social conservatism in relation to individual freedom, a position that has influenced the Court's reasoning well into the 21st century. In a lengthy confidential 1971 memorandum to the U.S. Chamber of Commerce prior to his appointment to the Court, Powell equated challenges to the unilateral dominance of capitalism as "a threat to individual freedom" (p. 32). To overcome criticism of capitalism, one front among many would be the creation of "action programs, tailored to high schools" that "would become a major program for local chambers of commerce" (p. 20). With a clear ideological strategy, Powell contended that there should be no "reluctance to penalize politically those who oppose" unregulated capitalism (p. 30). Justice Powell's stance was emblematic of an authoritarian streak that runs through social conservatism. Powell's position also foreshadowed the rise of neoliberalism as a public policy and as "a particular social form of class rule within capitalism" (Albo, 2002, p. 48).

Neoliberalism and Security. The concept of *neoliberalism* captures the political economy orientation of contemporary social conservatism. Neoclassical liberalism originally took the idea of negative freedom and applied it to economic activities. With Adam Smith's invisible hand, markets without government interference would hypothetically protect social interests. By 1980, neoliberalism—or "the new ultraliberal wave" (Piketty, 2014, p. 491)— became the modern form of this ideology but with a stronger and more intense emphasis on reductions in direct governmental spending on social goods under the claim that private markets would provide cost-savings to the public. Correspondingly, public funds are redirected or outsourced to private groups for the provision of public services such as K–12 education, prisons, highway maintenance, and armed military personnel. Framed as a more efficient fiscal policy than the public sector, an ideology of neoliberalism also actively pursues the selling off to the private sector of such public goods as a municipality's drinking water. Furthermore, under neoliberalism, private charities and religious organizations, rather than governmental agencies, would provide many of the basic social services. *Privatization of public services* refers to this move from the public to the private in tandem with tax cuts.

Neoliberalism is a form of negative freedom or *freedom from* outside interference to pursue individual self-interest. To maximize the common good, individuals and corporations should be left alone to compete in a market that is "free" and unregulated. Police and military expenditures for the protection of private individual interests are the primary arenas for legitimate governmental involvement under neoliberalism.

Consequently, the spending category for which social conservatism does find support for government involvement and public spending is for national security. William F. Buckley Jr. (1955/2003), the founder of the conservative periodical *National Review*, captured this belief of social conservatism: "It is the job of a centralized government (in peace-time) to protect its citizens' lives, liberty, and property. All other activities of government tend to diminish freedom and hamper progress" (p. 201). To this day, social conservatism views the main purpose of government as the protection of citizens against personal harm and threats to private property. Emphasizing the security importance of military funding, President Ronald Reagan (1983/2003) declared, "I urge you to speak out against those who would place the United States in a position of military and moral inferiority" (p. 360). Friedman (1962/2003) further summed up what the ideological extent of government should be in the public sphere: "The scope of government must be limited . . . to protect our freedom both from the enemies outside our gates and from our fellow-citizens: to preserve law and order, to enforce private contracts, to foster competitive markets" (p. 69). In summary, political economy priorities under neoliberalism are well-funded police and military security systems with duties that include the domestic and global protection and advancement of capitalism and neoliberal policies.

Diversity and the Market. Social conservatism opposes any diversity claims regarding economic redistribution as a right. Social conservatism is against, for example, equity demands for an expansion of social services under an assumption that this will take financial resources from those who have accumulated their private wealth due to their individual merit. Diversity for social conservatism is located instead in the marketplace wherein individuals can assert their unhindered liberty to select, for example, schools of their choice without unnecessary public intrusion. This perspective of social conservatism "sees regulation by public agencies and legislatures as barriers to opportunity rather than guarantees of equal treatment, and assumes that a broad scope of individual choice will produce greater equity and higher levels of achievement" (Orfield, 2013b, p. 42). From this orientation, parents are not subject to the arbitrary power of the state but instead are free to act as private individual citizens in the interests of their children. In this construction, parents are consumers who make market decisions about which schools support their individual preferences.

In response to public claims of racial, sexual, and gender discrimination, social conservatism assumes the state should not coercively challenge private tastes of a business or an individual. For example, U.S. Senator Rand Paul defended private business discrimination on the basis of the First Amendment's protection of free speech and the value of "controlling property" (as cited in Millhiser, 2012, para. 3). Hence, according to social conservatism, workplaces and schools should manage or discourage cultural diversity and multiculturalism and focus on cultural preferences and languages of consumer markets and trading partners.

Common Exclusionary Culture

Social conservatism views culturally diverse groups as potential traitors to a common culture. This is a result of conservatism's instrumental conceptualization of cultural diversity when expressed publicly. Representing this view, for example, a general in U.S.-occupied Afghanistan explained that knowledge of culturally different practices of an enemy necessitated the use of "culture as a weapon system" (Hogg, as cited in R. Davis, 2010, para. 1). A strand of anthropology that privileged "the American nation-state ideology" supports this view (Chicago Cultural Studies Group, 1992, p. 552; Price, 2011).

Social conservatism considers multiculturalism "as a misguided policy and ideology which victimizes cultural, gendered, racial, and ethnic groups while demonizing primarily white males" (Coates, 2008, p. 317). Social conservatism believes that "rather than leading to greater individuality and freedom, multiculturalism has become another vicious form of bias" (p. 317). Hence, diversity per se among groups is irrelevant under conservatism because group identities are considered a false construct that undermines the preeminence of autonomous individuals located within a nationalistic common culture. Because the expectation is for individuals to assimilate into a common culture, social conservatism dismisses group assertions of marginalization as divisive. The premise of assimilation requires surrendering ethnic and cultural bonds in order to experience the freedom of individual citizenship (Banks, 2013). Therefore, social conservatism supports public education to the extent that young people are socialized into a homogeneous common culture.

The basic conservatism of neoliberalism and religious fundamentalism can bolster each other's economic and cultural orientations. Religious fundamentalism intersects with neoliberalism's market fundamentalism in support of a common, divinely inspired culture protected from cultural and economic differences. This hierarchical worldview excludes the validity of other moral and economic systems because they obstruct the development of a common culture framed through a particular Christian tradition that gave rise to capitalism and Protestantism.

Gutmann and Thompson (2012) point to a "mindset" tendency in social conservatism that displays an unwillingness in practice to compromise on principles closely connected to material interests. An unbending position can "block some decent compromises that improve on the status quo" (p. 79). Conservatives fear a loss of their own liberty with an extension of equality and democracy (Robin, 2011). Because the ideology of social conservatism favors tradition and, therefore, a common exclusionary culture, this position is reluctant to consider alternative orientations that can alter the status quo in more inclusionary ways.

LIBERAL MULTICULTURALISM

The heritage of liberal multiculturalism stems from a history of liberalism that considered "itself as the opposite of conservatism . . . and proclaimed itself universalist" (Wallerstein, 2011, p. 5). Liberalism and more specifically liberal multiculturalism positions itself in the political center, but in practice the center is actually "an abstraction" because any ideology can discursively define the extremes in which to locate itself (p. 6). Liberal multiculturalism, which emerged out of the cauldron of movements for self-determination and civil rights as described in Chapter 1, fits within this tradition of ideological positioning by fashioning itself as politically in the center between perceived extremes of social conservatism and critical multiculturalism. By its acknowledgment of diverse group identities, liberal multiculturalism attempts to moderate social conservatism. On the other hand, in comparison to critical multiculturalism, liberal multiculturalism takes a gradualist approach to diversity and inclusion.

The Public Sphere, Positive Liberty, and Individualism

Whereas individualism remains a primary value, autonomy is tempered in a liberal multicultural orientation by acknowledgment of a person's location in the public sphere. With a recognition of cultural groups, liberal multicultural-ism brings diversity out of the private sphere and into the public to "celebrate diversity" with an additive conception of multiculturalism to the common culture of a homogeneous nation-state. This aspect of liberalism focuses on diversity as appreciating cultural differences among groups, highlighting individual contributions from cultural groups, and accepting cultural tolerance as foundational to a liberal democracy.

From this orientation, liberty can necessitate public interventions for the freedom to lead a particular way of life. Rather than denying the legitimacy of diverse group identities, liberal multiculturalism accepts the need in selected cases for public policies that allow groups to express their freedom to not only exist but participate publicly in liberal society. Freedom, therefore, is not just limited to private cultural practices but is a safeguard for diverse public expressions.

Positive liberty is asserted in tension with negative liberty. Berlin (1958/1969) explained that positive liberty entails external interventions as "*not freedom from, but freedom to*–to lead one prescribed form of life" (p. 133, emphasis added). Under positive liberty, "the real self may be conceived as something wider than the individual . . . as a social 'whole' of which the individual is an element or aspect" (p. 132). For example, support for affirmative action under liberal multiculturalism represents a form of positive freedom or positive discrimination as a gradual reform measure that acknowledges group-based racial and gender inequalities.

Political Economy and Social Welfare

Liberal multiculturalism claims that governments may need to moderate inequalities created by the state's political economy. Rather than an absolute adherence to the privatization orientation of social conservatism, liberal multi-culturalism acknowledges that under certain circumstances some degree of public intervention is necessary to curb the detrimental harm of unregulated private interests.

The roots of economic liberalism that underpin liberal multicultural-ism take into account Adam Smith's caution about the effects of inequality on the working class that springs from the relationship between capital and labor. While social conservatives claim Smith for their own purposes, they ignore his social welfare concerns. Smith (1776/2001) stated that inequality "is the state into which the labouring poor, that is, the great body of the people, must necessarily fall, unless government takes some pains to prevent it" (p. 1041). More broadly, Smith contended, "When the institutions or public works which are beneficial to the whole society…cannot be maintained altogether," the state should provide public revenues (p. 1090). Liberal multiculturalism accepts Smith's observation that government intervention in the affairs of society may be necessary to provide equal opportunity and protection of the human rights and well-being of an economically disadvantaged group. Therefore, such hardships cannot always be placed on the back of the individual and left to the private sector alone to solve.

Inequality and Personal Responsibility. Whereas liberal multiculturalism, like social conservatism, privileges meritocracy to explain economic well-being, liberal multiculturalism nuances this view by incorporating group-based discrimination. President Obama reflected liberal multiculturalism's political economy orientation between public policy intervention and private individual responsibility for economic well-being. In his State of the Union address, President Obama (2013a) highlighted a shortcoming of a conception of individual responsibility based on a system of meritocracy under current capitalist practices:

> There are millions of Americans whose hard work and dedication have not yet been rewarded. Our economy is adding jobs—but too many people still can't find full-time employment. Corporate profits have skyrocketed to all-time highs—but for more than a decade, wages and incomes have barely budged. (para. 4)

Despite this naming of stagnant job opportunities and declining wages while wealth redistribution moved upward, a few months later at the conclusion of a college commencement address, Obama (2013b) stated,

> Success may not come quickly or easily. But if you strive to do what's right, if you work harder and dream bigger, if you set an example in your own lives and do your part to help meet the challenges of our time, then I'm confident that, together, we will continue the never-ending task of perfecting our union. (para. 55)

In that speech to a group of college graduates, the president applied the ideology of meritocracy and personal responsibility as he emphasized that when people work hard and apply their talents, they can be successful in meeting their economic aspirations.

These two presidential speeches by Obama provide an example of how liberal multiculturalism seeks simultaneously to (a) support publicly funded economic programs to help individuals from historically marginalized groups and (b) maintain both an ideology of individualism and meritocracy presented as personal responsibility. Throughout his political career, as an illustration of liberal multiculturalism, Obama has reflected a "vision of the civil rights struggle as one of individual initiative and self-transformation" based on a "profoundly individualistic understanding of the freedom struggle" (Sugrue, 2010, pp. 14–15).

Liberal multiculturalism rejects the notion that economic inequalities are inherently systemic in a liberal democracy. Because liberal democracy's creed of egalitarianism regards inequality differentials as exceptions to the norm, equality of opportunity remains ideologically privileged over diversity. Hence, liberal multiculturalism grapples with a continuing quandary to preserve an egalitarian ideal within an existing socioeconomic stratification that liberal democracies permit.

> ***The Public, Markets, and Choice.*** Liberal multiculturalism values public–private collaborations in meeting the demands for public goods. For example, the ideology of liberal multiculturalism lends support to charter schools that operate like deregulated private schools but are financed with public funds, especially when this perspective frames such schools as innovative sites to improve academic achievement for children who live in disproportionally poor neighborhoods. This approach represents a search for a political economy equilibrium "to resolve the conflict between the aggregate impact of individual [private] choices and the common [public] needs that no individual or group of individuals acting separately can fulfill" (Orfield, 2013b, p. 56). Unlike social conservatism, liberal multiculturalism places limitations on direct transfers of tax dollars from public education to private school options.

Liberal multiculturalism views choice through charter schools as promoting a means to advance racial and economic equality. For instance, the Obama administration declared, "The Federal Government should focus its attention and available resources on improving the quality of public schools for all students. Private school vouchers are not an effective way to improve student achievement" (White House, 2011). Rather than choice being an end in itself, liberal multiculturalism also frames choice through racial integration. Orfield (2013b) explains that in theory "the idea is, as much as possible, to give students from segregated, high-poverty neighborhoods access to predominately white and Asian schools, which research shows, are likely to be better in crucial respects" (p. 62). Demographic diversity in this orientation is both racially desirable for a multicultural society through school choice policies and a pragmatic way to advance the life opportunities of children of color from low-income families.

Common Inclusionary Culture

Liberal multiculturalism accepts tolerance for culturally diverse groups as fundamental to a common culture of a liberal nation-state. With the exception of Canada, Australia, and New Zealand, however, majority opinion in liberal democracies across Europe and the United States is wary about or opposed to supporting policies that would expand ethnic and religious diversity ("Canadians Endorse Multiculturalism," 2010; Gallup Muslim-West perceptions, 2011; "Global Views on Immigration," 2011; Kymlicka, 2010; Marszalek, 2013; Newport, 2006; Tan, 2012). In response, the liberal Council of Europe (2010), for example, made calls for tolerance and dialogue in an attempt to calm conservative perceptions that diverse identities are threatening majority economic and moral interests.

Liberal multiculturalism generally recognizes group identities as fixed and considers diverse cultures as relatively equal. The concept of multiculturalism becomes recognition and respect of cultural diversity as a shared value of the larger society. Liberal multiculturalism assumes that through recognition of diversity, despite some public accommodation of differences, groups will assimilate into an existing common culture. Liberal multiculturalism endorses a civic identity in which diverse cultural groups share the common good of a liberal democracy while also seeking their own individual goals. Liberal multiculturalism assumes that recognition and accommodation of ethnic and gender diversity deepens and protects human rights and democracy while decreasing hierarchies based on diverse identities (Kymlicka, 2007). Equality under liberal multiculturalism, nevertheless, tends to reduce differences to issues of culture (Juteau, 2008). The emphasis on an inclusive common culture for liberal multiculturalism is on equalizing *recognition* of diversity rather than on equitable *redistribution* of political, economic, and social rights based on cultural, ethnic, or gender identification.

Whereas religious fundamentalism assumes a modern nation-state based on a particular interpretation of Christian values, liberal multiculturalism sees such advocacy as a breach of separation of church and state and contends that truth can exist in other religions and other diverse cultural systems within a common culture. Although liberal multiculturalism privileges Judeo-Christian moral beliefs and cultural practices over those of other religions, it advocates inclusion to fold diverse beliefs into an existing common culture. Thus, a liberal multicultural orientation supports public policies for diverse religious groups as long as they do not harm the material interests and maintenance of a common culture.

Liberal multiculturalism values compromise to create a more inclusive common culture and improve the condition of diverse groups. While social conservatism holds steadfast on principles, liberal multiculturalism is more accommodating in its attempts to find common ground with opposing opinions. Gutmann and Thompson (2012) refer to this strategy as "economizing on disagreement" to defend a "preferred proposal in a way that minimizes rejecting the positions they oppose" (p. 117). The assumption is that "it increases the chances of producing a desirable compromise and thereby creating the conditions for cooperation that lead to future compromises" (p. 117). Decades earlier, Reisman (1964/1993) warned that compromise with social conservatives is "an illusionary operation since the [political] right can always go still further right and will" (p. 95). Liberal multiculturalism is more likely to seek compromise with social conservatism than with critical multiculturalism, the latter a position that liberal multiculturalism often ignores or dismisses as a legacy of the "culture wars" of the 20th century and labels "radical," "polarizing," or "extreme" (Reifowitz, 2012, p. 29.).

CRITICAL MULTICULTURALISM

Critical multiculturalism stands in opposition to social conservatism and liberal multiculturalism. Based on critical theory, critical multiculturalism brings to the forefront such concepts as resistance, power, knowledge construction, class, cultural politics, and emancipatory actions. Through "educational criticism" that "is not only deconstructive but reconstructive," critical multiculturalism within the broader domain of critical theory actively "build[s] possibilities" that are dismissed or ignored by dominant ideologies (Leonardo, 2009, p. 147).

Critical multiculturalism contends that wealth and academic achievement gaps among classes are inherently unjust along racially diverse categories. Critical multiculturalism speaks against the naturalizing of hierarchical differences and supports a multiethnic and gender-fair society in which the tensions of differences are central to what makes a society's culture common. Pincus (2006) labels this approach "conflict diversity" (p. 4). Critical multiculturalism explains diverse cultural practices and identities as fluid rather than fixed or reducible to a market commodity. Critical multiculturalism analyzes "institutional inequities" that include issues of race, ethnicity, class, and gender and investigates them for intersections in relation to power and privilege (May & Sleeter, 2010, p. 10).

Critical multiculturalism emphasizes historical perspectives to understand contemporary conflicts over diversity. It rejects conservative proclamations of an end of history with no alternatives to neoliberalism's project of privatization of public services in the name of progress. For critical multiculturalism, diverse histories of discrimination serve as a basis for contemporary claims of recognition and redistribution of rights, including indigenous sovereignty.

The Public Sphere, Democratic Liberty, and Society

Unlike the individualism of social conservatism and liberal multiculturalism, critical multiculturalism examines individuals in relation to their social location in groups within society. Unlike former conservative British Prime Minister Margaret Thatcher's (1987/2013) declaration, "There is no such thing as society" (para. 78), critical multiculturalism responds that society exists and is more than a simple aggregate of "individual men and women and . . . families" (para. 76). Whereas conservatism and liberalism start with the individual as the primary unit of analysis, critical multiculturalism embraces an understanding of *society* as an entity that independently precedes individual relationships and their subjectivities. Recognized as more than a collection of private, autonomous individuals and their families, society highlights an obvious existence of the public sphere (cf. Pfaffenberger, 2008).

According to critical multiculturalism, both conservative negative liberty and liberal positive liberty place limitations on the potential of freedom and liberty in a participatory democracy. According to Berlin (1958/1969), "Yet it is not with individual liberty, in either the 'negative' or in the 'positive' senses of the word, that desire for status and recognition can easily be identified" (p. 158). Instead liberty is "a desire for something different: for union, closer understanding, integration of interests, a life of common dependence and common sacrifice" (p. 158). The individual is part of a vibrant, interactive whole. Liberty is recast, away from an ideology of individualism toward a societal perspective.

In the end, however, Berlin rejected this view because he believed that "where the self to be liberated is no longer the individual but the 'social whole'," individuals will submit themselves to the authority of dictators (p. 159). A critical multicultural emphasis on deepening and expanding democratic participation, however, precludes Berlin's conclusion. Instead, critical multiculturalism captures a concern that excessive individualism ignores erosions in public participation in a democracy. In summary, according to critical multiculturalism, a participatory democracy can create a more equalitarian world that honors individuality and creativity. Such a worldview is possible under a concept of liberty that emanates from a society based on socioeconomic equity that actively facilitates the full political participation of its diverse populations.

Political Economy and Equity

Critical multiculturalism rejects conservative and liberal assertions that equate democracy with corporate capitalism. Critical multiculturalism represents a vision of democracy that goes beyond normative citizenship participation in voting and public hearings as performance and looks instead to democratic inclusion in economic decisionmaking. Critical multiculturalism is economically oriented toward expansion of the public sphere through socialism and opposes systems of capitalism that historically ravaged marginalized diverse groups. Critical multiculturalism supports socialism as a political economy alternative to capitalism. As an alternative, socialism is a democratic system in which "the economy's resources should be used in the interests of all its citizens" (J. Black, 2003, p. 434). The goal is an equitable and just allocation of society's resources to meet fundamental human needs as an inherent aspect of the common good.

An economic model of democratic socialism emphasizes an expansion in material comfort and social justice for all. With this aim, democratic socialism supports the individuality and creativeness of the local, small business sector and targets the undemocratic effects of a financial and corporate oligarchy that concentrates wealth and important political decisions in the private hands of the few. Rather than markets guided by a metaphysical invisible hand, basic social needs are met through a democratically designed system of production and distribution. Some economists describe this type of political economy as a *participatory economy* that can provide *economic justice* for the vast majority of people who are currently excluded from economic decisions that affect their daily existence and well-being (see Albert, 2003; Hahnel, 2012).

Critical multiculturalism contends that the economic policies of conservatism result in the exploitation of diverse subordinate groups. Moreover, a political economy of liberalism provides diverse populations insufficient economic protection and opportunities under capitalism. In summary, the socialism of critical multiculturalism is democratically redistributive in contrast to conservative and liberal ideologies of capitalism that, in the name of individual economic self-interest, tolerate and promote a distorted income distribution that favors the wealthy.

In response to conservative and liberal parading of images of totalitarianism under mislabeled "socialist" governments, critical multiculturalism uses socialism as a democratic expression of the will of the vast majority of people for its potential to reduce material suffering and raise the living standard of all. A "movement toward socialism" works democratically through a political economy intended to meet human needs (Amir, 2014, p. 27).Twenty-first century experiments in the implementation of democratic socialism, however, face two major challenges.

During the Cold War, from the late 1940s to the early 1990s, some self-designated socialist governments had an undemocratic and dictatorial record in which economic redistribution policies were oppressive and often unproductive. Democratic socialist Michael Harrington (1976), whose writings introduced poverty in America to the Kennedy administration and helped fuel the 1960s War on Poverty (see Chapter 5), explained how communism during the Cold War became conflated with socialism in popular culture: "Communist society is not socialist, but bureaucratic–collectivist" (p. 174). More problematic was that "a movement calling itself socialist socialized poverty, not wealth, and since there was not enough to go around, classes developed despite the pretentions to classlessness" (p. 175). As an ideological strategy, conservatives have used this history to label contemporary economic reforms designed to benefit historically marginalized populations as "'socialism' to forestall their enactment" (J. Anyon, 2011, p. 67).

The other challenge for movements toward socialism is the nearly 150 years of a capitalist propaganda campaign to demonize political economy alternatives to the dominance of corporate capitalism. Capitalist interests and the federal government collaborated to marginalize and suppress democratic socialist political and labor movements (Zinn, 2003). This collaboration also reduced the social use value of a family's home to a capitalistic exchange value, often with dire consequences. Legislative and executive actions supporting capitalist land development have a long history of displacing poor and vulnerable diverse populations. For example, in 1969 during the first year of Richard Nixon's presidency, the administration's Council of Economic Advisors reported,

> Investing in new housing for low-income families—particularly in big cities—is usually a losing proposition. Indeed the *most profitable investment* is often one that demolishes homes of low-income families to make room for business and high-income families. (as cited in Harrington, 1976, p. 224, emphasis in original)

During the Great Recession (2007–2009), a population disproportionately elderly and of color further experienced dispossession through shady home-loan practices. Geographer David Harvey (2014) explains that

> tactics of eminent domain, along with the brutal foreclosure wave that led to massive losses not only of use values (millions rendered homeless) but also of hard-won savings and asset values embedded in housing markets, to say nothing of the loss of pension, health care and educational rights and benefits, all indicate that the political economy of outright dispossession is alive and well in the very heart of the capitalist world. (p. 58)

For other nations that deviated from the dictates of capitalist policies that prioritize profit accumulation, U.S. foreign policy with the support of mainstream media was intent on replacing democratically elected socialists ("Hugo Chávez Departs," 2002; McCormick, 1995; Wilpert, 2007). This hegemony permits capitalist governments to present opposing views as "evil" and "to silence critics at home and to overthrow governments not to the liking of business interests" (Hunt, 2003, p. 221).

Influenced by the legacy of Dr. Martin Luther King Jr. (1967/1991c), critical multiculturalism stands in opposition to conservative and liberal foreign policy political economy positions that privilege military expenditures and an expansive for-profit weapons industry over the domestic social needs of its citizens, especially the poor. Both conservatives and White and Black liberals, however, criticized King for his dissent against U.S. foreign policy and the connections he made with public expenditure priorities. In the spirit of Dr. King, critical multiculturalism incorporates the problematic intersections of U.S. foreign policy, domestic economic policies, and racial justice for the well-being of diverse groups.

"Why Socialism?" During the 20th century, such venerated public figures as Helen Keller (1912/2002) and Albert Einstein (1949/2002) advocated for socialism. In his essay "Why Socialism?" Einstein was not only percipient about the post–World War II political economy but also remarkably accurate in foreseeing our contemporary era's concentration of wealth and erosion of democracy. Einstein expressed concern over

> an oligarchy of private capital, the enormous power of which cannot be effectively checked even by a democratically organized society. This is true since the members of legislative bodies are selected by political parties, largely financed or otherwise influenced by private capitalists who, for practical purposes, separate the electorate from the legislature. The consequence is that the representatives of the people do not in fact sufficiently protect the interests of the underprivileged sections of the population. (pp. 60–61)

Keller and Einstein recognized that capitalism and the established political order did not benefit the struggling poor or democracy.

Educator George Counts (1932/1978) criticized capitalism for devastating the livelihood of millions of people. In his classic *Dare the School Build a New Social Order?*, which he wrote in the midst of the Great Depression of the 1930s, Counts advocated "some form of socialized economy" (p. 45). He called on teachers to take political leadership: "The times are literally crying for a new vision of American destiny. The teaching profession, or at least its progressive elements, should eagerly grasp the opportunity which the fates have placed in their hands" (p. 50). Today, the challenge remains as educators face a neoliberal offensive to privatize public education and to delegitimize teacher unity and bargaining power.

Movement toward socialism prioritizes and redistributes governmental expenditures to fully fund public education to meet the needs of *all* children. With a governing system focused on the redistributive values of socialism, critical multiculturalism envisions a political economy in which an expansive diversity of citizens participate democratically in deciding the direction of society's economy. This approach contrasts with political economy practices that grant the weight of decisionmaking to capitalists and their political representatives.

The Economic Surplus and Choice. A basic tenet defining the rise of civilization was the ability to create an economic surplus for its population.

Without a surplus, economic growth is not possible. The existence of a surplus comes down to decisions on how to use it and who controls it. To illustrate, consider the events of the Great Recession and the continuing economic crisis of the 2010s. The ideological orientation of conservatism and liberalism led mainstream politicians to privilege society's economic surplus for capitalists affiliated with large financial institutions rather than for a population that became increasingly unemployed or underemployed and homeless. A critical multiculturalism perspective understood this decision as one that prioritized an inherent elitism in capitalism over the democratic values of socialism.

Despite the ongoing economic crisis, both social conservative and liberal multicultural orientations hold sway in public discourse on school choice in its slow but steady diversion of a government's economic surplus away from public schools. Critical multiculturalism stands opposed to the ideology of choice that drives the privatization and deregulation of charter schools because this trend to transfer the public surplus enables efforts to privatize K–12 schools with public, tax-generated funds. Economists MacEwan and Miller (2011) explain that this transferring-of-funds phenomenon is "in effect, giving away the public's money without public control" (p. 217). For example, in 2010–2011, New York City schools increased funding to charter schools by 9% in funding while decreasing funding to public schools by 4%. A Department of Education spokesperson explained that obligations to charter funds created a situation in which the department finds itself owing "our charter schools more money than we have to give" (as cited in Gonzales, 2011, para. 17). In this instance the use of an economic surplus represented a trend to privatize schools through a transfer of public funds.

Critical multiculturalism recognizes school choice as an ideological strategy that "posits a one-way causation from the problems of the schools to the problems of society. It largely ignores the impact of our society's great economic inequalities on what happens in schools" (MacEwan & Miller, 2011, p. 216). This neoliberal policy blames K–12 schools and teachers for a capitalist economic crisis in order to build a governing consensus favoring school choice. Under critical multiculturalism, an economic surplus priority would instead address such human needs as childhood poverty, food insecurity for struggling families, and adequate housing for all children and their families, which could, in turn, improve the schooling and life opportunities of young people.

A Critical Reading of Adam Smith. Chomsky (1996) counters the selective reading of Adam Smith by both conservatives and liberals and states, "What we would call capitalism he [Smith] despised" (p. 162). Smith (1776/2001) only mentions "invisible hand" once in his huge treatise and that was in regard to guiding producers to favor domestic industries over foreign ones (p. 593). Smith did not imagine the 21st century scenario in the United

States where domestic producers had already moved and "outsourced" their industries to countries with cheap labor, in effect deserting its domestic working class. Further problematic for critical multiculturalism is the basis of Smith's invisible hand theory, which is contingent on "an article of blind faith" that "absolves us from the conscious burden of building a common world" (Rollert, 2012, paras. 14–15).

In actual practice Smith (1776/2001) was concerned about the effects of repetitive labor developing in the early stages of industrialization. Taken to its logical end, Smith feared that workers would become "stupid and ignorant" and unable to appreciate, let alone participate in, the public sphere of civil society (p. 1041). For the new laboring class Smith supported a form of a living wage that an appropriate remuneration could provide, both for its provision of necessary leisure time and worker efficiency. Smith stated, "Where wages are high, we shall always find the workmen more active, diligent, and expeditious than where they are low" (p. 119).

Smith's (1776/2001) theory assumed that equality of liberty would lead to perfect competition in economic markets. Smith reserved equality for the merchant and producer classes, not the vast numbers of disenfranchised people. Yet Smith contended, "The wise and virtuous man is at all times willing that his own private interest should be sacrificed to the public interest of his own particular order or society" (p. 213). Smith set aside private interests in favor of the common good because he recognized that the few could use governmental power for their own interests rather than for the "popular will" (Chomsky, 1996, p. 162).

In summary, critical multiculturalism asserts that a fair society must rein in and eliminate material inequalities inherent to capitalism, not voluntarily through decisions based on private actions, but through forceful public policies committed to equity. Opposed to a political oligarchy that determines the material fate of diverse populations, critical multiculturalism advocates public regulation of an economy's resources and its surplus for use in the interests of all citizens. This orientation argues that such critical advocacy and outcomes serves the common good for the vast majority of people, including those from diverse groups who have not experienced equity in material benefits promised under a liberal democracy.

Common Multiculture of Differences

To some extent critical multiculturalism overlaps with liberal multiculturalism in that they both imagine a unified culture in which diversity flourishes. Critical multiculturalism, however, assumes that individuals are inseparable from society and can find liberty through the social union of common multicultural differences based on equitable redistribution of rights and privileges. Unlike the way liberal multiculturalism essentializes culture as static and fixed, critical multiculturalism sees culture as dynamic and ever changing. Critical multiculturalism names and avoids the assimilationist pitfalls to promote a common culture that strives to "legitimize the social order through racial harmony and a national identity based on the 'Americanization' of marginalized cultures" (McLaren & Farahmandpur, 2005, p. 114).

Critical multiculturalism envisions a society that incorporates differences found within and between diverse cultures. This orientation opposes conservative and liberal constructions of identities within a nation-state's dominant definition of common culture. May (2012) explains that a critical multicultural approach "recognizes that one's identity choices are inevitably structured by class, ethnic, and gender stratification, objective constraints, and historical determinations" (p. 475). Critical multiculturalism presumes that cultural systems are an extension of belief systems and that no one group can make a priori claims that one cultural orientation is dominant over or superior to others. Incorporating antiracism as a premise of a common culture of differences, this orientation also directs attention to "new 'cultural racisms,' which emphasize culture or religious differences as a basis for legitimating discrimination" (p. 474). Furthermore, critical multiculturalism highlights global cultural hybridity over neoliberal versions of global homogeneity that mirrors market standardization. The goal here is to reimagine a common culture that reduces and eradicates hierarchies of recognition and privilege so that multiple cultures can thrive together.

Critical multiculturalism counters liberal positions about civil society where dominant forces characterize cultural diversity as a distraction from significant material and cultural inequalities and marginalization. Banks (2008) observes that when a homogeneous application of citizenship is applied by a society divided hierarchically by status categories of differences but operating under a liberal ideology of equal opportunity, individuals from diverse groups are limited in exercising their full citizenship rights. To resist this second-class treatment that contests the legitimacy of diverse identities, critical multiculturalism posits that differentiated rights in a common multiculture of differences can eliminate historical inequalities and injustices.

In summary, critical multiculturalism attends to diversity in relation to the exercise and distribution of recognition, power, and wealth in a social hierarchy of inequality. Because individuals and groups begin their quest for equality from unequal starting points, critical multiculturalism emphasizes the perspective of equity as fairness of outcomes more than equality of opportunity. Critical multiculturalism turns its focus away from liberalism's individualist ideology of meritocracy and equal opportunity and instead looks to claims for justice, equity, and community by historically marginalized groups. This standpoint accepts diversity conflicts as a necessary part of political struggles over power and allows democratic equivalencies among various group demands without attempting to eliminate differences.

SHIFTING POSITIONS WITHIN A SPECTRUM OF WORLDVIEWS

This chapter presented an overview of social conservatism, liberal multiculturalism, and critical multiculturalism as ideal types across a spectrum of worldviews. The interdisciplinary explanation of the viewpoints in the typology focused on ideological orientations toward diversity through history, political theory, political economy. A premise of this book is that people are capable of change and can shift positions among these three typologies.

Dorothy Day provides an example of the permeability of an ideal typology in practice. Day was female, White, a Christian, and a socialist, identities that when taken together do not lend themselves to an easy ideological categorization. We recall Day's (1952/1981) direct involvement during the Great Depression with "the poor, the dispossessed, the exploited," (p. 204) which included African Americans at a time the Federal Bureau of Investigation equated advocacy for racial justice with anti-Americanism. In her autobiography Day explained, "My very experience as a radical, my whole make-up, led me to want to associate myself with others, with the masses, in loving and praising God" (p. 139). This example of Dorothy Day indicates how deep Christian religious beliefs can be compatible with social justice, an orientation that contrasts with conservatism's religious fundamentalism (see Chapter 7).

Despite the fluidity across worldviews in practice, each orientation in the typology represents valid patterns and trends—despite instances that are exceptions and blur ideal viewpoints together. The purpose of these comments is to remind ourselves that we are examining ideal categories as a way to understand contested diversity. In this exploration the categories help us better grasp why such divisions exist over diversity in our current era.

From the perspective of these three major worldviews—social conservatism, liberal multiculturalism, and critical multiculturalism—that inform the current conflicts over diversity and multiculturalism, the following chapters provide specific examples and analyses of diversity issues in education. The first area we examine is the construction of race and ethnicity and its effects on children and youth.

CHAPTER 3

Color Consciousness and Color Blindness

Color is not a human or personal reality; it is a political reality.

—James Baldwin, *The Fire Next Time*

The most contentious diversity topics originate from interpretations about the social, political, and economic impact of racial and ethnic identification. This aspect of how people consider diversity defines who is included within a nation's identity and who is seen as an outsider, regardless of citizenship status. As discussed in the previous chapter, contested diversity centers on different interpretations of what constitutes a common culture. Hence, a group's racial or ethnic identification is a significant factor tied to the identity of a nation.

To understand this aspect of diversity, the chapter differentiates and clarifies the terms *race* and *ethnicity*. We see how biological race is a modern creation that lingers ambiguously in our current moment. The chapter describes how a spectrum of ideological worldviews weighs and interprets the importance of race and ethnicity. Then we turn to the changing meanings and implications of *color consciousness* and *color blindness*. The chapter critiques underlying orientations of judicial opinions of U.S. court cases that have affected decisions about educational policy regarding racial and ethnic diversity. Folded into this discussion is the mutual relationship between neighborhood housing patterns and diversity in public schools. The chapter concludes with an examination of the value of racial diversity in schools and neighborhoods in a multicultural society. Drawing from social psychology, we consider for both Whites and people of color the effects of racially isolated communities and the corresponding resegregation of public schools in the 21st century.

DIFFERENTIATING RACE AND ETHNICITY

Shortly after World War II the United Nations reported that because "there is great confusion on the notion of race," an expert panel of scientists would produce "an authoritative declaration on the race problem" (United Nations

Educational, Scientific, and Cultural Organization [UNESCO], 1950, p. 2). The panel concluded that race as a biological entity did not exist nor was there a difference in intelligence between different groups of people identified historically by race. In this 1950 report, *The Race Question*, the authors collectively concluded that "it would be better when speaking of human races to drop the term 'race' altogether and speak of *ethnic groups*" (p. 6, emphasis in original).

Into the 21st century the biological concept of race lingered. More than 6 decades after the UN report, the Human Genome Project further confirmed the UN's conclusion and added that "no consistent patterns of genes across the human genome exist to distinguish one race from another. There also is no genetic basis for divisions of human ethnicity" (U.S. Department of Energy, 2013, para. 2). Characteristics that today may be mistaken for biological race or ethnicity are actually superficial physical appearances or phenotypes such as skin color, hair texture, body structure, and facial features. Yet the *socially produced* concept of race continues to carry significant impact on life opportunities.

Modern Creation of Race

Prior to the colonization of the Americas, Europeans used the concept of race in conjunction with an individual's geographical origin or ancestors. During this precolonial era, race did not have the same meaning as it would later and was interchangeable with ethnicity. In standard usage, the concept of *ethnicity* attempts to capture a people's shared cultural elements, such as religion, language, customs, and laws (Baum, 2006).

British colonialism in the Americas marks the development of race as a fixed entity. Specifically, the phenotype of skin color became equated with biological race. Up until the late 1600s, poor indentured servants from England and slaves from Africa generally shared a similar status. When these two groups united against the colonial aristocracy, the planter class in particular took notice and began the process of legally and extralegally separating people on the basis of recognizable skin color differences (Harris, 1993). Eventually British colonizers asserted that all people of African descent, regardless of ethnic differences, were one race, "Negro." It is during this era that "White" as a racial category emerged to signal who "the people" would eventually be in a new nation, the United States of America (Baum, 2006).

Twenty-First-Century Racial Ambiguity

In the 21st century nationalistic tension over who racially represents "the people" found expression in the controversy that erupted surrounding the election of Barack Obama over whether the president met the requirement of natural-born U.S. citizenship, despite legal documentation by his birth state,

Hawaii. Besides his birth certificate noting the specific hospital in which he was born, his mother's birthplace is listed as Wichita, Kansas, and her race as "Caucasian." His father's birthplace is entered as Kenya, East Africa, and his race as "African" ("Certificate of Live Birth," as cited in Pfeiffer, 2011, para. 3).

The use of "African" as a race harkens back to the colonial era of designating dark-skinned people of African origin as "Negro." Africa as a continent, however, contains more than a thousand different ethnic and language groups and refers to a geographic origin rather than a specific race or ethnicity. The origin of "Caucasian," too, rests on a geographical location, and in the context of American racial classifications the term has historically been equated with "White." The use of Caucasian globally is indeterminate, and in parts of Russia today it not only does not apply to Whiteness but is actually used as a slur for darker-skinned people (Baum, 2006). The term Caucasian has changed in meaning over time from an origin story of a particular biological race tied to Whiteness to a concept that is unreliable for identifying either race or ethnicity. Although Caucasian is not a legal term, as recently as 2013 a U.S. Supreme Court judge used Caucasian to describe a plaintiff (Dewan, 2013). According to Harvard's Jennifer Hochschild, mainstream jurists "really don't want to use the word white in part because roughly half of Hispanics consider themselves white. White turns out to be a much more ambiguous term than we used to think it was" (as cited in Dewan, 2013, p. 4SR).

Returning to President Obama and the ambiguity in racial identification, various options on the 2010 population census existed for noting one's race. Since 2000, the U.S. census has allowed individuals to mark more than one racial category or enter multiple configurations of racial identity. Obama, therefore, had an opportunity to select a mixed-race category based on his White mother and his Black father. Or he could have just chosen White given his maternal lineage. Instead, he checked one census category, "Black, African Am., or Negro" (Roberts & Baker, 2010, para. 3). The category Obama selected refers to the phenotype of skin color and to a geographic origin but not to an ethnicity or biological race. Nevertheless, the salience of race as a politically identified category based on phenotype remained for the president as well as other U.S. citizens.

IMPLICATIONS FOR DIVERSITY

Social conservatism, liberal multiculturalism, and critical multiculturalism have differing orientations on the meaning of the United States as a nation-state and correspondingly who constitutes "the people" on the basis of racial and ethnic identity. "In fact," as Balibar (1991) pointedly notes, "the discourse of race and nation are never very far apart" (p. 37).

Social Conservatism

The position of social conservatism, as discussed in Chapter 2, holds to a homogeneous conception of a common culture characterized by strict exclusionary parameters within national borders. Social conservatism historically excluded non-Whites from its conception of a common culture. Throughout U.S. history, this meant that the legitimate representatives of a common culture were members of the "White race." The origins of modern conservatism in the 1950s contained a racialized view of a common culture. In a 1957 editorial for William Buckley's *National Review*, conservative intellectuals justified White southerners' opposition to an expansion of African American civil rights because "the white community is so entitled, for the time being, it is the advanced race" (as cited in Bell, 2002, p. 460).

The interpretation of the results of the 2012 presidential election illustrate the staying power of social conservatism in tying race to a common culture. In that national election when nearly three-fourths of all voters identified as White, a popular socially conservative television commentator and author stated after the reelection of Obama, "The white establishment is now the minority. . . . *It's not a traditional America anymore* (O'Reilly, 2012, para. 24, emphasis added). Even in an era when an individual who identified as Black was elected twice as U.S. president, a significant proportion of the population who identify as White likely holds this position. This reflects a half-century pattern when a majority of White males have not voted for a Democratic party presidential candidate since 1964 (Calmes, 2014). For example, exit polls from the 2012 presidential election indicated that among all White voters, only 39% voted for President Obama. This was the case for all age categories of White voters, except 18- to 29-year-old Whites; 44% of this group voted for Obama ("President: Full Results," 2012). This reflects a trend confirmed in research findings that a significant number of Whites believe that "the pendulum has now swung beyond equality in the direction of anti-White discrimination" (Norton & Sommers, 2011, p. 218).

Despite the election outcome, polling data suggest that a majority of Whites are socially conservative regarding race. Four years after Obama's first election, there was an increase of racial bias against both African Americans and Latinos (Ross & Agiesta, 2012). Anti-Black sentiments cut across mainstream political parties, with "sizeable proportions" of both Republicans and Democrats expressing such attitudes, although these sentiments were more dominant among Republicans, who generally lean toward social conservatism (Pasek et al., 2012, para. 1).

Social psychologists use explicit and implicit measures of an individual's attitudes to determine the presence of racial bias. For an attitude to be considered explicit, it must be a "consciously endorsed" viewpoint, whereas an implicit attitude is one for which an individual does not have "conscious, intentional control over the processes of social perception, impression formation, and judgment that motivate their actions" (A. G. Greenwald & Kreiger, 2006, p. 946). Using both explicit and implicit measures, attitudinal indicators point to an increase from 2008 to 2012 in the number of people demonstrating negative attitudes toward African Americans.

Specifically, 51% expressed explicit, unambivalent attitudes against African Americans in 2012, whereas 48% had done so in a similar 2008 survey. Implicit or unexpressed anti-Black attitudes increased to 56% from 49% 4 years earlier. In regard to Latinos, a 2011 survey recorded that 52% held explicitly anti-Latino attitudes, whereas 57% expressed negative attitudes on an implicit test (Ross & Agiesta, 2012). A. G. Greenwald and Kreiger (2006) explain that such beliefs result in actual racial discrimination because "implicit biases are predictive of discriminatory behavior and implicit-bias measures do a significantly better job than explicit-bias measures in predicting behavioral indicators of discrimination" (p. 966). Thus, an individual with an implicit racial bias can unconsciously or unintentionally support practices that are racist.

The racialized historical origins of the U.S. and contemporary data on racial attitudes are indicative of a socially conservative ideology concerning who are legitimate representatives of a homogeneous common culture. The growth of political and cultural influence by non-White populations is contrary to U.S. social conservatism. Verkuyten's (2010) research finds that "the more majority-group members identify with their own group the more they can be expected to try to protect their group's interests and status position" (p. 155). Hence, the orientation of social conservatism perceives the rise of multiculturalism as a betrayal of the common culture and a potential threat to majority privileges.

Social conservatism constructs outsiders as infringing not only on a common culture but ultimately on territory claimed under nationalism. The moral value of loyalty to an exclusive common culture is generally associated with *ethnocentrism*, a belief that one's own cultural group's characteristics are superior to those of another group. Ethnocentrism results in the conflation of race and ethnicity with national identity. In summary, the orientation of social conservatism privileges Whiteness within an exclusionary common culture. Ideologically, social conservatism accomplishes this by reducing physical or phenotypic differences to biological race to justify a hierarchy of differences among racially identified groups (Haidt & Kesebir, 2010; Hooghe, 2008).

Liberal Multiculturalism

For most of U.S. and modern European history, the universal values of liberty, freedom, and equality served as ideals in the midst of oppression and inequality faced in the daily lives of people of color. Liberal multiculturalism began a break from classical liberalism's one-dimensional ideology that naturalized racial discrimination. Liberal multiculturalism emerged as a response to the contentious and violent struggles of anticolonialism and the U.S. Civil Rights Movement of the 1950s and 1960s. As a means to keep nation-states from splintering, liberal multiculturalism offered an alternative to the exclusionary absolutism of social conservatism.

Liberal multiculturalism recognizes racial and ethnic diversity as long as it does not decenter a common culture and practices. This position of inclusivity, based on a model of assimilation, postulates that all people benefit from the moral values of Western European civilization. Racially and ethnically identified individuals and groups traditionally not part of the common culture can be included on the premise that dominant cultural norms and practices prevail. Whereas social conservatives distrusted and vehemently opposed a political order determined by individuals who may not have inherited positions of privilege, liberals were not entirely opposed to including new groups under an umbrella of "all men are created equal" as a means to temper the influence of social conservatism (Wallerstein, 2011).

The late Harvard historian Nathan Huggins (1991) posited that a "master narrative of American history" is founded on "a conspiracy of myth, history, and chauvinism . . . [that] could find no place at its center for racial slavery, or racial caste which followed Emancipation" (pp. 25–26). Consequently, contemporary liberal multiculturalism differentiates "the presence of racism *within the state* from an (official) state racism" (Balibar, 1991, p. 39). Under liberal multiculturalism, the maintenance of unity and a common culture can compromise the civil rights of people of color.

In contrast to the United States, Canada is an example of a liberal democracy that has an explicit multicultural policy designed to protect the civil rights of racial and ethnic minorities. The Canadian Multicultural Act (1988) proactively commits Canada's government to recognizing and promoting "the understanding that multiculturalism reflects the cultural and racial diversity of Canadian society" and acknowledging "the freedom of all members of Canadian society to preserve, enhance and share their cultural heritage" (3.1.a). In an effort to manage diversity, the government of Canada (2012) acknowledged that the nation "is not immune to the kinds of debates witnessed elsewhere in the world" ("Approaches to Multiculturalism," para. 5). Although racial and ethnic social and economic discrimination remains a fact of life in Canada (Canada, 2010; Environic Institute, 2012), the Canadian government (2012) designed a variety of programs to recognize and promote diversity. Compared to other liberal democracies, a significant majority of Canadians generally hold positive attitudes toward immigrants.

Nevertheless, Canadians have increasingly become ambivalent about how well newcomers integrate into society. In 2012, 70% of Canadians expressed concern that immigrants were failing to assimilate to "Canadian values," reflecting a level of unease not seen since the 1990s (Environic Institute, 2012, p. 46). This liberal multiculturalism tension over assimilation corresponds to those captured by social conservatism. Joshee (2009) relates the rise of neoliberal-oriented politicians to a growing official Canadian emphasis on tolerance of difference that casts diversity and equity "to refer primarily, if not exclusively, to groups that are having trouble with the existing school system" (p. 101). Hence, for liberal multiculturalism and social conservatism, diversity per se remains the problem rather than one of the existing political economy and social structures that critical multiculturalism highlights.

When liberal multiculturalism compromises with social conservatism over such interpretations as to the nature of assimilation in a common culture, it is generally framed in the name of national unity and maintenance of the existing social order. The racialized compromise of liberal multiculturalism negatively affects the full expression of the rights of people of color. By taking an assimilationist approach in the name of unity, liberal multiculturalists tend to share a similar disposition with social conservatives on the United States' being "color blind" or "postracial" in regard to charges of racial discrimination, a topic taken up later in this chapter.

Critical Multiculturalism

Critical multiculturalism goes beyond recognition of diversity and differences and supports a redistribution of racial and ethnic political power in order to create a more equitable society. Critical multiculturalism identifies with a history of battles led and fought by people of color against racism and disenfranchisement. The contemporary roots of this antiracism orientation trace to the mid-20th-century international anticolonialism movements in Asia, Africa, and Latin America and domestic civil rights struggles. In the United States, critical multiculturalism is historically rooted in the actions of African Americans and other non-White groups to gain full citizenship rights and experience economic justice.

Critical multiculturalism finds expression in opposition to the restrictive racial and ethnic policies and practices of both social conservatism and liberal multiculturalism. In both Europe and the United States, when a critical multiculturalism orientation solidified in social movements away from the claimed neutrality of liberalism, both the conservative right and the liberal "center" reacted against the critical left. For example, in a powerful combination of social conservatism and liberalism that often resulted in the suppression of political activism, the federal government and mainstream media throughout most of the 20th century perceived organizations that worked on behalf of full citizenship rights for African Americans as political subversives (Blackmon, 2008; Nelson, 2010; Olson, 2001).

Critical multiculturalism stands in opposition to mainstream avoidance of candid political economy analyses of race and racism and draws attention to color-blind discourse, our next topic.

COLOR-BLIND WORLDVIEWS

Color blindness is a dominant belief that "race should be ignored in public policy and everyday exchange" (Heyes, 2012, "Race," para. 2). Advancement of color blindness strives to create an invisibility of skin-color identification. Color blindness exists in conflict with color consciousness in public policy. Historically, social conservatism moved from overt racist color consciousness to a contemporary color-blind ideology. Ignoring the ramifications of racial discrimination, social conservatism contends that people are best judged on their individual merit because racial and ethnic group identification in the 21st century is an irrelevant distraction. When liberal multiculturalism finds itself affirming color blindness, it is based on an assumption that discrimination on the basis of skin color is an aberrant problem of the past. Law professor Kimberlé Crenshaw (1997) explains, "Color-blind discourse almost singularly achieves its mighty mission by simply suspending traditional signs of race and racism" (p. 103).

A discourse of color blindness persisted after Obama's election. Some liberals used this 2008 event to declare the arrival of a "postracial" society as a realization of Martin Luther King's most cited speech in which he imagined a future world where skin color would not determine social status. In turn, conservatives used an excerpt from King's 1963 speech to justify a pursuit of color-blind policies. Calling forth King's reference to judging people on their character rather than their skin color, President Reagan in 1985 was the first major conservative to use King's speech to justify color blindness in public policies. Often forgotten, as a rising political conservative in the 1960s, Reagan spoke out against the Civil Rights Act of 1964 (Blake, 2013).

Critical multiculturalists contend that conservatives in the name of White victimization misappropriate King's (1963/1991a) quotes and ignore that his purpose was "to dramatize a shameful condition" of racial segregation in housing and education (p. 217). King put this in the context of daily acts of discrimination against African Americans at the hands of Whites that included "unspeakable horrors of police brutality" (p. 218). Moreover, those adhering to social conservatism skipped King's analysis of problems that stem from channeling away public monies from job creation and underfunded schools. Hence, today, an ideology of color blindness rather than overt White supremacy is voiced in opposition to programs for affirmative action and redistribution of material resources for diverse groups.

Postracial claims in combination with color-blind discourse create an invisibility of race that affects how diverse populations of children and youth experience their education. To better understand the effects on public education, an overview of a history of color blindness, color consciousness, and citizenship rights follows next.

COLOR AND CITIZENSHIP RIGHTS

Color consciousness and color blindness originate from a history of a racially explicit political economy. During the U.S. founding, a political compromise between the new liberal class and social conservatives was most evident in the framing of the Constitution. In order to count slaves for the purpose of congressional representation and to appease a southern planter class, liberals helped to craft a compromise whereby free persons in Article 1 were Whites and "three-fifths of all other Persons" were slaves of African origins. Hence, slaves, who had no right to vote, were constructed as worth 60% of a White person for the purpose of increased representation by a White plantation class. Unstated was the profitable benefit of slave labor to both southern elites and northern merchants and industrialists.

In 1790 the U.S. Congress enacted and incorporated race and color consciousness in its limitation of citizenship to "white persons" only. Four years prior to the Civil War, the chief justice of the U.S. Supreme Court declared from the bench that people of African descent "had no rights which the white man was bound to respect" (*Dred Scott v. Sandford*, 1857, p. 15). The court added that "the Declaration of Independence . . . show[s] that neither the class of persons who had been imported as slaves nor their descendants, whether they had become free or not, were then acknowledged as a part of *the people* (p. 16, emphasis added).

It would take a civil war that claimed 750,000 lives for the 1868 passage of the 14th Amendment to provide constitutionally protected citizenship rights for African Americans, a change in status from property to person. This was preceded by the 13th Amendment to end slavery and followed by the 15th Amendment to give African Americans the right to vote. Despite the 13th Amendment, not until the 1940s did the federal executive branch provide law enforcement to end what has been called the era of neo-slavery (Blackmon, 2008). Before Congress enacted legislation to give any significant enforcement to the 14th and 15th Amendments, another 100 years would elapse.

U.S. Supreme Court actions from 1896 to the present provide a lens to view a shift from explicit privileging of White perspectives of color consciousness to color blindness. Despite the passage of Reconstruction era constitutional amendments, *Plessy v. Ferguson* (1896) solidified the practice of White supremacist state segregation laws by declaring that under the Constitution public facilities could be "separate but equal" and not be considered discriminatory against people of color. The court's decision eventually served as the constitutional basis to legally segregate public school students by race.

In 1906 President Theodore Roosevelt signed into law a naturalization act that continued to limit applications for citizenship on the basis of racial eligibility. Writing for the National Archives about this act, Marian Smith (2002) notes that "by mixing references to color and geographic origin, the law displayed a then-popular confusion, or equation, of race with nationality" (para. 15). Smith cites a district court clerk who was confused over the racial descriptors used under the 1906 Naturalization Act and asked if the term "white person" referred to "only those whose color is actually white or does it further include all persons of what is ethnologically known as the white or caucasian race" (para. 18)? The problem of indeterminacy surrounding official racial and ethnic identity continues into the 21st century for state and federal officials (M. L. Smith, 2002).

Using the 1906 citizenship law, the Supreme Court in *Takao Ozawa v. United States* (1922) ruled against a Japanese man who met all the naturalization requirements except for his racial identification and contended he was not of Caucasian origin. A year later in *United States v. Bhagat Singh Thind* (1923), the Court ruled against the citizenship request of an Oregon man who was an Indian Sikh. In this case, Thind argued that as an individual originally from India he could trace his linage to the Caucasian race. The same court denied the validity of the origins argument that it had supported earlier and color-consciously concluded, "It may be true that the blond Scandinavian and the brown Hindu have a common ancestor in the dim reaches of antiquity, but the average man knows perfectly well that there are unmistakable and profound differences between them today" (p. 2).

Following these Supreme Court decisions, Congress passed the 1924 Immigration Act, which "meant that even Asians not previously prevented from immigrating—the Japanese in particular—would no longer be admitted to the United States" (U.S. Department of State, n.d.). This closed the circle of anti-Asian immigration that originated in 1882 with the Chinese Exclusion Act. With the 1924 Immigration Act, Congress also codified the notion that individuals from Eastern and Southern Europe were not fully White and limited their immigration while expanding access to individuals migrating from Western Europe and Britain. Overt color-conscious polices that privileged the rights of White citizens in wealth accumulation over people of color continued after World War II in discriminatory access to federal home ownership with loans provided through the Federal Housing Administration and Veterans Administration (Loewen, 2005). All racial and ethnic stipulations for citizenship were eventually dropped in a revision to immigration law in 1965, a result of the Civil Rights Movement and a new multicultural discourse.

COLOR CONSCIOUSNESS/BLINDNESS
AND DIVERSITY IN SCHOOLS

In 1954 a liberal U.S. Supreme Court declared unanimously in *Brown v. Board of Education* that racial segregation in public education was unconstitutional, signaling an end to de jure segregation. This was an era when "the growing black civil rights movement had created an ever more critical legitimation crisis for . . . white elites" (Feagin, 2012, p. 67). During the Cold War era, the former Soviet Union brought international attention to Jim Crow laws of racial segregation in public facilities and influenced the Court's movement toward recognition of African American citizenship rights where desegregation was "seen as a necessity to improve the image of the United States abroad" (DeJong-Lambert, 2007–2008, p. 67). The Court initially did not set an implementation timeline and in a follow-up ruling stated only that desegregation should proceed with "all deliberate speed" (*Brown v. Board of Education*, 1955, p. 4). With Congressional committees controlled by conservative Southern segregationists, Congress failed to pass a civil rights bill shortly after the *Brown* decision that would have provided anti-discrimination enforcement against segregation in voting booths and public facilities, including schools. A decade later, political pressure from expanding civil rights protests led to the eventual passage of the Civil Rights Act of 1964 and the Voting Rights Act of 1965.

In 1973 the Supreme Court ruled in *Keyes v. Denver School District* that the district "had engaged over almost a decade after 1960 in an unconstitutional policy of deliberate racial segregation" (p. 192). For the first time, U.S. law included Latinos with African Americans as a protected class with respect to racial discrimination. Rather than counting schools with just Latino and African American students as integrated, the Court ordered the district to desegregate their schools, because the two student groups of color "suffer identical discrimination in treatment when compared with the treatment afforded Anglo students" (p. 5). According to Horn and Kurlaender (2006), Keyes "meant that desegregation was now mandated in the North and that it extended to whole districts, not just single schools" (p. 3).

Due to the slow progress of school desegregation spurred by a White backlash, the courts turned to busing students between formerly segregated schools. In *Swann v. Charlotte-Mecklenburg Board of Education* (1971), the Supreme Court affirmed the constitutionality of busing students out of segregated neighborhoods to create integrated schools as imagined under the *Brown* decision. The Court, however, was unwilling to tackle the long history of residential segregation in wealthier White suburbs that surrounded poorer central cities whose populations were disproportionately Black.

By 1974, the Court concluded in *Milliken v. Bradley* (1974) that to impose a multidistrict desegregation plan on White populated schools outside a central city, in this case the Detroit metropolitan area, was not justified by the *Brown* decision. Instead, emphasis was placed on local control of individual school districts because, the Court majority argued, there was "no showing of significant violation by the 53 outlying school districts and no evidence of any interdistrict violation or effect" (p. 4). In a dissenting opinion, Justice Thurgood Marshall, a lawyer who had argued for the *Brown* decision and was the first African American to serve on the Supreme Court, stated,

> Desegregation is not and was never expected to be an easy task. . . . In the short run, it may seem to be the easier course to allow our great metropolitan cities to be divided up each into two cities—one white, the other black—but it is a course, I predict, our people will ultimately regret. (p. 33)

However, in subsequent years Marshall's critical dissent and prediction failed to gain mainstream political traction.

Sociologist Joe Feagin (2012) explains that the White majority of justices on the Supreme Court "intentionally limited the enforcement" of school desegregation by excluding "arguments showing institutional and systemic racism" (p. 102). By the decade of the Reagan presidency (1981–1989), the nation's attorney general opposed busing for school integration if a student had to travel more than 15 minutes or 5 miles (Wicker, 1982). Notably, in the early days of the Reagan administration, John Roberts, conservative Supreme Court Chief Justice since 2005, served as a special deputy to the attorney general and opposed any further enforcement or advancements in civil rights laws, including efforts to desegregate schools (R. J. Smith, Becker, & Goldstein, 2005). It was during the 1980s that the Reagan administration's "white racial framing and associated administrative efforts was catastrophic" for reducing racial inequalities (Feagin, 2012, p. 102). From this period to the present, neither prominent conservative nor liberal public officials framed school desegregation as a fundamental moral standard for a liberal democracy.

Contemporary Color Blindness and School Resegregation

By the 1980s, the ideology of color-blind justice sought to deny past and present skin-color discrimination. Color-blind discourse moderated overt racial imagery and comments and substituted the language of White-oriented rights and equal opportunity. Groups declaring *reverse racism*, a "white-coined conservative term" (Feagin, 2012, p. 149), claimed that Whites now suffered discrimination and, therefore, any racially based affirmative action programs should end.

Under color blindness, remedies for past racial injustices were not relevant. For example, in *City of Richmond v. Corson* (1989), the Supreme Court majority was unequivocally against any claim that "past societal discrimination alone can serve as the basis for rigid racial preferences" (p. 3). Consequently, the Court reasoned that this "would be to open the door to competing claims for 'remedial relief' for every disadvantaged group" (p. 18). Reflecting an ideology of individualism and meritocracy, the Court concluded, "The dream of a Nation of equal citizens in a society where race is irrelevant to personal opportunity and achievement would be lost in a mosaic of shifting preferences based on inherently unmeasurable claims of past wrongs" (p. 19). In other words, to determine human cost of past racial discrimination is contrary to a color-blind ideology in which race is not a factor in individual success. Law professor Cheryl Harris (1993) identifies *City of Richmond v. Corson* as the Court's modern expression of "full-blown hostility toward any infringement of white interest" (p. 1773). In his dissent in this 1989 case, Justice Marshall acknowledged how color-blind justice undermined "race-conscious remedies" and stated that the "decision marks a deliberate and giant step backward in this Court's affirmative action jurisprudence" (*City of Richmond*, p. 27). Integration efforts for diverse student populations within school districts felt the effects.

Decline of Judicial Support for Diversity in Schools

In 1997, White parents reopened the case that led to school busing, *Swann v. Charlotte-Mecklenburg School* (1971), and argued that busing unfairly harmed their children. In 1999 a federal court agreed; in 2002 the Supreme Court let the federal court decision stand. The era of busing to achieve school integration had officially ended at a time when racial segregation between and within schools was increasing (Irons, 2002). The 1973 *Keyes v. Denver School District* court-ordered desegregation plan to integrate Latino and African American students with White students ended in 1995, and by the 2000s Denver had returned to a pattern of more racially isolated schools.

In the 2000s the Seattle School District sought to increase racial diversity in its schools. In *Parents Involved in Community Schools v. Seattle School District* (2007), however, the Supreme Court struck down Seattle's plan. Chief Justice Roberts claimed that "racial balancing" in public schools would make sure that "race will always be relevant in American life" (p. 15). Justice Stephen Breyer, however, pointed out in his dissent how one Seattle high school had an 80% population of color in 1999 but under the school district's diversity plan in 2000 it was 60%. In the stay of implementation of the Seattle plan, as the case went through the judicial system, Breyer further noted that the same school was resegregated by 2005 and had a 90% population of color.

Using a color-blind rationale to rule against the Seattle School District's plan to racially diversify its secondary schools, Roberts concluded, "The way to stop discrimination on the basis of race is to stop discriminating on the basis of race " (*Parents Involved*, 2007, p. 21). Seven years later Justice Sonia Sotomayor, the first

Latino to serve on the U.S. Supreme Court, stated in a dissent to a majority ruling in favor of Michigan's higher education ban on affirmative action in admissions,

> The way to stop discrimination on the basis of race is to speak openly and candidly on the subject of race, and to apply the Constitution with eyes open to the unfortunate effects of centuries of racial discrimination. (as cited in Liptak, 2014, p. A12)

Critical race legal scholars Devon Carbado and Cheryl Harris (2008) explain how color blindness in college admission processes is only possible when applicants' personal statements suppress how their own racial and ethnic identities have affected their development. In effect, this process gives preference to those who choose to suppress their racial and ethnic identities, especially when Whiteness is normalized as part of a common culture.

Through a circular color-blind argument, the conservative Supreme Court essentially sanctioned school segregation by claiming that racial identification and diversity were not an important priority in a multicultural society. Civil rights scholar Gary Orfield (2013a) notes that the claim that the United States is a color-blind society is "an intellectual lie" made possible by "ignoring the obvious." Instead, Orfield explains, to end systemic racism and school segregation, critical color-conscious policies are necessary. Nevertheless, despite color-blind and postracial assertions, skin-color discrimination remains a documented fact of contemporary life (R. E. Hall, 2008), data that underpin the orientation of critical multiculturalism in its examination of structural racism.

Residential Segregation and Diversity in Schools

Segregated schools are largely a function of residential segregation and the decline in busing to achieve diversity in schools (Roberts, 2012). Whereas people regularly cross school district boundaries for personal needs, such as shopping and entertainment, the parameters of school districts are strictly bound. Yet, where most large-scale school integration plans "were well accepted by locals," the effect "had a clear tendency to increase stable residential desegregation" (Orfield, 2013b, p. 61). Court decisions against school diversity plans along with individual school-choice policies, however, undermine efforts toward residential diversity. Orfield (2013b) explains, "Color-blind choice plans permit whites to transfer out of integrated communities into more-segregated white communities, speeding white flight just like the urban open-enrollment plans of the 1960s" (p. 61).

Socioeconomic class differences generally favor Whites in making school choice decisions. While wealthy investors support choice for poor children of color in central cities, the rich "are rarely willing to allow choice for all in their schools or housing markets" (Orfield & Frankenberg, 2013, p. 260). Yet, choice options that disallow poor students of color to transfer to affluent White neighborhood schools represent "a long history of hostility to inner-city residents in suburban schools" (Rury & Mirel, 1997, p. 97). Research continues to find that for Whites the presence of other Whites in a neighborhood is more important than the quality of housing when making a neighborhood evaluation (University of Illinois, 2008). White hostility likely relates to a perception that people of color threaten norms and values of the exclusivity of White space. Nevertheless, both conservatism and liberalism explain residential segregation by race as a natural function of the invisible hand of capitalism. Hence, individualistic color-blind worldviews explain segregated neighborhood schools as simply "outcomes of the free market rather than products of a modern state-sponsored system of racial apartheid" (Lassiter & Crespino, 2010, p. 14).

With exclusionary housing patterns and tight controls over access to schools, the predominately White upper classes offer little or no choice within their own schools. Affluent neighborhoods vigorously oppose affordable housing options that spur diversity. Furthermore, people of color disproportionately were victims of bogus home loans in housing discrimination that led up to the Great Recession of 2007–2009. Substantial declines of wealth as a function of home ownership alongside a continuing economic crisis exacerbated a wealth gap between people of color and Whites. From 2007 to 2010, Latinos experienced a 40% decrease in wealth and African American wealth fell by 31%. In comparison, Whites saw a decline of 11%. During this same period, Whites, however, experienced a 9% increase in retirement savings, whereas Africans Americans and Latinos saw respective declines of 35% and 18% (McKernan, Ratcliffe, Steuerle, & Zhang, 2013). Such a dramatic loss of wealth and savings significantly affects the housing mobility of affected populations of color and, in turn, diminishes hopes for an increase in student racial diversity in public schools.

THE VALUE OF RACIAL DIVERSITY
IN SCHOOLS AND NEIGHBORHOODS

Large metropolitan regions are where an increasing number of young people live and go to school. Despite modest gains in residential diversity in metropolitan regions during the 1990s and 2000s, racialized spatial separation persisted within these areas and accounted for an estimated 75% of residential segregation between Whites and populations of color that include Latinos, African Americans, and Asians (Britton & Goldsmith, 2013; Roberts, 2012). Segregated schools of color in segregated neighborhoods have, on average, fewer resources and fewer experienced teachers than predominately White-populated schools (Orfield, Kucsera, & Siegel-Hawley, 2012). Students of color who live and learn in racially integrated schools, however, generally experience higher academic achievement than those in segregated schools (Horn & Kurlaender, 2006), a point that Justice Breyer unsuccessfully argued in his dissent against the Court's denial of Seattle's diversity plan.

Importantly for a multicultural society, research finds that reductions in prejudice and racial stereotypes and increases in civic engagement "are more likely when children experience integration from an early age" (Frankenberg, 2013, p. 552). Racially integrated communities are more accepting of diversity. In comparison to White-isolated areas, integrated communities have less expression of racism and are more open to creative opportunities in entrepreneurship and the arts. Young Whites who stay in enclaves of Whiteness generally perpetuate intergenerational White racist attitudes and espouse conformist attitudes that are opposed to differences that include alternative lifestyles (Loewen, 2005). Furthermore, teachers with a critical multiculturalist orientation who work in historically White school districts and who try to move their White student "to an anti-racist position fight an uphill battle, at best succeeding one student at a time" (Loewen, 2005, p. 333). On the other hand, adolescents who attend integrated schools and reside in diverse neighborhoods are more likely as young adults than their peers who graduated from segregated schools to move to diverse communities (Britton & Goldsmith, 2013; Frankenberg, 2013).

One week after the 1968 assassination of Dr. Martin Luther King Jr., President Lyndon Johnson signed into law the Fair Housing Act. The legislative intent was to end policies and practices that created and perpetuated racially segregated housing that negatively affected the mobility and life opportunities of people of color. Despite various efforts by the U.S. Justice Department, Frankenberg (2013) notes, "Enforcement of the Fair Housing Act has never been seriously monitored" (p. 563). She suggests that enforcement could help create more diverse neighborhoods. Additionally, a move to more "county- or regional-level school districting" can increase diversity in schools where residential segregation appears intractable (p. 562). Metropolitan regions with significant enclaves of White populations resist such redistricting plans in their conservative opposition to desegregation and the diversity it brings (Loewen, 2005). As long as both liberals and conservatives fail to provide political avenues to create more diversified neighborhoods and integrated schools (Roberts, 2012), we can anticipate that racial segregation and the accompanying isolated contact between the vast majority of Whites and people of color in schools and neighborhoods will likely remain a feature of American life into the 2020s. Critical multicultural critiques continue, nevertheless, to incorporate 21st-century racial and economic apartheid in housing and schooling into standpoint analyses that seek to overturn such entrenched practices.

Next, we turn to the relationship between an individual's racial or ethnic identification and the criminal justice system and how this relationship has filtered into public school disciplinary practices.

CHAPTER 4

The Color of Criminalization and School Discipline

> What turns me cold in all this experience is the certainty that
> thousands of innocent victims are in jail today because they had
> neither money nor friends to help them. . . . There is desperate
> need of nationwide organizations to oppose this national racket of
> railroading to jails and chain gangs the poor, friendless and black.
>
> —W. E. B. Du Bois, *In Battle for Peace*

Worldviews differ on interpretations of what constitutes *a crime* and *a just punishment*. To better understand how dominant ideologies develop a legal framework to determine criminality in relation to racial identification, this chapter begins with a descriptive history that constructed African Americans as criminals. The historical record of arrests and incarceration in the United States is worthy to recall in order to grasp the racial disparities that exist in public school suspension and expulsion rates and their connections to a *school-to-prison pipeline*.

To explain the process of criminalization since the end of the Civil War, we consider a neo-Confederate narrative of Black criminality and White victimization along with racial profiling. We then examine, in a context of racial disparities and the effects on children, reasons behind the United States' having the world's highest rates of incarceration. The school-to-prison-pipeline analysis follows an inquiry into the lasting effects of juvenile justice on arrested and incarcerated youth. These sections survey attitudes and practices of dominant political orientations, beginning with a historical perspective.

HISTORICAL PATTERN OF CRIMINALIZATION OF AFRICAN AMERICANS

Dating back to the North American British colonies, laws separated White populations and people of African descent. In *White by Law*, López (2006) explains that law-making processes attached racial meanings to individual phenotype or physical features. The 1600s in the colonies marks the beginning of the criminalization of dark-skinned populations. Legalized corporal punishment could result from evidence of any cooperation or relationships between the White English and Black African populations.

Black slaves were legally constructed as a criminal class, a category eventually extended to all people of color. The colony of Virginia set the tone for the next 4 centuries by justifying physical punishment of African Americans, including disciplinary actions that could result in death. A 1669 Virginia law specified that if a slave "should chance to die" in the process of "correction" by a White person, the African American's "death shall not be accounted a felony, but the master (or that other person appointed by the master to punish him) be acquitted from molestation" ("Virginia Slave Laws," para. 10). The 1705 Virginia Slave code added that such a murder at the hands of a White person would be as if it "had never happened" (Virginia General Assembly, 1705, p. 459). If, however, any person of color, free or slave, "lift his or her hand, in opposition against any Christian, not being negro, mulatto, or Indian, he or she so offending, shall, for every such offence . . . receive on his or her bare back, thirty lashes, well laid on" (p. 1459). By the mid-1770s, "the main result of slave insurrections, throughout the Americas, was the mass execution of blacks" (Horsmanden, 2013, para. 4). The colonial and then U.S. rule of law denied African American self-defense testimonies. In 1853 an abolitionist lamented that it appeared as if "civil government were designed for human demoralization and torture" (Goodell, 1853, p. 308).

In 1861 southern states declared their independence from the United States, formed the Confederate States of America (CSA), and sought international recognition as the only explicitly *proslavery* nation-state formed in the modern era. Jefferson Davis, the president of the CSA and a former U.S. senator and secretary of war, contended that people of African descent were incapable of governing themselves. The CSA constructed slaves as "*domestic enemies* against whom the state adopted a posture of self-protection" (McCurry, 2010, p. 219, emphasis added).

Shortly after the Civil War, the southern planter class was pardoned by President Andrew Johnson and allowed to retain their land. White political leaders sent warnings to the North to be wary of freed slaves as unwelcome and criminal refugees. Southern states enacted laws on vagrancy and used contracts in an effort to keep freed slaves on plantations and under White control. Many former slaves were now landless and forced to enter contracts for their survival. The nature of these contracts continued to restrict the civil liberties of African Americans (e.g., Freedmen's Bureau Online, n.d.). African Americans who remained in former slave states and ended up working on plantations were subjected to peonage, a system similar to slavery in its restrictions of basic freedoms. Under peonage, plantation owners put former slaves into a debt system in which they could rarely repay what they supposedly owed for such items as room, board, and farming supplies.

From the Reconstruction era to World War II, law officials systematical-
ly arrested African Americans for such charges as being homeless or unemployed and in numerous instances returned them to a condition of slavery.
Essentially, police in former slave states arrested African Americans for nearly
any charge; judges then found the African Americans guilty and required
them to pay a fine. When payment of a fine was financially impossible, a
convict leasing system permitted private owners of lumber camps, farms, and
mines to pay the fine and then place the now criminalized Black person in
a private prison to work off his fine. Rarely did these incarcerated African
Americans escape from what were essentially 19th- and 20th-century slave
labor death camps. Douglas Blackmon (2008), author of the Pulitzer Prize–
winning *Slavery by Another Name*, summarized that Blacks under such arrest
conditions were incarcerated in "free labor camps that functioned like prisons,
cotton tenancy that equated to serfdom, or prison mines filled with slaves"
(p. 300). Apparently this history is too telling, so much so that in 2011 state
officials denied a White Alabama inmate access to Blackmon's book on the
grounds that it was "too incendiary" and "too provocative" (Robertson, 2011,
para. 8).

Throughout much of the 20th century, state and town laws and practices
across the United States criminalized freed African Americans if they entered
spaces reserved for Whites such as partitioned areas in public libraries, theaters,
hospitals, restaurants, and public schools. Moreover, states such as Mississippi
made advocacy for social equality among the races illegal: a person "guilty of
printing, publishing or circulating matter urging or presenting arguments in
favor of social equality or of intermarriage between Whites and negroes, shall
be guilty of a misdemeanor" and could be subject to a $500 fine and 6 months
in prison (National Park Service, 2013, para. 28). Well into the 20th century,
every state had towns in which Whites could legally terrorize Blacks who were
present after sunset (Loewen, 2005). Not until the mid-1960s did the federal
government begin to periodically intervene to protect some of the civil liberties
of African Americans.

NEO-CONFEDERATE NARRATIVE OF THE BLACK CRIMINAL

Thomas Dixon's (1905) *The Clansman: An Historical Romance of the Ku Klux Klan*
was a work of fiction that presented freed male slaves as criminals who preyed
on White women. After White audiences watched *The Clansman* performed as
a play, terrorism against Blacks often ensued. *The Clansman* served as the basis
for the 1915 silent film *The Birth of a Nation* (Griffith, 1915/2002), a film widely
praised and studied in colleges today for its groundbreaking editing techniques
and cinematography. Similar riots ensued after the film was shown in such cities

as Boston and Philadelphia. Dixon was pleased to learn of these White riots and confessed, "The real purpose of my film was to revolutionize Northern audiences that would transform every man into a Southern partisan for life" (as cited in Wormser, 2002, para. 2).

Quoted in *The Birth of a Nation* is President Woodrow Wilson (1913–1921), who had reinstituted racial segregation in the federal government and had earlier rationalized that the Ku Klux Klan (KKK) "began to attempt by intimidation what they were not allowed to attempt by the ballot or by any ordered course of public action" (Wilson, 1902, p. 59). Projected in this film was the president's quote that "white men were roused by the mere instinct of self-preservation . . . until at last there had sprung into existence a great Ku Klux Klan, a veritable empire of the South, to protect the Southern country" (pp. 58, 60). Dixon, Wilson's good friend and former college classmate, arranged for *The Birth of a Nation* to be the first film shown in the White House. In that film the KKK marches proudly past the White House (Stokes, 2007).

A widely circulated neo-Confederate narrative is a mythic story in which Whites are the benevolent providers for African Americans. Charles Blow (2013), a commentator on contemporary popular culture, observes how this trope finds rearticulation today—even by a costar of a widely viewed "reality" television show whose interview statements "conjure the insidious mythology of historical Southern fiction, that of contented slave and benevolent master, of the oppressed and the oppressor gleefully abiding the oppression, happily accepting their wildly variant social stations" (p. A19). The problem, according to a neo-Confederate narrative, is the upsetting of the social order by the Civil War and the Civil Rights Movement. With the racial hierarchy askew, African Americans supposedly turned on the Whites who "cared" for them. In this telling, Whites were victims of Black crime.

Aspects of a neo-Confederate discourse are useful within social conservatism as a justification for "law and order." This narrative contrasts with the actual historical actions of White males, especially those associated with the planter class, who raped and impregnated Black women and murdered Black males with impunity (Blackmon, 2008; Harris, 1993). Between 1877 and 1966 in Georgia, for example, only one White man was ever found guilty of killing a Black man despite numerous instances of murders that included lynching (Blackmon, 2008). (In 2005 the U.S. Congress officially apologized for the lynching of African Americans.) By the 1960s, a

> pro-white strategy emphasized the interests of whites in southern states as well as in much of suburbia in all states, with influential and widely used code words like "states' rights," "busing," "racial quotas," and "crime in streets," all of which explicitly or implicitly referenced antiblack images, stereotypes, or narratives from an old white framing of society. (Feagin, 2012, p. 70)

Emblematic of a neo-Confederate discourse, these "narratives from an old white framing" continued to find traction into the 2010s through mainstream media and various political circles.

The staying power of a neo-Confederate narrative in social conservatism switches the historical realities to that of White victimization. An explanation for this curious but significant storytelling rests on the upheaval of centuries of White supremacy and privilege. African American struggles for human and civil rights disrupted a socially conservative world of White power normalcy that held people of color in various forms of subordination. The social change that upset this authoritarian arrangement eventually resulted in a type of "social amnesia" (Werz, 2004, p. 221) that facilitated denial of centuries of a complex history of racialization and White nationalism. From a critical perspective, nationalism and "ethnic or religious fundamentalism are always bound up with the experiences of historic defeats" and contribute to the formation of a new identity that "is based on forgetting" (p. 221), in this case a neo-Confederate identity that circulates across all regions of the United States.

A neo-Confederate narrative contributes to the perception that a White-led power structure must watch and control African Americans and other people of color. This narrative justifies school and police actions that detain individuals on the basis of their skin-color phenotype, a practice commonly referred to as racial profiling.

Parameters of Racial Profiling

Racial profiling is "the targeting of individuals and groups by law enforcement officials, even partially, on the basis of race, ethnicity, national origin, or religion" (Amnesty International, 2004, p. v). The UN (2009) describes two specific forms of racial profiling in the United States. Most common is "the practice [that] targets predominantly African American or Hispanic minorities, generally but not exclusively in stops and searches by local and state police" (p. 16). A second form is domestic "antiterrorism" actions that primarily target "people of Arab, Muslim, South Asian or Middle-Eastern descent" (p. 16). Representing approximately 11% of the U.S. population, 32 million people reported racial profiling experiences (Amnesty International, 2004). An orientation in critical multiculturalism contends that racial profiling today is an extension of the legacy of White supremacist legal and extralegal practices. The result is an unprecedented number of incarcerated U.S. citizens relative to the rest of the world.

World's Largest Prison Population

With 5% of the world's population, the United States holds 25% of the planet's incarcerated population (National Association for the Advancement of Colored

People [NAACP], 2013). The U.S. prison and jail population soared during the 1980s, and this expansion continued into the 2010s (Schmitt, Warner, & Gupta, 2010). In 2012, according to the U.S. Department of Justice, 6,937,600 adults constituted the correctional population. This breaks down to 1 in every 35 adults in the United States, or 2.9% of adult residents, on probation or parole or incarcerated in prison or jail–the same rate recorded in 1997 (Glaze & Herberman, 2013, p. 1). As the mid-2010s approached, 2,870 adults per 100,000 residents were currently under some form of correctional supervision (p. 2).

In comparison to all other nations, the United States has the highest percentage of its population imprisoned. The United States incarcerates its adult citizens at a rate of 753 per 100,000 residents, significantly more than second-place Russia at 629. When comparisons are limited to nations that are part of the Organisation for Economic Co-Operation and Development (OECD), second place falls to Poland at a distant 224 (Schmitt et al., 2010). Among those with the lowest incarceration rates, Japan has just 63 per 100,000 and Germany has 90 (Schmitt et al., 2010). In 2009, 80% of the 1,660,000 U.S. drug arrests were for simple possession (Zakaria, 2012).

A data analysis by Schmitt et al. (2010) reveals that increases in crime alone cannot explain the historically unprecedented rise in incarceration. Using 1980 as a base year, they note that by 1992 there was a 44% increase in violent crime and a 7% increase in property crime. Yet, during the same time period, 1980 to 1992, the incarceration rate jumped more than 150%. Even with a drop in violent-crime rates below population growth from the late 1990s to 2008, incarceration rates continued to increase. From 1980 to 2008, the number of incarcerated individuals grew by 350% in comparison to a 33% increase in the total population.

Incarceration rates remain at this high level despite a U.S. Justice Department report that noted 2010 represented the nation's first annual decline–a miniscule 0.03%–in its prison population since 1972 (Goode, 2013; Guerino, Harrison, & Sabol, 2012). Criminal justice observers are not in agreement as to whether a small decline is a function of budgetary concerns or a reflection of less punitive approaches to violations of the law. A critical observer of the criminal justice system contends that the changes in overall incarceration rates were "relatively modest compared to the scale of the problem" (Mauer, as cited in Goode, 2013, p. A10).

The Reagan administration's "war on drugs," initiated during the 1980s, explains how the United States developed the highest rates of incarceration in the world and criminalized individuals for nonviolent drug possession and use. From 1980 to 1997, drug arrests rose nearly 1,000% (Zakaria, 2012). During the more than 30-year period of the war on drugs, young people of color were disproportionately singled out or profiled for arrest and jailing. For the year 2010 alone, Blacks were four times more likely than Whites to be arrested for marijuana possession (Urbina, 2013). Furthermore, "drug offenses committed near the urban areas that contain many communities of color are prosecuted more harshly than similar offenses in rural communities populated largely by whites" (Mauer & King, 2007, p. 17). Additionally, "zero tolerance" policies and mandatory sentencing laws for nonviolent crimes contributed to this difference.

Prison or School Funding? As an aspect of the drug war, federal agencies provided police and private prisons with incentives for arrest and conviction quotas. Police departments received surplus military hardware and other material rewards for drug-associated arrests. Based on the number of inmates that they house, including detained immigrants, private prisons in particular profit with this transfer of public funds (Alexander, 2010; Jarecki, 2012; Levine, 2013; Urbina, 2013). If, however, just half of incarcerated nonviolent offenders were moved to probation or parole, the public would realize an estimated *savings of $16.9 billion*, a figure that represents 22.8% of all spending on incarceration (Schmitt et al., 2010, p. 11).

The U.S. Supreme Court deemed as "cruel and unusual" overcrowding in California prisons. Instead of redirecting the savings from the early release of nonviolent prisoners, liberal governor Jerry Brown sought to use the funds to build new prisons. He also diverted a publicly supported proposition that raised taxes to provide needed funding for schools to an expansion of privately run prisons. This political economy decision is in the context of a state that is 49th in spending per student (Bezabler, 2013).

Race and Incarceration. Racial disparity exists within the population of those incarcerated. Census data indicates that Whites make up 64% of the U.S. general population but constitute just 39% of the total incarcerated population. In contrast, Blacks represent 13% of the general population yet comprise 40% of those imprisoned, a difference 5 times higher than Whites. Overall, this translates into the United States incarcerating Whites at a rate of 450 per 100,000. This figure compares to 831 per 100,000 Latinos and 2,306 for every 100,000 Blacks (Sakala, 2014). Looking just at males 18 to 64 years old, the rate of incarceration is 1.1% for Whites, or 1 in 87; 8% for Blacks, or 1 in 12; and 2.7% for Latinos, or 1 in 36. Most telling are the figures for 20 to 34-year-old males without a high school diploma or its equivalency. For that age bracket of individuals who have not graduated from high school, the rate of incarceration is 12% for Whites, or 1 in 8; 37.1% for Blacks, or 1 in 3; and 7% for Latinos, or 1 in 14, (Pew Charitable Trusts, 2010).

The U.S. government has acknowledged to the international community that a racial disparity exists within the criminal justice system. In a report to the UN, the U.S. Department of State (2007) noted that "the reasons for the disparities in incarceration rates are complex" but contended that this was not due to "differential handling of persons in the criminal justice system" (p. 59). The UN (2009) noted that U.S. police conducted traffic stops at similar rates for individuals from different racially identified groups. Nevertheless, "black and Hispanic drivers were approximately 2.5 times more likely to be searched [than White drivers]; the rate of arrests was two times higher for blacks and 50 percent higher for Hispanics; blacks were 3.5 times more likely and Hispanics were almost 2 times more likely to experience use of police force" (pp. 14–15). The UN report further chronicled research that indicated the existence of racial discrimination in sentencing and "that individuals belonging to minorities tend to be disadvantaged in terms of the decision to incarcerate or not and in receiving harsher sentences than white individuals with comparable social and economic status" (p. 15). The UN findings confirm an overall pattern of racial profiling in the United States.

THE CRIMINAL JUSTICE SYSTEM AND YOUNG PEOPLE

Research reveals material and developmental harm to children of incarcerated parents. As a result of having an incarcerated parent, an adolescent is likely to experience negative development in regard to "working productively with others," controlling "expressions of emotions," developing a "cohesive identity," resolving "conflicts with family and society," and engaging "in adult work and relationships" (Travis, McBride, & Solomon, 2005, p. 3). The repercussions for such children can create a legacy of intergenerational exposure to the criminal justice system.

The juvenile criminal justice system mirrors the adult system but often with less protection afforded than in adult due-process procedures. Adolescents of color experience significant disparities within the juvenile justice system. African Americans account for 16% of the youth population but represent 45% of juvenile arrests—a nearly 300% difference (NAACP, 2005). The UN (2009) observed that for juveniles

> the rate of African Americans serving life without parole sentences is on average 10 times higher than whites, relative to the state population. In California, the rate is 18 times that of white youth. Even after controlling for differences in murder arrest rates, racial disparities remain. (p. 16)

Moreover, the U.S. juvenile system generally treats young people more harshly and commits more human rights violations, on average, in comparison to other countries.

Human Rights Violations of Children

Along with other members of the UN General Assembly, the United States supported an international human rights principle that states, "Deprivation of the liberty of a juvenile should be a disposition of last resort and for the minimum necessary period and should be limited to exceptional cases" (UN, 1990, article 2). The UN (1990) resolution explicitly declares,

> All disciplinary measures constituting cruel, inhuman or degrading treatment shall be strictly prohibited, including corporal punishment, placement in a dark cell, closed or solitary confinement or any other punishment that may *compromise the physical or mental health of the juvenile* concerned. (article 67, emphasis added)

The U.S. juvenile justice system, however, regularly violates this agreement. Human rights violations of children include life sentences without parole, solitary confinement, shackling, and the lack of legal representation in judicial hearings.

Life Without Parole. In the 21st century the United States remained as the only nation in the world that sentenced individuals under the age of 18 to life in prison without the possibility of parole (Human Rights Watch, 2012b). The U.S. Supreme Court in 2012 did rule unconstitutional *mandatory* life sentences for certain crimes committed by a minor. However, life sentences in general without parole for juveniles were not ruled unconstitutional (DiLeonardo, 2012; Pomy, 2013).

Solitary Confinement. Even without a life sentence, young people are irreparably harmed and denied human rights protections in the juvenile justice system. In violation of the UN agreement that the United States signed, children reside in solitary confinement for multiple days, weeks, and months for 21 to 24 hours per day (Human Rights Watch, 2012a). In some instances school-age individuals reside in solitary confinement *before* conviction of a crime; in extreme cases this has extended for nearly 2 years. In one known case, a convicted 13-year-old Latino spent the next 15 years in solitary confinement (Solitary Watch, 2012). Human Rights Watch (2012a) reports that "the conditions that compound the harm of solitary confinement (such as lack of psychological care, physical exercise, family contact, and education) often constitute independent, concurrent, and serious human rights violations" (p. 5).

In comparison to the general population, adolescents in solitary confinement are 19 times more likely to commit suicide (Solitary Watch, 2012). In one instance a youth incarcerated for the nonviolent crime of stealing a bicycle took his own life while in solitary confinement (Hanna, 2013). International legal bodies that include the UN Committee on Torture consistently call for a reduction in the length of solitary confinement or the outright abolition of what many legal experts understand as cruel and inhumane treatment. At a fundamental level, human existence involves social contact with others. Solitary confinement goes developmentally against this basic social-psychological human need, especially under conditions that unconstitutionally deny young people meaningful due-process reviews (Lobel, 2008).

Shackling. Although shackling in the 19th century punished boys in particular, today it is not technically a punishment but rather a method of restraint. Hence, the juvenile justice system can place children in custody in shackles. Regardless of the risk a young person may pose, the majority of states permit the use of mechanical restraints such as chains on the hands, waist, and feet. Just five states "give defendants the right to a hearing on whether they should be shackled" (Ecenbarger, 2012, p. 251). The National Defender Center describes the effects of shackling as "repugnant, degrading, humiliating, and contrary to the stated primary purposes of juvenile justice system and to the principles of therapeutic justice" (as cited in Ecenbarger, 2012, p. 250). Furthermore, legal and child advocate opponents of shackling note that "routine shackling practice is punishment before a finding of guilt" (Gallagher & Lore, 2008, p. 460).

Lack of Legal Representation. Accused children and their parents often do not understand the educational and life opportunity consequences of juvenile incarceration and waive their rights to legal representation. Only three states "totally forbid juveniles to decline legal representation" (Ecenbarger, 2012, p. 248). Moreover, closed hearings designed to protect a young person's privacy can result in unfair outcomes for an accused child when legal counsel is absent.

Developmental Implications. Courts and legislatures are gradually beginning to acknowledge the effects of juvenile arrests and incarcerations on the social and psychological development of young people. Specifically, in the case of mandatory life sentences, some judges recognize that "three fundamental features of youth—lack of maturity, vulnerability to negative influences and capacity for change—make children 'constitutionally different' from adults and 'less deserving of the most severe punishments'" (Moriearty, 2012, para. 3). Writing in *Clinical Psychology Review*, Lambie and Randell (2013) reviewed factors that hinder the development of incarcerated youth and point out that

> incarceration, isolation, boredom, bullying, and victimization are pervasive stressors and, given the permeable and transitory nature of adolescent identity and self-esteem, incarceration can have a negative long-term effect on a young person's sense of self and self-worth. (p. 453)

When adolescents are moved to an adult facility, their mental health further deteriorates. Although educational programs have a rehabilitative effect on adolescent offenders, these programs do not provide an equal education, especially "for incarcerated youths, who are characterized by significant learning, behavioral, and cognitive problems" (p. 454). For adolescents released from incarceration, the return to society is difficult because incarceration disrupted a high school education necessary for gainful employment. Returning to unstable social environments without a diploma and with possible learning challenges along with an arrest and conviction record combine to make it nearly impossible to secure gainful employment and transition into civic life.

The criminal justice system for both adults and juveniles reflects racial disparity consistent with racial profiling, a practice that spilled into public schools.

School-to-Prison Pipeline

The school-to-prison pipeline "refers to the policies and practices that push our nation's schoolchildren, especially our most at-risk children, out of classrooms and into the juvenile and criminal justice systems" (American Civil Liberties Union, 2008, para. 1). What once was normal childhood and adolescent misbehavior at home or in school today can be grounds for arrest and placement in a juvenile detention center. A review of recent research indicates that suspended or expelled students have a 300% higher likelihood than their peers of having a direct experience with the juvenile justice system within 1 year (Koon, 2013).

Between 1973 and 2010 the number of students suspended from schools more than doubled, with millions of students affected annually (Koon, 2013). Accentuating this increase was *zero tolerance*, "a policy of mandatory punishment for given offenses without regard to the special circumstances of the individual" (Ecenbarger, 2012, p. 39). During the 2009–2010 academic year, California school administrators alone suspended 400,000 students. Despite color-blind polices of zero tolerance for misbehavior and an overall peak in the rate of suspensions and expulsions during the 1990s, the rate for African American youth increased during the past 20 years. Native Americans and Latinos were also overrepresented in school suspensions (Koon, 2013).

Low-economic status is associated with racial disparities in suspensions and expulsions, especially in urban school districts that serve poor neighborhoods. Nevertheless, "the racial discipline gap tends to be the same size or even larger in wealthier suburban school districts" (Koon, 2013, p. 5). Schools with a high population of students of color have gone "from rehabilitation and services to criminalization" (p. 3). The presence of police in schools is associated with "a surge in arrests or misdemeanor charges for essentially non-violent behavior . . . that sends children into criminal courts" (Eckholm, 2013, p. A1). In making this change from a focus on providing young people with counseling and using other nonpunitive methods of handling disciplinary complaints, schools operate tacitly under a neo-Confederate narrative that has increased schools' "use of crime control technology, personnel, and procedures, paralleling a larger political shift in public policy" (Koon, 2013, p. 3).

The significance of this is that a school that places an increased emphasis on punishment affects achievement. Compared to other students, suspended students miss more classroom instructional time and are more likely to drop out of school. On the other hand, low suspension rates were generally related to schools that support students in meeting high academic standards (Gregory, Cornell, & Fan, 2011). Only recently have large urban school districts started to rethink policies that criminalize students for minor infractions of school rules (Alvarez, 2013).

IDEOLOGICAL PERSPECTIVES ON CAUSES OF CRIMINALIZATION OF YOUTH

Social conservatism's stance on crime and punishment fits within an ideology that places the protection of private property through a very strong police and military as one of its highest priorities for public expenditures. According to social conservatism, the disproportionately high number of people of color in U.S. prisons is a result of strict enforcement of laws, reasoning that extends to the infraction of school rules. Social conservatism strongly supports the use of physical punishment in schools (cf. Republican Party of Texas, 2012).

Liberal multiculturalism throughout most of the 20th century acquiesced to conservatism's tough-on-crime position under a discourse that claimed the fairness of the criminal justice system and the rule of law. Notwithstanding critiques offered from a perspective of critical multiculturalism, decades passed during which ideologies of social conservatism and liberal multiculturalism allowed systemic violations of internationally recognized principles of equal and humane treatment before the law. In a liberal democracy, when human rights violations go unchecked, profits for private prisons and governmental corruption go unnoticed. For example, in one of the most extreme abuses of the system, two juvenile court judges received an estimated $2.8 million from 2003 to 2008 through a kickback scheme that unfairly incarcerated youth in privately run detention centers (Ecenbarger, 2012).

Misapplication of Political Psychology

Apparently individuals influenced by conservatism or liberalism are susceptible to specious arguments such as "the genetic basis of criminal behavior is now well established" (Raine, 2013, para. 9). For example, a federal judge's perspective that "racial groups like African-Americans and Hispanics are predisposed to crime" demonstrates the internalization of this belief (Jones, as cited in Bronner, 2013, p. A17). Research, however, indicates that "the relationship between genes and brain structures does not remotely reflect a simple 'gene-for' model" (Churchland, 2013b, para. 13). Furthermore, claims that brain scans prove physiological differences between an identified criminal and a law-abiding citizen (e.g., Raine, 2013) apparently do not take into account that variability in brain structures do "not predict *anything* about brain function" (Churchland, 2013a, para. 6; also, cf. Chapter 1, this book).

The contemporary misuse of political psychology compares to the eugenics movement of a century ago that also espoused a genetic basis for criminal behavior. In 1989, mainstream journalists introduced this fear-based, neo-Confederate narrative by referring to criminalized youth of color as a "new breed" of adolescents who were "wilding" their behavior" (Moriearty, 2010, p. 851). Ideologically conservative and liberal genetic color-blind explanations for criminal behavior, however a society defines it, are suspect. From a critical multicultural perspective, genetic explanations merely serve as distracting masks for the actual reasons that lie beneath racial disparities in arrests and sentencing.

A Shift in Liberal Multiculturalism

For those oriented toward liberal multiculturalism, an attitudinal shift took place by the 2010s. During this period, a melding of concern of liberal multiculturalists with more critical perspectives emerged over a racial disparity in arrests and convictions. Representative of this change is Michelle Alexander (2010), author of the best-selling book *The New Jim Crow: Mass Incarceration in the Age of Colorblindness*. Alexander, an African American law professor, admits to how an orientation based in liberal multiculturalism helped her initially dismiss a historical pattern of Black criminalization. She originally considered such claims as "absurd" and simply too "radical" (p. 3). Over time, however, Alexander critically reflected, "Quite belatedly, I came to see that mass incarceration in the United States had, in fact, emerged as a stunningly comprehensive and well-disguised system of racialized control that functions in a manner strikingly similar to Jim Crow" (p. 4). Liberal multiculturalism's belief in slow but steady advancements in race relations had the effect of making a racially disproportional U.S. prisons population appear "well-disguised" ideologically. Approaches of liberal multiculturalism allowed decades of a color blindness that passively responded to claims of out-of-control violent youth.

White Color Blindness. Because the huge growth in arrests and incarceration stemmed from possession of small quantities of marijuana and because victims of these arrests were overwhelming young and of color, many Whites were shielded from awareness of the approximately 10 million marijuana arrests from 1997–2012, an average of 700,000 each year. Sociologist Harry Levine (2013) explains, "The news media don't report on these cases," which "makes it difficult for many white Americans to believe so many people are being arrested" (p. 20). Added to this White-privileged color blindness is a shielding of arrest and incarceration data by police, prosecutors, and democratically elected officials (Alexander, 2010; Levine, 2013). Furthermore, liberal scientists and groups advocating for decriminalization of marijuana possession–who are nearly all White–publicly express what psychologist Carl Hart (2013) considers "apathy about pot arrest racism" (p. 17).

Under a critical multicultural analysis, the prison system is racist and far from color blind (Burton-Rose, Pens, & Wright, 1998; A. Davis, Magee, the Soledad Brothers, & Other Political Prisoners, 1971; Samuels, 2010). As early as 1970, critical theorist Herbert Marcuse critiqued the discourse on crime of both conservatism and liberalism:

> The language of the prevailing Law and Order, validated by the courts and by the police, is not only the voice but also the deed of suppression. This language not only defines and condemns the Enemy, it also *creates* him; and this creation is not the Enemy as he really is but rather as he must be in order to perform his function for the Establishment. (p. 74)

Marcuse called attention to the established dominant political order created under conservatism and liberalism that criminalized marginalized populations outside the mainstream as an "enemy" of the state.

"Super-Predator" Youth. Over time, young people of color were constructed as criminals–enemies to avoid and lock up. Based in part on a 1990s mainstream narrative of youthful criminals as "super-predators," nearly every U.S. state passed laws that permitted a child arrested for certain crimes to be tried as an adult (Moriearty, 2012, para 5). Political science professor John Dilulio (1995), a driving force behind this assertion, proudly announced,

> No one in academia is a bigger fan of incarceration than I am. Between 1985 and 1991 the number of juveniles in custody increased from 49,000 to nearly 58,000. By my estimate, we will probably need to incarcerate at least 150,000 juvenile criminals in the years just ahead. In deference to public safety, we will have *little choice but to pursue genuine get-tough law-enforcement strategies against the super-predators.* (para. 41, emphasis added)

Operating from an ideology of social conservatism with a neo-Confederate framing, Dilulio concluded that the basic cause of juvenile crime was due to "moral poverty" and that the solution was the Judeo-Christian tradition because "churches can help cure or curtail many severe socioeconomic ills" (paras. 21, 35). Yet, from 1994 to 2011, murders committed by young people actually declined by two-thirds during Dilulio's predicted rise (Haberman, 2014).

Therefore, by the 2010s, liberal multicultural positions pushed back against the negative outcomes for young people of criminal justice policies and solutions offered under social conservatism.

The immediate concern of critical multiculturalism is the fate of children of color who live in a racialized liberal democracy where the odds are currently three to one that an African American boy's future includes arrest and incarceration. Historically, dominant conservative and liberal ideologies do not explain negative life opportunities for young people of color on the grounds of deficiencies in school discipline policies and the juvenile justice system. Instead, according to law professor Perry Moriearty (2010), mainstream worldviews construct juveniles of color as "inherently more deviant than their white counterparts" (p. 906).

TOWARD RESTORATIVE JUSTICE

The past 4 decades witnessed a privileging of socially conservative discourse and a relatively mild response under liberal multiculturalism to an ongoing legacy of civil liberty and human rights violations of people of color that date back to the colonial era and the founding of the United States. Operating under ideologies that disproportionately criminalized adults and youth of color, the school-to-prison pipeline reflects "the prioritization of incarceration over education" (ACLU, 2008, para. 1). Attempts from a critical multicultural orientation to seek nonpunitive *restorative justice alternatives* in juvenile and school systems of justice demonstrate some positive gains against the staying power of social conservatism (Ross & Zimmerman, 2014).

We conclude with 15 recommendations that originate from a combination of liberal and critical multicultural solution-driven orientations as a way to reverse the criminalization of youth in general and those of color specifically. Human Rights Watch (2012a) offers the following recommendations:

1. Prohibit the solitary confinement of youth under age 18.
2. Prohibit the housing of adolescents with adults . . . in jails and prisons designed to house adults.
3. Strictly limit and regulate all forms of segregation and isolation of young people.
4. Monitor and report on the segregation and isolation of adolescents.
5. Ratify human rights treaties protecting young people without reservations. (p. 6)

Based on a review of the negative effects of juvenile criminalization, this list also includes these additional recommendations:

6. Provide legal counsel in all juvenile arrest cases. (Ecenbarger, 2012)
7. Decriminalize recreational drug use, especially marijuana, as some states have initiated. ("Let States Decide on Marijuana," 2014)
8. Remove completely arrest and incarceration public records for nonviolent youth offenders.(cf. American Bar Association, 2012)
9. Educate legislators to cost savings when releasing just half of nonviolent offenders from prisons. (Schmitt et al., 2010)
10. Increase public school funding and educational opportunities for incarcerated youth. (Lambie & Randell, 2013)
11. Stop the criminalization of normal child and adolescent student behavior. (cf. Eckholm, 2013)
12. Promote meaningful educational and job training opportunities for prisoners. (Lambie & Randell, 2013)
13. Grant to all prisoners, including felons, the right to vote, to increase civic engagement. (Cha & Kennedy, 2014)
14. Provide former inmates necessary social supports to transition back into their communities when released from prison. (Lambie & Randell, 2013)
15. Institute restorative justice that focuses on the needs of both victims and offenders as a community alternative. (Lambie & Randell, 2013; Moriearty, 2010)

Despite the feasibility of these 15 recommendations, rarely are community-based interventions implemented despite the evidence-based research that "the retention of offenders in the community and provision of such interventions is likely to result in the most desirable outcomes for both the offender and the community" (Lambie & Randell, 2013, p. 456). Socially conservative get-tough-on-crime-through-"boot-camp" programs show no positive effects on recidivism rates and in some cases result in an increase in recidivism. Instead, Lambie and Randell advocate for restorative justice because

> involving family group conferencing processes may provide a means of processing juvenile criminal behavior whereby the needs and wishes of the victim are apparent, the rehabilitative needs of the offender considered, and an acceptable outcome is settled that considers values of both reparation and rehabilitation. (p. 456)

This is radically different from the punitive system that now faces diverse young people who get caught up in the criminal justice system initiated in their schools and neighborhoods.

Poverty often correlates with criminality, an economic condition that disproportionately affects populations of color. We therefore turn next to socioeconomic class and culture as causes for differentiated treatment.

CHAPTER 5

Bad Math:
Equating Culture and Class

The most difficult cultural processes to examine are the ones that are based on confident and unquestioned assumptions stemming from one's own community's practices.

—Barbara Rogoff, *The Cultural Nature of Human Development*

The concept of diversity includes the interrelated concepts of culture, economic well-being, and educational achievement. In 2010 a front-page headline in the *New York Times* declared, "'Culture of Poverty' Makes a Comeback" (P. Cohen, p. A1). The *Times* report was in response to a special issue of the *Annals of the American Academy of Political and Social Science* in which sociologists revived studies that link poverty with culture by looking at microstructural conditions to explain why poor people, especially those who are of color, struggle economically and educationally (see Small, Harding, & Lamont, 2010). The concept of a culture of poverty equates *culture* with socioeconomic *class*, the latter signaled by access to economic resources. Multicultural studies often reference the differential effects of socioeconomic class on schoolchildren. Yet, the relation between class and economic conditions and the worldviews that contribute to the *formation of different classes* is a relatively unexplored diversity and multicultural topic.

Gorski's (2013) extensive review of research reveals that "*there is no such thing as a culture of poverty*" (p. 55, emphasis in original). Then, we have to ask, why assert a culture-of-poverty thesis against objective data? To explore this question, we are interested in the ideological connections among culture, economic status, and academic achievement. Educators, sociologists, economists, anthropologists, psychologists, policymakers, and political commentators offer various perspectives about the underlying importance of culture and class in relationship to educational and vocational prospects. Studying various worldviews unravels different explanations about culture and class and their combined ideological linkages to economic and educational circumstances.

Because many public school students come from families trying to meet basic economic needs, the immediacy of this diversity topic is germane to the future of millions of our children. From 2000 to 2010, for example, American children in the United States living in poverty increased by 57% (Institute for Children, Poverty, and Homelessness, 2013). Twenty-two percent of all children, or 16 million, live in poverty. When combined with low-income families, *45% of all children live in economically poor families.* For the families of these 34 million children, research indicates that economic resources are inadequate to meet some of their most basic needs. The percentages of children within racial categories who are poor are just over 30% for Whites and Asians and approximately 65% for Blacks, Latinos, and Native Americans (Addy et al., 2013). At the same time, the U.S. Congress reduced by $5 billion a food program that served 47 million Americans who experience food insecurity (Nixon, 2014). Yet, not all people perceive this condition as a crisis or as unnatural.

To better understand how different orientations view culture and class, including economic indicators of poverty, we return to our typology of social conservatism, liberal multiculturalism, and critical multiculturalism. Any discussion of varying orientations toward diversity and differences must, however, first wade into the murky definitional concept of culture. Following this, we examine cultural justifications for inequality that include the role of academia alongside the origins and applications of social Darwinism. This leads us to consider the effects of the culture-of-poverty concept on both economic and educational policies and practices. Finally, we reconsider the Civil Rights Freedom Budget and the progress the United States has made today in meeting the objectives of that proposal and what this means for the future of our children.

CONCEPTUAL ORIGINS OF CULTURE

Like the concept of diversity, culture is equally contested. Conflated in various ways with diversity, *culture* gained academic usage during the 19th century to explain European and U.S. colonial encounters with people of color. Early studies of anthropology used culture in a seemingly neutral way to capture "the sense of the totality of society's knowledge and beliefs, growing through innovations and intergenerational transmission" that included "the fundamental values guiding human behavior" (Wallach, 2005, p. 14). A common mainstream element to definitions of culture incorporated racialized identifications attached to population groups. The conquering White Europeans and Americans devised hierarchies of savagery and barbarism in contrast to what constituted "civilization" and "culture," both understood as European in origin (Adams, 1995; Wallach, 2005).

One reason contemporary researchers continue to investigate culture as a cause of poverty "is to develop and clarify exactly what they mean by [culture]—regardless of whether they believe it helps explain an outcome" (Small, Harding, & Lamont, 2010, p. 10). As students of culture quickly learn, "*culture* is slippery in meaning" (Erickson, 2012, p. 560). This is not a new conceptual challenge. In 1952 researchers used hundreds of pages, "describing, distilling, and assessing the many definitions of culture that anthropology had employed to date, only to leave the reader overwhelmed by the sheer number of issues . . . that cultural concepts had attempted to capture" (Small et al., 2010, p. 24). By the 2010s, academic disciplines had "produced entirely new vocabularies . . . that would make an updated version of that [1952] volume even more overwhelming" (p. 24).

Despite the indeterminacy of the concept of culture and efforts to link culture with levels of economic well-being, ideological associations between culture and class remain. By unraveling this ideological process, we can gain clearer insights about the effects on children from diverse backgrounds, especially students of color and those from low-income neighborhoods.

CULTURAL JUSTIFICATIONS FOR INEQUALITY

During the 19th century, the socially conservative Englishman Herbert Spencer (1864) borrowed Darwin's *biological* theory of evolution and applied it *socially* to the diverse cultures of the world. In his biology textbook, Spencer wrote about natural selection or "the survival of the fittest" among human beings evident in physiological structures of "the civilized races, as contrasted with the savage races" (p. 455). Out of Spencer's work came the ideology of *social Darwinism* in which "the survival of the fittest" explained differences in cultural attainment that included the arts, education, and political and economic institutions.

The invention of social Darwinism provided both conservatism and liberalism with an explanation as to why some people are rich and others are poor as well as why some people are "fit" to govern and others are not. Economist Nancy Folbre (2009) points out, "Proponents of social evolution, like Herbert Spencer, seemed to argue that poverty and inequality were the outcome of necessary, natural processes" (p. 223). As a result of an ideological orientation that justified poverty and inequality as a fundamental aspect of nature, Spencer and other prominent conservatives who dominated political discourse opposed any public assistance to the poor. This orientation saw social welfare programs as a waste of money under the assumption that the poor would simply pass on a genetic disposition that inhibited their children from overcoming their own poverty.

Wealth Accumulation as Gospel

In combination with academic theories about racial hierarchies, Spencer's notions about who were the genetically fittest found an audience with the post–Civil

War Southern plantation class and Northern business interests (Baum, 2006). For example, the wealthy industrialist and philanthropist Andrew Carnegie (1889) justified his wealth accumulation as a law of nature on the basis of social Darwinism. He did this with a fervent Protestant religious framing that led him to conclude that "the true Gospel concerning Wealth . . . is destined some day to solve the problem of the Rich and the Poor, and to bring Peace on earth, among men of Good-Will" (p. 18).

In his 1889 essay "The Gospel of Wealth," Carnegie explained the social value in accommodating capitalist competition. Economic competition provided the necessary "friction between the employer and the employed, between capital and labor, between rich and poor" so that society can make material advances (p. 4). Although this law of competition that determined the fittest "may be sometimes hard for the individual," Carnegie contended that capitalism and oligarchy, not democracy, was best for the continuation of the human race. Hence, the public must accept "*great inequality* of environment, the concentration of business, industrial and commercial in the *hands of a few* (p. 5, emphasis added). Socialists and others who challenged disparities in wealth accumulation and the inequality generated by capitalism and economic rule by the few should "be regarded as attacking the foundation upon which civilization itself rests" (p. 6).

According to social conservatism's rationale for enormous wealth concentration, only "good" has resulted to the human society "from the accumulation of wealth by those who have the ability and energy that produce it" (Carnegie, 1889, p. 6). Carnegie is also remembered as a philanthropist who funded public projects such as libraries. There is no question that private philanthropies have been used to relieve human suffering and provide services available to the public. Nevertheless, capitalists justify fundamental inequities by appearing charitable as long as it is voluntary and the balance of power and privilege remains unaltered.

This conservative justification remains to this day. Specifically, in 2012 the top 10% of income earners acquired over 50% of the United States' total income while the top 1% alone had more than 20% of the total income. In what is labeled "a new Gilded Age" (Lowrey, 2013, p. B1), income concentration among the very rich is similar to or higher than during the lead-up to the Great Depression of the 1930s.

Academic Praise of Capitalists

Carnegie could find defense for a status quo view on class, civilization, and culture from the professional class in higher education. The writings of William Graham Sumner, considered a founder of modern sociology, provided academic legitimization of the sentiments of Carnegie. Sumner lauded the capitalist and claimed in his 1883 *What the Classes Owe Each Other* that the "greatest step forward in this struggle [for human survival] is the production of capital which increases the fruitfulness of labor and provides the necessary means for an advancement of civilization" (as cited in Goldstone, 2011, pp. 68–69). Sociology's origins naturalized class differences and inequalities and served as an academic defense against socialist critiques of huge wealth disparities and worker complaints over the unfairness of wages and labor conditions under capitalism (Wallerstein, 2011). In our current era, academic advocates for wealth accumulation by capitalists surfaced 130 years after Sumner through a public exposure of "financial ties among professors promoting speculation and the banks and trading firms that profit from it" (Kocieniewski, 2013, p. B7).

Sumner basically claimed that culture could not be considered neutral and that a group's culture served as "an engine of social selection" (as cited in Goldstone, 2011, p. 70). Goldstone explains, "By linking the industrialists of the North with the planter class of the South, social Darwinism also helped solidify a national socioeconomic elite" (p. 72). In this paradigm, African Americans as a group were proof that their inferior social status and overall poverty were a result of their culture. Hence, the capitalist class and wealth itself became proof of the fittest.

From sociology and anthropology the concept of functionalism, as its name implies, assumes each person has a certain function or role to fill to meet a societal need. With a social Darwinian view of natural selection among human beings, individuals fulfill various roles and jobs based on their respective merit because some people are assumed more fit or capable than others to accomplish different socially necessary tasks. The meritocracy assumptions of functionalism exclude economic and social background. Under functionalism, social order is preserved without social conflict. Moreover, schools are expected to efficiently socialize students into their future places or functions in society (Bennett & LeCompte, 1990). Some scientists envision genetic engineering aiding this process (Specter, 2014).

Search for the Fittest Race

Conservatism's interpretation of class differences by an application of social Darwinism eventually spilled over into the 20th century and contributed to the creation of the eugenics movements. Eugenics borrowed from botany concepts of selective breeding of pea plants and attempted to apply it to creating the fittest race. The declining health of many Blacks who lived in poverty led a widely disseminated, scientifically framed 1896 insurance report to conclude that African Americans would eventually be extinct (Adelman, 2003). Financed primarily by capitalist philanthropists with the support of the U.S. federal government, eugenics eventually found its biggest support in the practices of Adolph Hitler and the Nazis' quest to create a superior race during the 1930s and 1940s (E. Black, 2003).

Social Darwinism provided another rationale to differentially finance racially segregated schools through state and local funding formulas that discriminated against Blacks, Latinos, and the poor and favored Whites and the relatively financially well-off. In the early 1900s, for example, when Georgia's overall White and Black populations were nearly equal (Gibson & Jung, 2002) and the state maintained racially segregated schools, school districts allocated just one-sixth as much per Black elementary school student when compared to average expenditures per individual White students. A 1917 study found counties in the South spent $22.22 per White pupil compared to $1.98 per Black student, or 11 times more on White children (Watkins, 2001). A similar pattern remains a century later for children of color who are disproportionally poor. In 2013 the U.S. Department of Education observed, "It is clear that students in many high-poverty districts receive less funding that those in low-poverty districts" (p. 18).

Despite documented funding differentials for schools, a 21st-century mainstream discourse forwards the premise that public schools have "failed" and that members of the capitalist class are the fittest to determine the future of K–12 education under the direction of "business round tables" and charter schools (Fabricant & Fine, 2012; Vavrus, 2002). Concordant with claims of failed schools are persistent assertions that students of color are less fit for academic success and fail due to their inferior culture despite the presence of effective culturally responsive instructional approaches (cf. E. G. Cohen, 1994; E. G. Cohen & Lotan, 2004; Vavrus, 2008). Such claims contribute to a disproportional placement by school officials of students of color in special education "as a structure for managing diversity and difference" (Y. Anyon, 2009, p. 53).

Although some critical anthropologists challenged the racial superiority assumptions that were foundational to mainstream studies of cultural groups, the federal government during the mid-20th century steered funding away from these scholars of culture who provided alternative structural explanations for patterns of human behavior (Price, 2004). It would take both the Civil Rights Movement and a book by a democratic socialist (Harrington, 1962/1969) in the early 1960s about the overlooked poor, however, to stir the conscience of the governing status quo to acknowledge poverty as a *public* problem alongside a "culture of poverty."

CULTURE OF POVERTY

The phrase *culture of poverty* originated in the late 1950s with Oscar Lewis's studies in poor neighborhoods of Mexico City. Under inadequate living conditions, the poor created cultural adaptations to survive. Although some "adaptations were self-defeating" by contributing to intergenerational poverty, Lewis never intended to place the blame for Mexican urban poverty on its low-income inhabitants (Erickson, 2012, p. 561). In 1962 socialist Michael Harrington borrowed the concept of a culture of poverty in his study of pockets of poor people hidden from mainstream discourse. When Harrington (1962/1969) stated, in *The Other America: Poverty in the United States*, "The poor are caught in a vicious circle; or, The poor live in a culture of poverty" (p. 15), he did not use the phrase in a culturally based, closed-circle manner as Lewis had (Isserman, 2009).

In contrast to an ideology of social conservatism, Harrington (1962/1969) contended that it was up to the public to step in to relieve victims of poverty: "Only the larger society, with its help and resources, can really make it possible for these people to help themselves" (p. 16). Because local governments did not consider poverty elimination a public policy obligation, Harrington focused on federal intervention. He came to this conclusion based on an assessment of opposition to public assistance for needy populations: "All the forces of conservatism in this society are ranged against the needs of the other America. The ideologues are opposed to helping the poor because this can be accomplished only through an expansion of the welfare state" (p. 172). In other words, Harrington challenged the social-good premise of both social Darwinism and the logic of wealth accumulation by the few.

Institutionalized Poverty

Rather than claiming that people were poor due to their genes or culture, Harrington turned to economic racism to explain inequality. The poor who were living in a so-called culture of poverty did not create their own poverty but were locked in "institutionalized poverty" in a racist society (p. 71). To overcome generational cycles of poverty, Harrington argued that "this can be done by offering real opportunities to these people, by changing the social reality that gives rise to their sense of hopelessness" (p. 167).

The UN Human Development Programme (2004) echoed Harrington's opinion 40 years later by praising the positive effects of national policies that reduce "identification of race with economic function" (p. 70). Instead, governments should focus on poverty reduction through alteration of structural conditions that contribute to economic disparities. The solution to a culture of poverty from Harrington's and the UN's perspective is not by a focus on the cultural characteristics of the poor per se but through a significant redistribution of public expenditures that would be directed to poor communities, a position that finds voice through critical multiculturalism.

Effect on Liberal Policy

By the mid-1960s, liberal multiculturalism expanded as an ideological expression as liberals confronted the relationship between racism and the nation's political economy. The historic 1963 civil rights "March on Washington" helped galvanize public attention to the plight of people of color. Deemphasized or excluded from both conservative and liberal recollections, the publicized purpose of the gathering at the Lincoln Memorial was "for Jobs and Freedom." Calls for living-wage jobs and nondiscriminatory hiring and promotion polices were the centerpiece of this famous event.

From the late 1950s through the 1960s, racial violence directed at African Americans who demanded basic human respect and rights was now impossible to avoid as televisions visually broadcast horrendous accounts of White terrorism on nonviolent protestors. For the burgeoning ideology of liberal multiculturalism, Harrington's work offered an analysis with a path toward solutions. Within a decade, policy liberals imagined engineering the end of poverty and the isolation of children of color from economic and social opportunities. This liberal optimism was amidst de facto segregated schools and urban ghettos.

Harrington's *The Other America* reportedly made it to the desk of President John F. Kennedy (Isserman, 2009). In 1963, shortly before he was assassinated, Kennedy was planning to have antipoverty legislation introduced. Kennedy's Council of Economic Advisors placed emphasis on public education as the primary solution to the culture of poverty: "Universal education has been perhaps the greatest single force contributing both to social mobility and to general economic growth" (as cited in Spring, 2010, p. 373). Breaking out of the culture of poverty through an emphasis on education impressed then vice president Lyndon Johnson.

A WAR ON POVERTY

In January 1964, in his State of the Union address after Kennedy's murder, President Johnson declared an "unconditional war on poverty" because "poverty is a national problem" (paras. 18, 20). President Johnson then identified solutions to escape the closed cycle of a culture of poverty that Harrington had described:

> Our chief weapons in a more pinpointed attack will be *better schools*, and *better health*, and *better homes*, and better training, and *better job opportunities* to help more Americans, especially young Americans, escape from squalor and misery and unemployment rolls where other citizens help to carry them. (Johnson, 1964, para. 23, emphasis added)

In the years immediately following this new national focus on poverty, Congress passed legislation to target a new surge in school funding and job training in low-income neighborhoods. Johnson's stated goal was to provide "special school aid funds as part of our education program, improve the quality of teaching, training, and counseling in our hardest hit areas" (para. 34).

To break the isolation of poor minorities in segregated neighborhoods and schools, Johnson signed an open housing law that made racial discrimination illegal in home purchases. Equal opportunity in well-paying employment, too, was a focus to counter White advantages and discrimination against people of color in hiring and promotions. Johnson proclaimed that economic and educational opportunities "must be open to Americans of every color" (para. 49). And, as Harrington (1962/1969) expressed, White racism aimed specifically toward African Americans had made them "classically the 'other' American, degraded and frustrated at every turn and not just because of laws" (p. 72).

Antipoverty Strategies

The month following the president's State of the Union address, Harrington began to work directly with the Johnson administration to craft a solution to poverty with a focus on unemployment. During his short tenure, Harrington worked with Daniel Moynihan, a U.S. Labor Department employee, who eventually became a Harvard professor, a member of Congress, and a U.S. ambassador. They both concluded that the solution was the creation of "massive public works projects to end unemployment and redistribute income to those most in need" (Isserman, 2009, para. 8). Influenced by the culture-of-poverty concept, Moynihan, within a year after Harrington's departure from the Labor Department, went on to author a federal report that advocated for jobs in a skewed context of cultural deficiencies of poor African Americans.

Pathological Culture of Poverty

Moynihan's report was entitled *The Negro Family: The Case for National Action* (U.S. Department of Labor, 1965). Although Moynihan clearly had an eye on eliminating workplace discrimination and expanding job opportunities for the poor, he reinforced the liberal perspective that education was in a causal relation with poverty: "Low education levels in turn produce low income levels, which deprive children of many opportunities, and so the cycle repeats itself" (p. 27). The fundamental source of the problem, Moynihan and many others believed, was the African American family structure that hindered educational attainment.

Using a disease metaphor, Moynihan contended that a cultural feature, a "family pathology," was a primary cause of intergenerational poverty (U.S.

Department of Labor, 1965, p. 19). This characterization fit with how conservative White anti-integrationist public officials labeled Black civil rights protesters during this era as pathologically angry and culturally deprived (Lassiter & Crepino, 2010). The identified source of the continuing culture of poverty was the Black female as head of household because "a matriarchal structure . . . seriously retards the progress of the group as a whole, and imposes a crushing burden on the Negro male" (U.S. Department of Labor, 1965, p. 29). The trope of the Black female parent as a cause of social problems would later become prominent in President Reagan's 1980s racializing discourse of mythic welfare queens and by the 2010s expand into a "cultural commonsense created by right-wing race-baiting: lazy nonwhites abuse welfare, while hardworking whites pay for it" (López, 2014, p. 73). The portrayal of women, especially of color, at the helm of a family as part of a cultural disease was for Moynihan and mainstream politics the key indicator that a "tangle of pathology is tightening" (U.S. Department of Labor, 1965, p. 45).

Critical Color Consciousness

Although Moynihan and others sought to eliminate poverty by "enhancing the stability and resources of the Negro American family" (U.S. Department of Labor, 1965, p. 48), critical perspectives pointed out how the strength of White racism would be an impediment to desired social programs. Harrington (1962/1969) had already emphatically noted this: "If all the discriminatory laws in the United States were immediately repealed, race would still remain as one of the most pressing moral and political problems in the nation" (p. 71). Despite claims of equal opportunity and congressional acts and Supreme Court verdicts that supported an extension of citizenship rights for African Americans, implementation was another matter in light of centuries of White supremacy at the expense of populations of color. Although supportive of a particular concept of an active citizen, liberal multiculturalism resisted the critical multiculturalism concept of what Banks (2009a) labels "transformative citizens" who take "actions . . . designed to promote values and moral principles—such as social justice and equality"—and sometimes must engage strategically in civil disobedience (pp. 316–317).

In the half century that has passed since Moynihan's report, dominant conservative and liberal ideologies set a policy tone on the relationship between culture and economic class. Liberalism contended that unsuccessful individuals from deficient cultures simply needed to change their behaviors to be successful. Research from social psychology documents that "high-status groups see themselves as having superior attributes and low-status groups as having inferior ones" (Fiske, 2011, p. 49). Yet, a series of research studies find that individuals with lower social class status are more generous and prosocial overall than those of higher status (Piff, Kraus, Côté, Cheng, & Keltner, D., 2010). Moreover, higher status groups hold "more favorable attitudes toward greed [that] can help explain their propensity toward unethical behavior" (Piff, Stancato, Côté, Mendoza-Denton, & Keltner, 2012, p. 4089). Nevertheless, a dominant hierarchical sense of cultural and racial superiority had shone a negative light on the private sphere of poor families, especially those of color, by bringing a culture of poverty into public policy. Despite liberal multiculturalism's attempt to treat cultural diversity neutrally, liberals saw cultural diversity as the cause of poverty.

CULTURAL DEFICITS AND EDUCATION

Despite Harrington's (1962/1969) plea for a massive infusion of public funding to help the poor and the Johnson administration's success in beginning to reduce poverty rates through governmental programs, an ideology of a sick culture of poverty filtered into the enactment of liberal multiculturalism in public school discourse. Throughout the last quarter of the 20th century, liberals constructed poor children, especially those of color, as disadvantaged by deficits in their cultural norms.

Ruby Payne's Approach

Public school educators sympathetic to liberal multiculturalism and an ideology of cultural deficits embarked on a mission to rescue poor children from their parents and communities. This approach became widely popular through Ruby Payne's (2005) *A Framework for Understanding Poverty*, which by the 2000s was in its 4th edition and was the basis for hundreds of professional development inservice workshops for teachers. In an effort to understand the problems of the poor and find possible solutions, mainstream educators latched onto her work. Gorski (2011) explains that the assertion of cultural deficits in Payne's work to account for academic achievement gaps stems from "the belief that inequalities result, not from unjust social conditions such as systemic racism or economic injustices but from intellectual, moral, cultural, and behavioral deficiencies assumed to be inherent in disenfranchised individuals and communities" (p. 154). In other words, according to Payne and like-minded educators, the problem resides in some notion of culture rather than being a function of existing political and economic structures that can reproduce inequality in schools.

Melding of Conservatism and Liberalism

Liberal multiculturalism, in its quest to celebrate diversity in public schools, found itself in partnership with Payne's (2005) socially conservative objectification and stereotyping of the poor. Following liberalism's ideology of individualism, Payne reinforced the belief that poor children primarily needed help to make better decisions that reflect behavioral norms associated with middle-class success. The solution for low-performing academic students who are poor and disproportionately of color apparently cannot be found through increased resources for their schools and neighborhoods. The effects of socioeconomic class inequities and systemic racism are outside Payne's ideological orientation (Gorski, 2006, 2011). Instead, as Chicago middle-school teacher Monique Redeaux (2011) concluded, Payne's discourse places "poverty within the dominant narrative of cultural deficiency and individual choice" (p. 195).

In a response to some of her critics, Payne (2009) answered that her purpose was not an analysis of poverty but instead to provide classroom teachers with practical ways to understand and teach poor children. She further responded to negative assertions that she advocated a deficit ideology by claiming her critics lacked a theoretical basis. Furthermore, Payne added, when critics assume "that my work is oppressive because it requires that people in poverty adapt to the middle-class environment or assimilate into it, I respond that *ignorance* is a brutal form of oppression" (para. 5). Hence, adopting middle-class schooling values in order to achieve in school becomes the primary vehicle to navigate an individual out of poverty. This echoes the ideological positions of mainstream political parties in the United States, whether Democratic or Republican, most evident in the 2012 televised presidential election debates when neither party offered anything of substance to alleviate poverty and provide help for the poor (Wessler, 2012). Thus, both dominant political parties ultimately rely "on education to solve the problems of unemployment and increases in poverty" rather than on significant increases in living-wage job opportunities (J. Anyon, 2011, p. 67).

Payne's approach is in line with liberal multiculturalism's emphasis on educational reform as the primary means to rise out of poverty. Because liberal multiculturalism "abdicates any recognition of unequal, and often untidy, power relations that underpin inequality and limit cultural interaction," it fits more easily into normative teaching practices (May & Sleeter, 2010, p. 4). Outside the purview of liberal multiculturalism is the structural basis of a skewed distribution of economic resources and institutional racism. Critical multiculturalism, however, finds a causal relationship between who has more economic resources and an individual's skin color. Racial discrimination in access to economic resources remains as a barrier to escaping a culture of poverty for poor children and their families and communities, especially the too often unacknowledged discrimination students outside the mainstream culture face within schools (Pollock, 2008; Vavrus, 2010).

THE FREEDOM BUDGET AND THE FUTURE OF OUR CHILDREN

Critical multiculturalism does not dismiss the potential of schools as sites to help poor children but acknowledges that "education bears far too much of the burden of our hopes for economic justice" (Marsh, 2011, p. 18). Because the influence of a political economy is inseparable from schooling practices, critical multiculturalism places a focus on social and economic redistribution of opportunities, rights, and outcomes in both the larger society and within the microcosm of schools. Critical multiculturalism, therefore, aligns with a political economy budget proposal from civil rights leaders and supporters that appeared in 1966.

"A Freedom Budget"

During the 1950s and 1960s, civil rights activists, including Martin Luther King Jr., worked on "A Freedom Budget for All Americans." Following the impetus of the 1963 March on Washington, this civil rights document for a new political economy was released in 1966. Although socialists saw it as an important movement toward a more democratic economic system, liberals viewed the plan as feasible within capitalism. The document was widely circulated to elected officials, religious leaders, and key civil rights activists (Le Blanc & Yates, 2013).

The advocates of this progressive budget faced two major barriers, however: (1) the financially costly Vietnam War that took a toll on public funds and (2) a conservative backlash. The ideologically conservative *Wall Street Journal's* reaction against the Freedom Budget called for "intelligent" policies, not a "poverty of thought" (as cited in Le Blanc & Yates, 2013, p. 96). Those with wealth, conservatives argued, should be proposing means to escape poverty because only "*private* policies can provide further assistance to the poor" (p. 96, emphasis added). Hence, a democratic, publicly led policy was antithetical to the ideological interests of the capitalist class.

Fifty years later it is worthwhile to review the budget's basic goals, which offered "a practical, step-by-step plan for wiping out poverty in America during the next 10 years"—that is, by 1976 (as cited in Le Blanc & Yates, 2013, p. 243)—by making comparisons to contemporary economic realities.

Freedom Budget Compared to Today

Economists generally agree that the War on Poverty helped add vital safeguards to protect millions from falling farther into poverty. Although failing to eliminate poverty, when combined with programs initiated during the 1930s, the contemporary social safety net helped millions. Individuals living in "extreme poverty," or on $2.00 a day, however, increased dramatically after liberal President Bill Clinton's 1996 support for legislation to reduce the number of people eligible for welfare assistance. Children living in extreme poverty grew from 8% to 10% in 1996 to upwards of 18% by 2011 (Shaefer & Edin, 2012). Social conservatism opposes government programs that transfer public funds to programs designed to help the poor and to keep families from falling into poverty. Liberal multiculturalism views the need to create more jobs (Lowrey, 2014) and more access to education. Neither conservatism nor liberalism, however, offer a holistic program to eliminate poverty as did the Freedom Budget.

With a 21st-century perspective, we can look back on objectives listed in the 1966 Freedom Budget and compare them to contemporary conditions. As part of a comprehensive document, five of the Freedom Budget's objectives are reproduced below and then followed by indicators of economic and social well-being in the 2010s.

1. To provide full employment for all who are willing and able to work, including those who need education or training to make them willing and able (as cited in Le Blanc & Yates, 2013, p. 244)

In 1964 when President Johnson declared his plan to attack poverty, the official unemployment rate was 5.6% and by 1968 was at 3.4%, its lowest level to date. As a percentage of the unemployed, the long-term unemployed during the Great Recession of 2007–2009 was 46%, the highest rate since the Great Depression of 1929–1933 (MacEwan & Miller, 2011). The official unemployment level in the mid-2010s hovered in the 7% range, down from 10% in 2009 (U.S. Department of Labor, 2014), or more than twice the 1968 rate.

2. To assure decent and adequate wages to all who work (as cited in Le Blanc & Yates, 2013, p. 244)

Wages have remained stagnant despite a rise in labor productivity. In other words, employment rates and wages declined along with reductions in antipoverty funding while profits rose exponentially. Meanwhile, White and Asian American poverty rates have remained historically low in comparison to the higher poverty rates for Latinos and Blacks. As a *Washington Post* analysis puts it, "Just as in Michael Harrington's day, the poverty rate for black and Hispanic Americans is much higher than for non-Hispanic whites and Asian-Americans" (Matthews, 2012, "It's Still Racially Concentrated," para. 1).

3. To assure a decent living standard to those who cannot or should not work (as cited in Le Blanc & Yates, 2013, p. 244)

The poverty rate at the beginning of 2014 for full-time workers was 3% whereas for the jobless it was 33%. The goal of a federally established living wage or a guaranteed annual income appears distant as political conservatives opposed raising even the minimum wage and instead contend that the problem of the poor is one of individual or personal responsibility (Lowrey, 2014).

4. To wipe out slum ghettos and provide decent homes for all Americans (as cited in Le Blanc & Yates, 2013, p. 244)

Not until the 1980s did the term "homeless" enter national discourse as it was not a widely observed phenomenon prior to conservative policies initiated during the Reagan Administration that cut housing subsidies ("Homelessness," 2013). By the 2010s, 1.6 million children, or 1 in 45, experienced homelessness. Poverty and unemployment are highly associated with housing instability. Largely due to predatory housing loans permitted under lax liberal oversight and conservative advocacy, foreclosures affected 10 million people during the late 2000s; families with children seeking access to homeless shelters increased significantly (Gottesdiener, 2013; MacEwan & Miller, 2011). The Institute for Children, Poverty, and Homelessness (2013) finds,

> Even when homelessness is not the final outcome, foreclosure has a detrimental impact on families with children, since the foreclosure process may involve *frequent moves and school transfers*. Combined with the stresses of financial insecurity experienced by parents, these tumultuous circumstances *negatively affect children's development, physical and mental health, and academic performance.* (p. 8 emphasis added)

In other words, children who experience unstable housing can face dire consequences in nearly all aspects of their lives.

5. To provide decent medical care and adequate educational opportunities to all Americans, at a cost they can afford (as cited in Le Blanc & Yates, 2013, p. 244)

Access to adequate health care is directly related to the economic status of U.S. families. As poverty has increased, so have declines in the health of the poor been recorded. As employers during the 21st century reduced health insurance for their workers, there was a significant increase in the poor seeking some form of public health insurance (Addy et al., 2013), an effect felt by all poor young people. Homeless children in particular are much more likely to suffer from illnesses, hunger, and nutritional deficiencies than children with housing. Homeless children are also "four times more likely to show delayed development [and] twice as likely to have learning disabilities as non-homeless children" (National Center on Family Homelessness, 2010).

Call to Reintroduce the Freedom Budget

Critical multiculturalism finds an urgency to reintroduce to the public the Freedom Budget objectives as a part of a guiding document that can serve all families today, especially those with school-age children. Wedded to a capitalist economy premised on private accumulation and concentration of wealth, social conservatism and liberal multiculturalism offer no meaningful structural answers to eliminate economically daunting conditions that low-income families and their school-age children face each day. The 45% of all children who grow up in poor families and often struggle to achieve academically in their under-resourced public schools are not helped by conservatism's disdain for families and communities in need and liberalism's policies of gradualism. For instance, the U.S. Department of Education's (2013) primary solution to problems of poverty and schooling that their research identified was an increase of parent involvement in low-income schools.

Critical multiculturalism instead offers a standpoint that advocates for a democratic economy that redistributes government funds so that every child lives without fear of food insecurity, uncertain housing, and a lack of comprehensive health care. The future of *all* of our children—not just those considered worthy and deserving by policymakers—can significantly change for the better if government transfers were a priority for poverty reduction programs and full funding of public education. For this reason, a critical multicultural orientation that strives to alter political and economic structural variables associated with the maintenance of poverty is the best hope for families struggling daily to make ends meet and to help their children succeed in school. To move dominant political orientations to stop using bad math that blames poverty on culture and to reverse the decline in the quality of life for increasing numbers of our children will require critically informed social action.

We now transition to the type of curriculum students of racially and ethnically diverse background experience and the place of ethnic studies and multicultural education in this process.

CHAPTER 6

Standoff over Ethnic Studies and Multicultural Education

> I heard an immigrant's voice . . .
> It pounded on its lover's breast,
> this voice
> demanding *where* is the dream?
> Where *is* the dream?
>
> It broke into tears at public urinals
> & spit on statues on the way home
> until sweat poured
> from the contour
> of their histories . . .
>
> —Naomi Ayali, "Immigrant's Voice"

Directly related to worldviews on diversity are attitudes and actions toward immigrant and indigenous populations and their various cultural practices. Perceptions of the value and necessity of ethnic and multicultural studies and minority language learning are hotly argued across a spectrum of diversity orientations. At one extreme is the belief that immigrants and indigenous people and their cultures and languages are a direct threat to the sovereignty and identity of a nation. An opposite belief is that ethnic and multicultural studies and languages that stem from the experiences of immigrant and indigenous populations enhance the vitality of a nation. Embedded within these perspectives is the fact that "citizenship is a contested site of social struggles . . . through which subjects become political" (Isin, Neyers, & Turner, 2009, p. 1).

This chapter explores a range of diversity viewpoints and why a settler nation such as the United States, which publicly prides itself on being a nation of immigrants, questions the value of immigrant and indigenous cultures and languages. The chapter first provides an overview of contemporary human migration patterns in the context of economic causes and the effects on immigrant youth. Next it explores how xenophobia and nativism help frame the perception that immigrants are a threat and how this ideology creates curricular tensions. Included in this chapter is the special case of indigenous cultures and education. A historical and political economy framework provides the context to account for the current condition of Native American youth. Following this, declines in language diversity and disputes over school instruction in nondominant languages lead to an exploration of bilingual education in the context of ethnic studies and multicultural education and the roots of antagonism to nontraditional curricula. Case examples from Texas and Arizona make visible ideological orientations that oppose ethnic and multicultural studies. Amidst these diversity debates, the chapter concludes by presenting a critical multicultural approach as a curricular alternative that can benefit the future of young people.

RECORD RATES OF HUMAN MIGRATION

The planet is in the midst of the highest recorded rates of human migration compared to any previous epoch. The significance of this trend is an unprecedented increase in ethnic and linguistic diversity for nations receiving immigrants. The estimated total of international immigrants by 2010 was 214 million, according to the International Organization for Migration (IOM) (2010b). Just 3 years later, the figure rose to a record 232 million people, which is equal to 3.2% of the world's population (UN News Centre, 2013). If the current pace of migration documented from 1990 to 2010 continues as anticipated, by the year 2050 the number of international migrants could rise to 405 million (IOM, 2010b).

With more than 40 million foreign-born people, the United States has the largest migrant population in the world. Although migration is a significant factor throughout the world, the largest region of international migration is between the United States and Mexico (IOM, 2010b). The percentage of immigrants entering the United States has significantly increased since 1965, when all racial and national-origin restrictions from a 1924 law ended. Nevertheless, by the mid-2010s the number of immigrants as a proportion of the total population was similar to the period of 1860 to 1930 (Dews, 2013).

Economic Cause

Most international migrants, 63%, end up in developed countries,* and taken together compose nearly 9% of the total population of those nations (Castles, 2009). The primary cause for human migration at record rates is economic, specifically as affected by capitalist globalization and wars. Within receiving countries and regions, migrant populations overwhelmingly find themselves in racially and ethnically segregated jobs and neighborhoods (Bacon, 2008; IOM, 2010a).

The use of migrant populations for irregular employment reflects "the continuing dependency of economies in many parts of the developed world on cheap, unprotected migrant labour" (IOM, 2010b, p. 11). In economic down-turns, such as the current global economic recession that began in the late 2000s, "migrants are often among the most vulnerable category of workers affected by job losses, as they *tend to be younger*, are more likely to be in temporary jobs, [and] have *less formal education* (p. 123, emphasis added). This is the case for the 400,000 children who annually work to harvest food in the United States. As migrant laborers, these young people fail to finish school at a rate 400% higher than the national average (Conde, 2012).

Immigrant Youth

Although a significant amount of migration results from efforts toward family reunification in the receiving countries, "it seems likely that an important proportion of children and young people are migrating independently" (IOM, 2010a, p. 117). Immigrants under the age of 20 represent 16% of the total world migrant population, or 33 million young people. The highest percentage of migrant youth globally are located in the United States (United Nations Children's Fund, 2012).

Right to Education. Immigrant children often end up in schools with relatively inferior resources and a high proportion of low-income students. Dominant policies and practices historically limited or rejected the enrollment of immigrant children in public schools. Holding to a belief that immigrant presence negatively influences the stability of a common culture, educational policies of many individual states denied undocumented immigrants the right to attend public schools. In 1982, however, the U.S. Supreme Court ruled in *Plyler v. Doe* that a state cannot deny undocumented immigrant children access to public K–12 schools. Hence, immigrant children have the right of "territorial personhood" that grants them access to a public education regardless of their official citizenship status (Song, 2009, p. 613). Nevertheless, "the dynamics of immigration and schooling are complex and potentially subtractive and linguistically and educationally restrictive" (Baquedano-López, Alexander, & Hernandez, 2013, p. 161).

Social Psychological Effects. With diverse cultural practices and languages, immigrant children often begin their education in their new countries at a distinct learning and emotional disadvantage compared to their domestic peers. Public schools and related social services generally lack "psychosocial support mechanisms" for indigenous and immigrant children (IOM, 2010a, p. 4). Moreover, the dominant narrative simply frames the social psychological adjustment of immigrant youth to their new settings as stages of child and adolescent development. Mainstream mental health providers work from liberal "theories of individuals' cognition and development [that] may not have much relevance to immigrant populations from non-European cultures" (Patel, 2013, p. 40). This individualistic approach reduces immigrant youth transitions to their physiology and in effect "close[s] off inquiries into contextual factors" (p. 40). To provide appropriate support, positions based on critical multiculturalism contend that public educators need to move beyond a one-dimensional emphasis on reduction in cultural dissonance and attend to the political economy in which indigenous populations and new immigrant families find themselves (Castles, 2009; Vavrus, 2002), factors which xenophobia and nativism obscure.

XENOPHOBIA AND NATIVISM

Historically, the United States resisted the inclusion of immigrants who were culturally and ethnically different than dominant groups of European Americans. *Xenophobia,* a fear and general hatred toward foreigners and those perceived as strangers and outsiders, finds expression in social conservatism and political reflection through *nativism.* Not to be confused with indigenous populations, the "natives" in this construction were originally people of English descent. Nativism as a visible political movement harkens back to the mid-19th century and is "a recurring social and political movement characterized principally by hostility to supposed foreigners" (Germic, 2008, p. 430). Furthermore, "as a form of ethnic discrimination," nativism "is closely related to racism but may be distinguished by its emphasis on language and the privileges of citizenship" (p. 430).

Social psychological research finds that in-group loyalty of social conservatism is correlated with racial intolerance, nationalism, and ethnocentrism (Haidt & Kesebir, 2010) and that "the more majority-group members identify with their own group, the more they can be expected to try to protect their group's interests and status position, for example by emphasizing assimilation" (Verkuten, 2010, p. 155). The emphasis on assimilation reflects both a socially conservative and liberal multicultural orientation to protect the status of mainstream groups. For social conservatism, "once threat is perceived, it leads to less support for immigrants and ethnic minorities" (p. 157). Because "perceived group threat is a key determination of tolerance" (p. 150), critical multiculturalism openly and positively recognizes ethnic differences by an acknowledgment of the importance of a fair and equitable democratic society based on those differences, a point discussed later in this chapter.

The Immigrant Threat

Social conservatism's xenophobia and nativism constructs immigrant cultures and languages in threatening terms: (1) *medically,* as constituting a "contamination" to a common culture; (2) *militarily*, as representing an "alien invasion"; (3) *psychological-ly*, as raising concerns about individual "capacity" or "fitness"; or (4) *politically*, as being inherently "un-American" (Behdad, 2005, pp. 118, 122, 124, 130). Within this context, the trope of racialized genetics and intelligence resurfaced in a 2013 report from a prominent conservative think tank that contended Latino immigrants were genetically inferior in intelligence in comparison to White Americans. A coauthor of the report based his findings on his 2009 Harvard doctoral dissertation in which he stated,

> Immigrants living in the U.S. today do not have the same level of cognitive ability as natives. No one knows whether Hispanics will ever reach I.Q. parity with whites, but the prediction that new Hispanic immigrants will have low-I.Q. children and grandchildren is difficult to argue against. (J. Richwine, as cited in A. Parker & Preston, 2013, para. 3)

In *The Mismeasure of Man*, Stephan Jay Gould (1996) theoretically and statistically debunked such research. Gould labeled contemporary research that conflates race and I.Q. as "anachronistic social Darwinism" (p. 367).

Social conservatism carries an ideological vigilance against immigrants as invaders and disrupters of an exclusive common culture. Writing in the influential mainstream journal *Foreign Affairs* against an increase of non-European immigrants into the United States, Huntington (1997) argued, "Reviving a stronger sense of national identity would also require countering the cults of diversity and multiculturalism" (p. 48). Conservative *New York Times* columnist David Brooks espoused on an NBC television news program that undocumented immigrants bring to the United States a "culture of criminality" (as cited in Dimond, 2005, para. 1). In this interpretation, immigrants are aggressors on U.S. soil who, if not stopped or contained, can bring down the nation's culture, health, intellectual capacity, and political institutions. As a seemingly passive solution, the socially conservative 2012 presidential nominee for the Republican Party advocated a policy of "self-deportation" for undocumented immigrants to leave the United States if "they can't get work here" (M. Romney, as cited in Boroff & Planas, 2012, para. 3).

Despite a business practice of employing undocumented immigrants, mainstream narratives present new immigrants as an economic threat for jobs and are linked in this ideology as a cause of high unemployment rates. In contrast to scapegoating immigrants, grounded experience suggests that immigrants can improve economies. For example, cities devastated by the Great Recession (2007–2009) and left with abandoned homes and lost businesses find new immigrants are willing to invest in housing and create new businesses (J. Preston, 2013). In 2011, immigrants created over 25% of new U.S. businesses. Texas alone "would see a $4.1 billion gain in tax revenue and the creation of 193,000 new jobs if its approximately 1.6 million undocumented immigrants were legalized" (Garcia & Fitz, 2012, para. 5). At the federal level, undocumented immigrants contributed $300 billion to Social Security funds which they cannot access (H. A. Goodman, 2014).

A Barrier Wall Against Immigrant Students

Nativist perceptions of immigrants led to social conservatism's political embracement of the construction of a 664-mile barrier wall along the Mexico–U.S. border (R. Jones, 2012). Public school classrooms reproduce this ideological stance. Both literally and metaphorically, nativists erect a wall to censor and criminalize nontraditional, interdisciplinary scholarship and practices associated with ethnic studies and multicultural education programs in public schools.

A symbolic wall minimizes or simply excludes, for example, the language of immigrant students, approximately 75% of whom speak Spanish as their first language (Stritikus & Lucero, 2012). Social conservatism characterizes nondominant language acquisition as a disability that poses a danger to an assimilationist concept of a common culture and the "traditional conception of the United States as a melting pot" (Minami & Ovando, 2004, p. 577). Even when a state incorporates into its educational policies a transitional bilingual requirement from preschool through high school, both politically conservative and liberal governments provide inadequate resources for the implementation of such policies (e.g., Puente, 2012). Because social conservatism envisions a homogeneous common culture, advocates of this position support the exclusive use of a politically dominant language in public schools—and work to erect walls to match this ideological orientation.

While liberal multiculturalism may acknowledge advantages in a diversity of languages, groups operating from this orientation are generally reluctant to financially support policies that would allow instruction in an immigrant or indigenous student's native language. Even in a liberal democracy such as New Zealand, where the indigenous Maori language coexists with English as an official national language, actual instruction in Maori language and culture remains sporadic (Hynds, 2012). In the United States, mainstream policymakers and educators rarely advocate or fund language restoration programs for indigenous populations.

Diversity and multicultural discourse often categorize Native American and other indigenous groups together with immigrants and people of color in a way that ignores the historical origins of indigenous people. For an estimated 10,000 to 12,000 years, indigenous people living in what is conventionally referred to as the Americas developed complex cultures and languages. We therefore shift our attention for the moment to unique historical and contemporary conditions that affect the lives and education of Native American young people.

INDIGENOUS CULTURES AND EDUCATION: A SPECIAL CASE

In contrast to social conservatism and liberal multiculturalism, critical multiculturalism does not essentialize culture devoid of political economy connotations. Explanations that reduce economic disparities to cultural diversity and deficits mislead. Instead, as human development psychologist Barbara Rogoff (2003) notes, "Misunderstandings and hostilities are much greater with groups that have a long history of competition for resources or poor treatment of one by another" (p. 334). Subordination and limited access to material resources characterize the historical relations between White dominant populations and people of color. This is particularly true for how mainstream ideologies and practices affect indigenous cultures and education.

From the standpoint of indigenous groups, culture is "the interrelated aspects" of shared values and practices expressed in communications, education, the arts, and other forms of representation "alongside the economic, political and social facets of life" (Genia, 2012, p. 657). Indigenous cultures struggle globally against *cultural appropriation* that takes place when outside groups claim "parts of a culture that is not [their] own" or simply adopt them "for [their] own personal gain or commodification" (p. 661). For protection against exploitation, indigenous cultures seek legal protection against capitalistic and academic patterns of cultural appropriation.

The UN's (2008) "Declaration on the Rights of Indigenous Peoples" articulated the relationship between culture and education. Specifically, the Declaration stated, "Indigenous peoples have *the right to the dignity and diversity of their cultures*, traditions, histories and aspirations which shall be appropriately *reflected in education* and public information" (p. 7, emphasis added). The Declaration also emphasizes an indigenous "right to establish and control their educational systems and institutions providing education in their own languages" as well as participation in public education "without discrimination" (p. 7). By the beginning of 2010, all nations had signed the "Declaration on the Rights of Indigenous Peoples," with the United States as the last signatory. President Obama (2010b) qualified U.S. support for the Declaration by noting that it was a non–legally binding *hope* for indigenous rights.

Critical indigenous perspectives make clear that the aim is neither structural inclusion in the nation-state nor just citizenship rights. Instead, the goal in the United States is to have congressionally ratified treaty agreements fully recognize tribal sovereignty in practice. Nevertheless, historically imposed barriers continue to negatively affect the exercise of indigenous cultural, educational, and economic rights, especially in the transmission of diverse cultural practices to future generations.

Indigenous Miseducation

Critical multiculturalism offers a contemporary perspective to place the cultures of indigenous children and their families in a historical and political economy context. Specifically, the U.S. boarding schools of the 19th and 20th centuries designed for Native American youth ideologically held an explicit goal to eliminate all cultural vestiges from indigenous children. Conditions in these schools often resembled prison camps in which forced labor of children was the norm. Disease and death of native youth were not uncommon in government boarding schools (Adams, 1995).

Mainstream worldviews contended that indigenous youth came from tribal regions that lacked a culture and needed to be brought into civilization. Critical multiculturalism calls attention to the legacy of racial superiority claims by a hegemonic European American Christian culture and the detrimental effects those claims have had for the full inclusion and academic success of Native American children. To this point, the UN (2013) highlighted negative effects of contemporary public education that serve as "a way of indoctrinating indigenous youth with the dominant culture while denying them access to their indigenous culture" (p. 6). In addition to this educational conservatism, the UN faulted public policies of liberal multiculturalism for its "melting pot" approach that "ignores cultural differences between groups, and thus strips groups of their cultural heritage" (p. 7). When schools do include indigenous histories, a sole focus on the historical past presents an image of an indigenous heritage disconnected from the lives of contemporary indigenous youth. Including cultures and more accurate histories of native people, the UN report argued, is "a key element in building understanding between indigenous peoples and society at large" (p. 7).

Effects on Contemporary Indigenous Youth

As the UN observed, native histories and culture are rarely included in the school curriculum beyond that provided through a master narrative. This exclusion of indigenous culture beyond relics of a distant past is associated with low school attendance and high drop-out rates among Native American youth. In the state of Washington, with 29 federally recognized Native American tribes, for example, nearly half of Native American youth do not graduate within 4 years of beginning secondary school or at all (Came & Ireland, 2012).

Conservative and liberal educational models combined with media stereotyping of indigenous people and their cultures negatively affect the psychological well-being of indigenous youth. The observations of a UN report reinforces critical multicultural critiques of both social conservatism and liberal multiculturalism: "Indigenous youth are often dislocated and disconnected from mainstream society because of discrimination and the negative way in which the dominant culture constructs indigenous identity" (UN, 2013, p. 8). Cultural dissonance in schools and stereotypical media images of Native Americans contribute to mental health challenges among indigenous youth.

Native American children have the highest suicide rate among all young people. For adolescents and young adults it is 2.5 times higher than any other group. Between the ages of 10 and 14 is when Native American suicide rates begin to skyrocket significantly (Crosby, Ortega, & Stevens, 2011). Figure 6.1, "Suicide rates by race/ethnicity and age group, 1999–2007," compares suicide rates among young people. Although the 2001 No Child Left Behind Act contained provisions to address suicides among Native American school-age children, the chair of the U.S. Senate Committee on Indian Affairs noted that "the hard fact remains that there has been no substantial decline in the youth suicide rate in Indian communities" (Dorgan, 2010, p. 216).

The degradation of indigenous culture, language, and education by a legacy of European American colonialism continues in the 21st century as an increasing number of languages become extinct, a subject we turn to next.

Figure 6.1: Suicide Rates by Race/Ethnicity and Age Group, 1999–2007

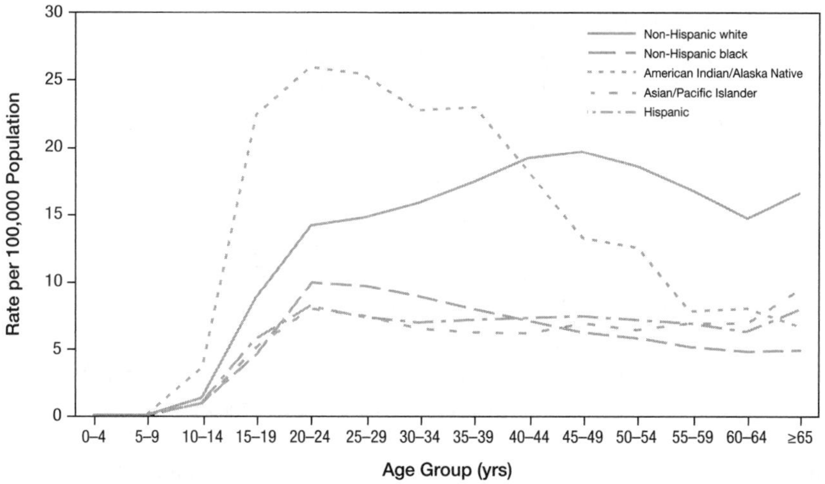

Source: Crosby, Ortega, & Stevens (2011, p. 58).

LANGUAGE DIVERSITY AND HOMOGENEITY

Languages historically have aided in "maintaining distinctive human identities by serving an important boundary-marker function between groups" (Romaine, 2009, p. 373). A specific language is never culturally neutral nor static but instead is a key characteristic of a culture. Cultural contact among groups altered languages throughout human history. When circumstances involve one ethnic group conquering a different cultural group, the language of a dominant group results in a decrease of language diversity. The decline of language diversity can best be observed in the colonizing of the Americas and its effects on indigenous languages (Rogoff, 2003).

Language diversity specifically refers to the number of languages spoken in a particular geographic region. For all the languages spoken in the world in the 35 years from 1970 to 2005, one-fifth were lost. In the 21st century the rate of decline in linguistic diversity accelerated in an era of expansive capitalist globalization and a corresponding emphasis on standardization and homogeneity. The greatest declines, nearly two-thirds, were recorded in North, Central, and South America (Harmon & Loh, 2010). Of the almost 7,000 languages that remain in the world, Canada and the United States together contain 6.5%, or 456 diverse languages of the world. Nevertheless, English is the dominant language globally (Romaine, 2009).

Oxford University's Suzanne Romaine (2009) emphasizes how the nation-state—with its arbitrary boundaries and need to establish a standard ruling language—is "the greatest threat to the languages, cultures, and identities of minority communities" (p. 374). If not completely exterminating a conquered people, the nation-state strives to eliminate the remaining vestiges of the culture and, therefore, the language of the subjected through policies aimed at assimilation to dominant norms. Justification stems from a belief in "common origins and culture," although "virtually no nation-state has ever actually been completely homogeneous and monocultural" (Castles, 2009, pp. 49, 53). As long as a nation struggles to find a common identity through one language and culture, the diversity of languages and cultures of immigrant and indigenous children will remain contested and compromised (Romaine, 2011).

In regard to the effects of assimilation policies, Romaine (2009) explains, "Eventually, the dominant language tends to invade the inner spheres of the subordinate language, so that its domains of use become even more restricted" and "traditional culture and identity is also lost when that language disappears" (pp. 375, 377–378). Despite the suppression or loss of an individual's first language, cultural identities cannot simply be tossed aside, all of which bring into play the role the nation-state chooses in prioritizing the importance of subordinated languages that remain. Formal educational policies and practices aimed at young people are one of the most visible ways in which nation-states enact cultural and language assimilation strategies aimed at creating a homogenized society.

The effects of educational discourse on immigrant and indigenous students, families, and communities influence the degree to which nondominant ethnic groups develop a sense of belonging and inclusiveness within the mainstream culture. When the language and cultural history of a particular group is either stigmatized or suppressed, immigrant and indigenous school children experience cultural exclusion and develop a belief that they and their cultural heritage are inferior. Research on immigrant youth who achieve academically, however, reinforces the importance of schools that demonstrate a caring atmosphere and are receptive to a diversity of ethnicities and their cultures (Suárez-Orozco & Suárez-Orozco, 2013).

To understand why differing worldviews support, oppose, or tacitly allow exclusions and marginalization of immigrants and their children, we turn to responses to ethnic studies, multicultural education, and bilingual language curriculum and instruction.

ETHNIC, MULTICULTURAL, AND BILINGUAL EDUCATION

The impetus for ethnic and multicultural education during the late 1960s and 1970s was to help diverse students of color, including young immigrants, find themselves in the school curriculum. This was spurred by the fact that ethnic inclusion in the United States after World War II had been successful for White European immigrants but outside the reach of people of color. Ethnic studies programs "are centered on the knowledge and perspectives of an ethnic or racial group, reflecting narratives and points of view rooted in that group's lived experiences and intellectual scholarship" (Sleeter, 2011, p. vii). Research indicates that such programs improve the academic achievement for both students of color and their White peers (Sleeter, 2011, 2012b).

As a school reform movement, multicultural education is broader than ethnic studies. A major goal of multicultural education is to have historically marginalized students see their histories and cultures reflected in school organization, personnel, policy, spending priorities, and general practices of the school, including the curriculum. In turn, an aim of multicultural education is to increase a sense of belonging for students of color within the school and broader society and to provide White students with a more inclusive and accurate perspective of their world (Banks, 2009b).

Both ethnic studies and multicultural education strive to incorporate nondominant languages in the organization of the school and the curriculum, especially those languages that immigrant children and their families have brought with them as part of their cultural heritages and identities. From the era of

North American British colonialism and throughout U.S. history, the dominant culture opposed the use of languages other than English within schools as a means to make immigrants into "Americans" (Spring, 2010). This historical pattern influences a "political atmosphere that makes bilingual education controversial" and affects "the types of programs offered, the extent to which bilingualism and biliteracy are promoted, and who will benefit from them" (Dabach & Faltis, 2012, p. 216).

Political practices oppositional to language diversity continue despite research that documents that "well-implemented bilingual education programs have a positive effect on the language development and academic achievement of students who enter and exit these programs" (Dabach & Faltis, 2012, p. 215). Moreover, recent research on immigrant children living in poverty finds that bilingualism contributes more positively than monolingualism to the development of "executive control" functions, an aspect of cognition that involves tasks such as "directing attention, focusing on relevant aspects of a problem, and filtering misleading information" (Engel de Abreu, Cruz-Santos, Tourinho, Martin, & Bialystok, 2012, p. 1369). The team of psychologists who conducted this study on bilingualism explain that "in spite of facing many linguistic challenges, bilingual immigrant children present important strengths in nonlinguistic cognitive domains that promote academic achievement" (p. 1369).

We next explore contemporary ideological expressions of nationalism and patriotism that oppose ethnic studies and multicultural education.

PATRIOTISM AND CURRICULUM STANDARDS

To public expressions of diversity that counter dominant narratives about a homogeneous common culture, a segment of conservatives reacted with populist cries, such as a U.S. congressman's contention that "if we don't control immigration, legal and illegal, we will eventually reach the point where . . . we will have to face the fact that we are no longer a nation" (Tancredo, as cited in Zeskind, 2009, p. 527). Such opposition is a form of White nationalism that glosses over the place of race and White privilege in the formation of the modern nation-state. Whites-as-victims is a familiar strategy for a dominant group who resists acknowledging that accrued economic and political advantages are normalized in the experiences and perspectives of Whites, including the mainstream school curriculum (Wise, 2005). Nevertheless, by the end of the 2000s the conservative position became U.S. federal policy through an act that privileged antidiversity grants for academic programs. The goal of this policy was to promote a monocultural ideology by privileging grants for "academic programs or centers" that emphasize values of classical liberalism as expressed through "traditional American history, free institutions or Western civilization" (P. Cohen, 2008, p. A22).

E. D. Hirsch (2009–2010) represents a mainstream anguishing over a curriculum that incorporates diversity. Hirsch couches his position on an assumption that since the United States founding era, schools have played a valuable role in peacefully assimilating diverse groups socially into a common culture while enabling different ethnicities to retain their private identities. Critical multiculturalists note that liberal claims of American exceptionality like Hirsch's continue to misread the history of schooling, which has been replete with conflict and public denunciations of diverse identities (Spring, 2010). In response, Hirsch labels those who oppose his ahistorical interpretations as "anti-curriculum" (p. 10).

Hirsch's conservatism in opposition to ethnic studies and multicultural education echoes positions expressed in previous decades by public intellectuals such as Sandra Stotsky (1999) and Samuel Huntington (2004), who contended that multiculturalism is a hateful threat against the moral values embedded in dominant common culture narratives. Stotsky contended that such programs lead to "the disappearing of an American culture as a whole" (p. 209). In a negative critique of multicultural scholar James Banks, Huntington framed the inclusion of ethnic studies as part of a curriculum that comes "at the expense of teaching the values and culture that Americans have had in common" (p. 173), a view that informs Hirsch's stance. According to Hirsch (2009–2010), only a common curriculum can rescue culturally diverse students in their struggle to close racially stratified achievement gaps. Absent from his discourse are the actual structural barriers and oppressive conditions that, critical multiculturalists point out, disadvantage diverse student populations in relation to academic and economic privileges of children from advantaged families.

Deep-seated opposition to multiculturalism as expressed by socially conservative elected officials and public intellectuals spills over into schoolhouse debates over diversity. For example, in 1994 a school board in Florida voted that teachers provide a curriculum that places American culture as exceptional and "superior to other foreign or historic cultures" (Rohter, 1994, p. 22). Nearly 20 years later, the state of Texas expressed a similar sensibility toward the curriculum K–12 students should receive.

The Case of Texas

The anxiety by social conservatives over ethnic studies and multiculturalism extends to interpretations of what should be included and excluded in the public school curriculum. Representative of this trend is how the state of Texas reworded its social studies standards to reassert common culture privileging of Christianity along with more favorable impressions of patriarchy, the Confederacy, capitalism, and the military. From a critical multiculturalism analysis, the standards represented a backlash against Islam and immigrants of color and overtly mute a history inclusive of slavery, political gains of

women, racial discrimination, labor unions, indigenous histories, and excess-
es of capitalism (Foner, 2010).

Cynthia Dunbar, a lawyer and a state board of education member, explained that it was necessary "to promote patriotism and to promote the free
enterprise system. There seems to have been a move away from a patriotic ideology" (as cited in McGreal, 2010, para. 4). Hence, the Texas standards state that
a purpose of social studies is to enable a kind of Americanism where "students
understand the importance of patriotism [and] function in a free enterprise society," which is synonymous with "capitalism and the free market system" (Texas
Administrative Code, 2011, pp. 2–3). Furthermore, a particular patriotic nationalism with a Protestant view of religion is present in the new standards because,
according to Dunbar, "There seems to be a denial that this was a nation founded under God" (as cited in McGreal, 2010, para. 4). The standards effectively
merge patriotism and nationalism with a divine sense that students understand
"the concept of American exceptionalism" (Texas Administrative Code, 2011,
p. 8). Such a worldview leaves little room to affirm diverse cultures, values,
languages, religions, and daily practices of immigrant and indigenous children
and their families.

The Case of Arizona

The U.S. state of Arizona, which borders Mexico, passed legislation to end ethnic
studies programs with a Latino emphasis in public schools. Acting on a philosophy of color-blind individualism, that state's conservative governor, Jan Brewer,
explained that her opposition to ethnic studies was because schoolchildren should
learn the values of individualism so that they will not express hostility toward
other races or socioeconomic classes (see Cambian Learning & National Academic
Educational Partners, 2011). Thomas Horne, the state's attorney general and former state superintendent of schools, claimed that a Mexican American Studies
(MAS) program in Tucson was "propaganda and brainwashing" (Horne, as cited
in Lacey, 2011, p. A1). Horne's position was within a larger context of nativist
anti-immigrant legislation and extralegal actions (Biggers, 2012).

In 2011 John Huppenthal, Arizona's superintendent of public instruction,
threatened to withhold $15 million from the Tucson School District if the school
board did not close the MAS program (Martinez, 2011). Huppenthal contended that the program violated state law and compared it to the indoctrination
that the Hitler Youth received in Nazi Germany (Biggers, 2011). An administrative judge concurred with the superintendent's assessments, and in 2012 the
local school board voted to shut down the program (Martinez, 2012).

The MAS program reflected an orientation in critical multiculturalism.
In diversity debates, the nativist nature of social conservatism strives to censor multiple perspectives that fall outside a master narrative. This disposition

resulted in a political strategy to deny Tucson students access to books in classrooms perceived as a threat to a common culture. Among the 81 banned books from classrooms with a Mexican American or social justice focus were *500 Years of Chicano History in Pictures*; *Pedagogy of the Oppressed*; *Rethinking Columbus: The Next 500 Years*; *Chicano! The History of the Mexican American Civil Rights Movement*; and *A People's History of the United States*. Also on the list was Shakespeare's *The Tempest* (Arizona Ethnic Studies Network, n.d.).

Arizona's Department of Education contracted with an independent organization to conduct an audit of the Tucson School District's MAS Department to determine the extent to which the ethnic studies program was in violation of a state statue that prohibits courses that

1. Promote the overthrow of the United States Government.
2. Promote resentment towards a race or class of people.
3. Are designed primarily for pupils of a particular ethnic group.
4. Advocate ethnic solidarity instead of treating pupils as individuals.
   (Cambian Learning & National Academic Educational Partners, 2011, pp. 4–5)

The 120-page report by the auditors concluded that "no observable evidence was present to indicate that any classroom within Tucson Unified School District is in direct violation of the law" (p. 50). Instead, the auditors found that "quite the opposite is true" (p. 50). The report noted, "Every school and every classroom visited by the auditors affirmed that these learning communities support a climate conducive to student achievement" (p. 50).

Specifically, both the district and the MAS faculty "agree that the academic focus of *culturally relevant coursework*, *critical consciousness*, and *authentic caring* is fundamental" (Cambian Learning & National Academic Educational Partners, 2011, p. 42, emphasis added), all conceptual elements of critical multiculturalism. The auditors further noted that "visual evidence presented within the classroom observation and instructional context demonstrated effective use of curriculum to support student achievement" (p. 42). Auditors also found the banned books acceptable for classroom use. Importantly, MAS students demonstrated higher graduation rates than non-MAS students from 2005 to 2010 (Cambian Learning & National Academic Educational Partners, 2011; Sleeter, 2011).

Based on another report that came to similar conclusions about the MAS program, especially in regard to academic achievement and graduation rates among students who participated in the program (Cabrera, Milem, & Marx, 2012), a federal judge in 2013 declared that the district should provide culturally relevant courses similar to those offered in the banned MAS program. The decision was part of a desegregation order that the judge declared the school district ignored for over 25 years (Nevarez, 2013). Books previously banned were reinstated by a narrow vote of the Tucson school board later that same year. Nevertheless, the future reinstatement of the MAS program remained uncertain as the state superintendent promised to continue to scrutinize the district's curriculum (Quinn, 2013).

A CRITICAL MULTICULTURAL ALTERNATIVE

Positions based in critical multiculturalism are not surprised to find that in the 21st century groups associated with social conservatism and liberal multiculturalism either oppose or give perfunctory support for ethnic studies and multicultural education. For example, Sleeter (2011) is clear in naming the marginalization of nondominant standpoints from the mainstream school curriculum that should be more accurately labeled "Euro-American ethnic studies" (p. vii). Such a curriculum and school organization can contribute to low graduation rates for students of color and to compromised social psychological experiences of ethnically diverse students. Sleeter explains, "As students of color proceed through the school system, research finds that the overwhelming dominance of Euro-American perspectives leads many such students to disengage from academic learning" (p. vii).

As an alternative orientation, critical multiculturalism embraces a diversity of cultures and languages that young people and their families bring into their communities and classrooms. Rather than finding the cultures and languages of immigrants and indigenous people a threat and in need of assimilation or token celebration, critical multiculturalism incorporates the concept of a *common multiculture of difference*. As used here, difference signals an affirming recognition and inclusion of underrepresented groups. Critical multiculturalism offers a clear choice to an absolutist social conservatism as to who can legitimately be included in and excluded from a nation's culture or the liberal multiculturalism assimilation conception of cultures and languages of immigrants and indigenous people simmering into a uniform and nondescript English-speaking melting pot.

Whereas social conservatism is quite clear about fears of difference, the individualistic ideology of liberal multiculturalism minimizes structural barriers to academic success and economic well-being for immigrant and indigenous students and their families. Critical multiculturalism, instead, highlights the structural challenges that these groups face and supports active resistance to exclusionary and assimilationist educational policies that marginalize minority ethnic groups. Critical multiculturalism aligns with current research on bilingualism for incorporation of immigrant and indigenous languages into the early years of schooling. Rather than ignoring language diversity through generally ineffective English-immersion programs, a well-constructed bilingual curriculum can provide a sense of belonging within the school alongside research-based instruction that can enhance academic learning. Critical multiculturalism favors a redistribution of public expenditures to this end and away from practices that continue to alienate and ill serve immigrant and indigenous youth.

Martha Nussbaum (2010) gives voice to critical multiculturalism when she observes that educators and policymakers who identify with dominant political economy goals "will not want a study of history that focuses on injustices of class, caste, gender, and ethno-religious membership, because that will prompt critical thinking about the present" (p. 21). Dominant groups oppose ethnic studies with a critical multicultural orientation by silencing "the damages done by nationalist ideals" (p. 21). The result, Nussbaum continues, is a curriculum that skews "national ambition, especially ambition for wealth, as a great good, and will downplay issues of poverty and inequality and issues of global accountability" (p. 21). Nussbaum's critical perspective captures the immigration and curriculum battles that provide national examples of social conservatism's political influence alongside liberalism's acquiescence. Within diversity debates over ethnic studies and multicultural education and the best interests of students from diverse backgrounds, the standpoint of critical multiculturalism remains a viable alternative to nativist approaches to difference that liberal multiculturalism is ineffective in countering.

Dominant White Christian patriarchy plays a significant role in opposition to ethnic studies and multicultural education. We next investigate how this orientation also affects intersections of diverse sexual and gender identities and minority religions.

NOTES

*The UN uses the phrase "developed countries" for statistical purposes. Developed countries include the United States, Canada, Australia, New Zealand, Japan, and nations in Europe (UNICEF, 2012).

CHAPTER 7

A Smog of Patriarchy:
Gender, Sexuality, and Religion

Religion is one of the most important multicultural issues in the
United States today—and possibly the most problematic.

—Philip Chinn, Religion, Culture, and Education in the United States

More than other religious faith Christian doctrine which condones
sexism and male domination informs all the ways we learn about
gender roles in this society.

—bell hooks, *Feminism Is for Everyone: Passionate Politics*

Religious and secular values influence moral interpretations of social and
political expressions of gender and sexuality in public schools. Although
commonly conceived as aspects of the private sphere, gender, sexuality, and
religion clearly exist in the public sphere. Building in momentum since the
1970s, diversity debates around gender, sexuality, and religion grew in complexity and intensity into the 2010s. Because these diversity issues contentiously range from the private sphere of the family and religious institutions to
the public sphere of civil rights, educators and policymakers find themselves
in a rapidly shifting terrain as to what constitutes a common culture and what
should and should not be included in a school's curriculum. In this atmosphere, many public school teachers enact curricula daily that leave students'
sexuality and gender identification concerns to school hallways, social media,
or dreaded and embarrassed silences. More than any other issues discussed in
this book, the diversity issues described in the following pages are in a rapid
renegotiation that is radically reshaping mainstream interpretations of gender
and sexuality. These diversity issues carry over to what is an acceptable religion in a national culture of a hegemonic Christianity.

This chapter does not attempt to cover all of these topics but instead highlights key diversity issues that face the public and what this can mean for the
education of children. Like differing societal attitudes toward race, ethnicity,
and immigration, worldviews expressed in homes, religious institutions, and
the public domain affect the responses of schools to youth sexuality, gender

identification, and religious expressions. A purpose of this chapter is to engage in a discussion of how these three aspects of identity that arise in diversity debates are intertwined with ideological orientations in the typology of social conservatism, liberal multiculturalism, and critical multiculturalism.

As a useful reminder, a typology represents categories of ideal types (cf. the Introduction and Chapter 2) and, therefore, does not suggest an essentialization of identities. Across ideological orientations, people who identify with a particular religion, such as Christianity, will differ in religious attitudes and practices—and have done so for centuries. The same is true in regard to gender identification and sexuality. For example, simply because an individual is identified as male, female, or transgender does not imply that people with those respective identities necessarily fall into the same camp in regard to gender identification discourse or religious attitudes. In summary, individuals with similar gender identities and religious preferences can find themselves in this analysis at different points along an ideological spectrum.

The chapter's organization is on the centrality of *patriarchy*, the disproportionate dominance of men in society. Discussed is the political economy commonality between slavery and patriarchal families, legal barriers to the full personhood of women, and gendered career opportunities. This leads to an examination of the modern origins and lingering effects of a patriarchal backlash against sexuality and gender in the school curriculum as a clash of ideologies rather than the more common assertion of a clash of cultures. The policing of sexual and gender boundaries in schools requires a clarification of terminology in this critique alongside an overview of the developmental ramifications for young people. A discussion of harassment and bullying of persons of diverse sexualities and genders segues into the relationship of patriarchy and patriotism and the consequences for Muslims since September 11, 2001. The chapter includes that event because many education students in the 2010s were too young to recall the continuing significance this act of terror had on people of the Islamic faith and the subsequent nationalistic fervor that found an unconstitutional home in public schools. The chapter concludes with a discussion of the effectiveness of hegemonic Christianity and the importance of naming and teaching about patriarchy.

A BRIEF HISTORY OF PATRIARCHY

The origins of diversity debates over gender, sexuality, and religion are located historically in systems of patriarchy, or male domination. Patriarchy is

> a social system in which men disproportionately occupy positions of power and authority, central norms and values are associated with manhood and masculinity

(which in turn are defined in terms of dominance and control), and men are the primary focus of attention in most cultural spaces. (Whisnant, 2013, para. 5)

Under such arrangements, women and children were legally property of their husbands and fathers without individual rights. The Christian concept of an all-powerful divine Father in heaven was equally applied to males as earthly societal and family leaders. Through the promise of eternal salvation, a patriarchal social order unified itself around a hierarchical social order premised on male superiority and female submission to male authority (Folbre, 2009).

Whereas male children could anticipate someday becoming independent of their patriarchal families of origin, female children were forever constructed as male property. A daughter transitioned from the status of her father's property to her husband's upon being given away for an exchange value. Under patriarchal arrangements, a woman was to submit to her husband's sexual demands and not attempt to avoid conception. Restricted from the public sphere of life, women were to marry with the blessing of the Church and to bear children for their husbands. Despite John Locke's (1690/2003) ideological influence on liberal concepts of individual liberty and equality, he made an exception when the subject included women. Drawing on a biblical interpretation of women that required them to submit to men in marriage as part of natural law, Locke intellectually separated the political domain from the private sphere of marriage:

> the power that every *husband hath to order the things of private concernment to his family*, as proprietor of the goods and lands there, and to have *his will take place before that of his wife* in all things of their common concernment. (p. 33, emphasis added)

Women who deviated from such patriarchal norms faced shame and, more severely, physical violence.

Commonality Between Slavery and Patriarchy

The treatment of slaves and women in patriarchal marriages shared certain similarities. A male-dominated social and political system created "the expectation of subservience" for both slaves and married women (Folbre, 2009, p. 76). Like slaves, married women could not legally claim a right to the product of their labor. Both slaves and women under patriarchy were unable to make a lawful claim to their own children. With religious approval and a patriarchal rule of law, White men could legally separate children from their mothers under slavery and during marriage. A sexual double standard existed for White married men who raped slave women or sought sex through prostitution whereas a woman adulteress faced punishment. In regard to the care of their slaves and wives, legally, "slave owners and patriarchs were required only to meet the subsistence needs of their dependents and could administer physical punishment without the close supervision of the law" (Folbre, 2009, pp. 75–76). This system of patriarchal control finds resonance in contemporary violence against girls and women (Valenti, 2013).

Many women in the movement to abolish slavery were also active in working to secure civil rights for women. Gradually state laws granted common ownership of property in marriages to both the husband and wife although men retained the legal right to manage and dispose of property. Only in the death of a husband could a woman legally manage her property ("Married Women's Property Laws," n.d.).

Legal Barriers to Full Personhood for Women

What had been religiously sanctioned coercion and control of women became institutionalized in legal doctrine in the 19th and 20th centuries. Political deliberations excluded women from policies that directly affected their participation in the public sphere and control of their own bodies. Despite a constitutional amendment in 1920 that provided women with the right to vote, U.S. women lacked full property rights or personhood. Their participation in the public sphere increased but was confined through legal decisions according to gendered norms of appropriateness for a woman.

Historian Alice Kessler-Harris (2001) notes that in the United States from the 1890s into the 1980s "special considerations of all kinds could prevent women from being persons under the law" (p. 171). Restrictions on definitions of persons varied in different states and over time. Although statutes would use the word *person*, the legal interpretation was *man*. Courts deferred to states to determine personhood on the basis of patriarchal custom that could exclude women from serving on juries and qualifying for traditional male careers and jobs. In the 1960s and 1970s "almost all [federally funded] job programs excluded or discriminated against women" (p. 270). Section 1 of the Equal Rights Amendment (ERA) that was passed by Congress in 1972 and sent to the states for ratification stated, "Equality of rights under the law shall not be denied or abridged by the United States or by any state on account of sex" ("Overview," n.d.). The ERA failed, however, to get the necessary number of state legislatures to pass the amendment. By the mid-2010s, U.S. women held just 18% of congressionally elected positions and 22% of statewide elective executive offices (Center for Women and Politics, 2014).

Gendered Career Opportunities

As a result of the Women's Movement, girls and women started to see expanded educational and career opportunities in the 1970s and 1980s. Nevertheless, within families and the larger society women carry the patriarchal responsibility to take care of others. Despite unprecedented gains for women in career opportunities, women find most jobs in the caring vocations. As necessary as these jobs are for a healthy functioning society, secular patriarchal ideologies serve to reward caring professions financially less than those deemed historically for men. Moreover, career advancement for women in traditionally male-dominated organization is often limited by a glass-ceiling effect, where a woman can aspire to higher levels of an organization but only in exceptional cases break through a seemingly impermeable barrier (Folbre, 2009). Predictive of patriarchal values, by the 2010s a significantly higher percentage of men than women held the highest paying jobs (Carnevale, Strohl, & Melton, 2011). Gendered career differences are a contributing factor to women's weekly earnings representing 81% of men's median earnings (cf. U.S. Department of Labor, 2011).

PATRIARCHY AND THE SCHOOL CURRICULUM

Critical multiculturalism brings attention to both gender balance and sexual health in the school curriculum. Because liberal multiculturalism emerged from Locke's (1690/2003) patriarchal interpretation of equality and liberty, this orientation takes tepid steps to gender and sexuality inclusion in the curriculum. Social conservatism remains resistant to altering patriarchy's legacy. Among these three ideological orientations, a fluid struggle continues over control of the place of gender and sexuality in public schools.

Social conservatism found voice in the 1970s in a backlash against gains in civil rights for women and people of color. A patriarchal social order reinforced by dominant Christianity was threatened—and social conservatism reacted with lasting effects. In order to appreciate this historic reaction, we turn to events in West Virginia that fueled a national religious movement to realign the school curriculum to its former monocultural status.

Clash of Ideologies

The 1974 case of the West Virginia Kanawha County textbook controversy set a political tone for the next 40 years over the place of religion and sexuality in the school curriculum. Although framed by conservatives and liberals as a clash of cultures, more accurately the events set off in the state capital of West Virginia were a clash of ideologies. In this instance, the ideology of social conservatism found support in massive protests against textbooks and curricular practices that went against dominant Christian patriarchal values.

The authoritarian and violent aspect of social conservatism appeared publicly in these ideologically driven political actions. As parents staged a school boycott that kept thousands of children home, protesters firebombed homes of textbook supporters and shot at school buses. Protestors also fired upon two schools and dynamited another. After a school board meeting, 15 sticks of dynamite exploded in the district's office building. Anti-textbook protesters physically attacked the school superintendent, assistant superintendent, and two school board members; this included a female protester's spraying disabling chemical mace on the superintendent (National Education Association, 1975/1991; Phillips-Fein, 2011).

The Kanawha County textbook backlash marks a rise of a conservative Christian social movement that forcefully asserted its orientation in school board elections and at hearings over textbook selections. The overriding claim of conservative protesters was that many of the district's books were "dirty," "Godless," and "Communist" (Franklin, 1974, para. 1). Parent protesters and their supporters complained about the inclusion in libraries and classrooms of texts that they believed reflected (a) a decline in sexual morals since the rise of the Women's Movement, (b) a distortion of literature with the inclusion of diverse racial voices emerging from the Civil Rights Movement, and (c) un-American attitudes of peace poetry as a reflection of an era of public opposition to the Vietnam War. Specifically, this religious fundamentalist uprising was accompanied by an "antifeminist backlash . . . set off not by women's achievement of full equality but by the increased possibilities that they might win it" (Faludi, 1991, p. xx).

The tipping point for socially conservative parents and their allies nationally was a more receptive environment to discussions and expressions of sexual norms. Sex education in the school curriculum "represented the extension of the new promiscuity to children and the loss of the rights of parents to protect their children from the 'immoral' changes taking place around them" (Kincheloe, 1983, p. 12). Moreover, for this particular diversity topic, no space existed for alternative viewpoints. In the words of the Kanawha County leader of the anti-textbook movement, "God is right—everything else is wrong" (as cited in Kincheloe, p. 30).

The Continuing Curriculum Battle

The lingering effects of this case remain today within the public school psyche. In many regards a socially conservative orientation is replicated in the contemporary cases of social conservatism's hegemony in Texas and Arizona over multicultural expressions and ethnic studies. In 2012, for example, the Texas Republican Party's platform mirrored the same social conservatism enforced in West Virginia 4 decades earlier. Claims that "public acknowledgement of

God is undeniable in our history and is vital to our freedom, prosperity and strength" lead those wedded to social conservatism to work at "dispelling the myth of separation of church and state" (Republican Party of Texas, 2012, p. 14). Moral absolutes of social conservatism based in a mission to remake the United States into a theistic nation through threats of violence and a climate of fear can effectively limit curricular actions school districts are willing to take.

Censorship. Patriotism, Christian fundamentalism, a claimed sanctity of the family unit of a married man and woman, and capitalism merge seamlessly in social conservatism (see National Education Association, 1975/1991). In the last decade of the 20th century, the American Library Association reported over 6,000 calls to remove books from schools. The most cited reasons were material that religious conservatives deemed "sexually explicit," containing "offensive language," "unsuited to age group," "promoting homosexuality," and including "nudity" ("Schools and Censorship," n.d., para. 6). An example of this conflicted milieu is a recent controversy over the banning of a Newbery Award–winning children's book—with some school librarians leading the censorship charge—for using the word "scrotum" as the identifying body part of a dog that had been bitten by a rattlesnake (Bosman, 2007). In the 2010s cautious school district textbook selection guidelines helped to serve as self-censoring mechanisms (Rickman, 2010). The overall ideological results are strategies by liberal multiculturalism to strike a cautious balance with social conservatism whereas critical multiculturalism's emphasis continues as a standpoint for full inclusion of gender and sexuality topics that serve the developmental needs of young people.

Opposition to Critical Thinking. Among the banned books in the 1974 Kanawha County school district were ones that encouraged students to reflect on their personal values. In a world of moral absolutes, no room exists for learning that leads to critical reflection. In 2012, under "Knowledge-Based Education," the Texas Republican Party platform stated, "We oppose the teaching of Higher Order Thinking Skills (values clarification), critical thinking skills and similar programs that . . . have the purpose of challenging the student's fixed beliefs and understanding of parental authority" (Republican Party of Texas, 2012, p. 12). The long arch of social conservatism from the 1970s to the 2010s is further illustrated in the platform: "We recognize parental responsibility and authority regarding sex education. . . . We oppose any sex education other than abstinence until marriage" (p. 13). In contrast, researchers for the Centers for Disease Control and Prevention find that the middle school years are when educators should introduce formal sex education and contraceptive options to prevent unwanted teenage pregnancies (S. Cox et al., 2014).

PATRIARCHAL POLICING OF SEXUAL BOUNDARIES

Social conservatives oppose sexuality education, other than abstinence before a marriage between a man and women, and fail to recognize diverse genders and sexual orientations. A liberal multicultural response is limited to instruction in human physiology and tolerance for nondominant gender and sexual expressions. To understand these restrictive curricular actions, a critical multicultural approach helps clarify attitudes that result from these two dominant orientations.

Unexamined terminology in public discourse holds significant implications for the ways in which educators treat young people and for the content of the curriculum students receive. It is important to clarify the language used to analyze intersections of gender, sexuality, and religion. Many of these terms found in mainstream discourse, popular culture, and new emerging definitions exist in tension with one another. The terms that follow are a significant aspect of debated diversity discourse where the private and public spheres overlap.

Sex and Sexuality

Conventionally *sex* refers to biological characteristics of male and female. Expanding this binary definition, *transsexual* denotes "having a gender identity that does not align with physical sex [alongside] changing one's self-presentation or one's body in order to arrive at a more satisfactory gender expression" (Meem, Gibson, & Alexander, 2010, p. 434), a standpoint that critical multiculturalism includes. In popular usage to *have sex* implies some kind of physical intimacy between at least two individuals. Social conservatism limits definitions of having sex to acts that can lead to human conception as part of a patriarchal expectation. Other forms of sexual intimacy between partners and a broader definition of sexuality fall within more liberal and critical interpretations. *Sexuality* refers to "any and all human qualities, behaviours, feelings and preoccupations of a sexual nature" (Cameron & Kulick, 2006, p. 3). Despite the fact that people vary widely in experiences of sexuality, sexual identities are socially and politically contested.

Differing ideological orientations across cultures "distinguish acceptable sexual acts, practices or relationships from those that are inappropriate, distasteful, disgusting, perverted or wicked" (Cameron & Kulick, 2006, p. 4). Whereas liberal multiculturalism springs from an impulse to limit discussions to individual sexuality in the private sphere, critical multiculturalism questions how young people can learn from adults if sexuality is only whispered about in private settings and not incorporated into the public sphere of the school curriculum. Such various worldviews account for how educational policies for provisions of sex education are fraught with social and political anxiety. The consequences of a hegemonic mix of social conservatism and liberal multiculturalism, nevertheless, hold significance for the welfare of children and their transition to adulthood.

Implications for Young People

Throughout their schooling years, children and youth experience physiological changes that affect their social-psychological identity and state of well-being (Maccoby, 2005), yet adult culture generally avoids helping young people to understand the social, emotional, and political dynamics that are associated with these physical and affective developments and desires. Developmental psychologists explain that

> as a domain of identity formation, sexuality is importantly unique . . . [and] is not a frequent topic of conversation between adolescents and their parents, peers, or school counsellors. As a society, we do not go out of our way to provide adolescents with opportunities to explore their sexuality. (Cole, Cole, & Lightfoot, 2005, p. 643)

This overall avoidance of meaningful discussions of sexuality between adults and youth occurs in an environment where, according to the National Center for Health Statistics, approximately 20% of young people in the United States engage in sexual intercourse before the age of 15 (Kelly, 2005). Furthermore, "88 percent of middle and high schoolers who pledge to stay virgins until marriage end up having premarital sex anyway. . . [and] are less likely to use contraception" (Kelly, 2005, "Teaching the Children," para. 2). School district responses range from a few newsworthy ones that include sexual orientation and condom use in their sex education programs (de Vise, 2007; Zemia, 2007) to those that advocate religious-informed "abstinence only" or "abstinence based" programs by disallowing directions on birth control, including condom applications (Buhain, 2007; Jayson, 2007). Based in a heterosexual discourse, such programs contribute to a negative school climate for students with diverse gender identities and sexual orientations (Kosciw, Greytak, Bartkiewicz, Boesen, & Palmer, 2012). This technical, "antisex" pattern is replicated not only in the United States but also in Canada, the United Kingdom, and Australia in contrast to the Netherlands's critical "emphasis on 'relationship' education" (Epstein, O'Flynn, & Telford, 2001, p. 131; Robinson & Ferfolja, 2007). The privileging of a technical notion of sexuality over the actual desires and experiences of young people represents what a critical standpoint identifies as "compulsory heterosexuality" (Rich, 1983). At the same time sex education remains contested, students with nondominant sexual orientations and diverse gender identifications face remnants of an unacknowledged patriarchal policing of behavior and curriculum.

PATRIARCHAL POLICING OF GENDER BOUNDARIES

Unlike biological sex, gender is a socially constructed category that holds political and economic consequences. Social conservatism does not overtly make a distinction between gender and biological sex. Only in 2012 did the mainstream American Psychiatric Association (APA) remove "gender identity" as a mental health disorder, a stigma that gave conservatives "rhetorical carte blanche to describe the entire trans community as disordered, delusional, and mentally ill" (Ford, 2012, para. 2). More accurately, the APA substituted "gender dysphoria" to identify the stress that can develop from "a marked incongruence between one's experienced/expressed gender and assigned gender" (as cited in Ford, 2012, para. 3). Both contemporary liberal and critical perspectives—despite significant variance—view sex and gender as separate categories.

At its basic meaning, *gender* is "learned behaviors and attitudes supposed to correspond with biological sex" (Meem et al., 2010, p. 432). Under this definition, all of us embody a socially constructed *gender identity*. Over time, people learn what it means to perform as a male or a female. Outside the boundaries of social conservatism, *transgender* breaks from this binary and blurs normative gender identities beyond dominant boundaries of a masculine–feminine dichotomy. Liberal multiculturalism requires a respect for the dignity of an individual but tends to stop short of full acknowledgment of the consequences of group-based discrimination of diverse gender identities. To better understand this issue, critical multiculturalism draws from the feminist concept of heteronormativity.

Taken collectively, identities and orientations of heterosexual, gay, lesbian, bisexual, transsexual, and transgender blur rigid distinctions between sex and gender. To capture this overlapping of identities and their material and psychological effects, critical multiculturalism incorporates the concept of heteronormativity. Cameron and Kulick (2006) define *heteronormativity* as "an overarching system for organizing and regulating sexuality, whereby certain ways of acting, thinking and feeling about sex are privileged over others," recognizing that "not all expressions of heterosexuality are equal" (p. 9). Conceptually, heteronormativity helps explain how mainstream social discourse places limits on the validity of gender and sexuality expressions.

Queering the Curriculum

In the context of heteronormativity, queer theory serves as "an inquiry into the nature and workings of heteronormativity, along with the 'queer' sexualities that heteronormativity produces by stigmatizing, silencing and or proscribing them" (Cameron & Kulick, 2006, p. 10). Cameron and Kulick carefully note that the use of *queer* is not intended to be equated with homosexual "but rather 'non- or anti-heteronormative' [because] straight people and heterosexual practices can also be 'queer' if they deviate from the heteronormative ideal" (p. 10). What appears reserved for the private sphere of sexual expressions can become an aspect of gender identification in the public sphere. Confounding this situation is the management of multicultural expressions in schools that can limit diversity issues, including sexuality and gender equity when they move beyond heteronormative boundaries.

The goal of queering the curriculum away from heteronormativity shares similarities with Banks's (1993) multicultural analysis of "positionality" and identity formation where "important aspects of our identity . . . are markers of relational positions rather than essential qualities" (p. 5). In his use of positionality, Banks was specifically interested in having teachers, especially those who identify as White, understand how an unspoken normalized White identity can perpetuate the costs of institutional racism while continuing to create negative consequences for students of color. A parallel purpose for queering the curriculum is found with educators who use a queer approach to make visible the harm of heteronormativity for gay and lesbian students as well as those who identify as heterosexual.

Hypermasculinity and Violence

Reactive patriarchy can result in violence against women and diverse gender identifications. To give language to this phenomenon, critical multiculturalism incorporates the heteronormative concept of *hypermasculinity*. As "an exaggerated form of traditional masculinity ideology," hypermasculinity is "characterized by a lack of appreciation of differences among males" (Aez, Casado, & Wade, 2009, p. 116). Based on a patriarchal ideology of male dominance, hypermasculinity displays characteristics of "dangerousness, acceptance of violence, and dominance, particularly over women" (Karp, 2010, p. 65). Compared to other men, hypermasculine men are less empathic to diversity and react with more anger to negative behavioral feedback (Vass & Gold, 1995). From his extensive research on masculinities and violence, Bowker (1998) concluded, "Violent men are notoriously difficult to socialize into prosocial lifestyles" (p. 1).

Hypermasculine men find refuge in social conservatism and its respect for male authority. Liberal multiculturalism views violence and abusive behavior of hypermasculinity as individual problems that are solved through such techniques as anger management. Because liberal multiculturalism is deeply invested in the individual as the primary unit of analysis, this orientation overlooks institutional causes. In contrast, critical multiculturalism returns to systems of religious and secular patriarchy as enablers for hypermasculinity. It is not only heterosexual men who are capable of expressions of hypermasculine violence. Bowker (1998) makes an important gendered distinction and explains that he does not equate biological men with masculinities of violence: "Anyone can play a masculine role" (p. 7). Systems of patriarchy contribute to a hypermasculinity in which any sex or gender identification is capable of violence against non-normative sexuality and gender expressions. Nevertheless, the manifestation of masculine violence rests primarily with men and institutionally with "political opposition to violence control by masculine elites who benefit from the violence in some way" (p. 14).

Federal law requires schools to have policies and practices to prevent school personnel from inflicting sexual violence on students. Although nearly 10% of all students are apparently victims of sexual abuse by school personnel, a U.S. Department of Education report noted that cases are underreported (Blad, 2014). In a smog of patriarchy that goes unacknowledged by the larger society, only in the 21st century has the practice of students' harassing and bullying other students—let alone school personnel's taking sexual advantage of vulnerable students—undergone a process of unpacking this normalized patriarchal behavior.

PATRIARCHAL BULLYING AND GENDERED HARASSMENT

Meyer (2009) explains that *gendered harassment* represents "behavior that acts to shape and police the boundaries of traditional gender norms" and negatively affects the recipient (p. 1). *Bullying* is "behavior that repeatedly and over time intentionally inflicts injury on another" (p. 2). While bullying targets a specific individual, harassment contributes to a hostile learning environment, especially for groups with minority sexual orientations and diverse gender identities.

Students in the United States who are outside heterosexual norms, such as lesbian, gay, bisexual, and transgender (LGBT) youth, report higher incidences of harassment and bullying than other students and lack confidence in school officials coming to their assistance (Gay, Lesbian, & Straight Education Network [GLSEN], 2005). Although overall levels of anti-LGBT language and experiences of harassment and assault remain high, a 2011 report of an annual survey sponsored by GLSEN found for "the first time . . . both decreases in negative indicators of school climate (biased remarks and victimization) and continued increases in most LGBT-related school supports" (Kosciw et al., 2012, p. 144). Despite this positive turn for LGBT students, the report's authors pointedly note, "*Schools nationwide are hostile environments* for a distressing number of LGBT students, the overwhelming majority of whom hear homophobic remarks and experience harassment or assault at school because of their sexual orientation or gender expression" (p. xiv, emphasis added). Over time, harassment and bullying take a toll on their young victims. Harassed and bullied LGBT students as well as those with non-normative gender expressions have higher levels of depression, lower self-esteem, higher absentee rates, and lower academic en-gagement and achievement than other students (Kosciw et al., 2012).

At the middle and high school levels, it is not unusual to hear educators and parents explain adolescent manifestations of sexuality and gender identity formation as simply a case of "raging hormones." This asserted folk-biological knowledge permits many adults to compartmentalize this developmental facet of young people outside the scope of schooling. This is a time when "heterosex-uality is expected to break out and yet remain taboo in the secondary school" (Epstein et al., 2001, p. 139). A study of graduate-level teacher candidates found that their own experiences of early adolescent years of middle school were "the most volatile and significant developmental experiences with gender and sexual identity formation. The change from elementary school to middle school was generally recalled as a dramatic shift" (Vavrus, 2009, p. 387). Reinforcing this finding, the GLSEN survey researchers also reported that LGBT middle school students "fared worse" than those at high school (Kosciw et al., 2012, p. xix). One explanation was limited school resources and support mechanisms avail-able for diverse gender identities and sexual orientations at the middle school level. Students apparently begin to experience the full impact of patriarchal heteronormativity during the early adolescent years.

Antibullying Legislation

By the mid-2010s, all but one U.S. state had passed some kind of antibullying legislation that required schools to create policies to halt bullying. The scope of the laws varied significantly among states. Some mentioned both sexual orien-tation and gender identity, some just sexual orientation, and others purposely disallowed mention of any protected category. Punishment for an apprehended bully ranged from no repercussions in five states to possible criminal prosecution in 12 (Clark, 2013; Sacco, Silbaugh, Corredor, Casey, & Doherty, 2012).

Socially conservative parents oppose laws intended to protect school-children from bullying, especially those who do not fit gendered norms. Using religious texts, these parents and their allies assert that homosexuality is a life-style choice and not a biological reality. For example, an analysis of state laws by the prominent conservative Christian political advocacy group Focus on Family in collaboration with the Alliance Defending Freedom (ADA) (2012) states that any school policies that mention "sexual orientation" or "gender identity" as a protected category are part of "a nationwide campaign to promote homosexual behavior to impressionable, school-age children" (p. 4). With religious echoes of the 1974 Kanawha County textbook protests, the ADA critique is clear in its advocacy of heteronormative curriculum and instruction. The effectiveness of this ideology can be measured by the fact that positive representations of LGBT-related topics in schools remains rare (Kosciw et al., 2012).

As part of its ideological strategy, the socially conservative ADA (2012) contends that private schools should be exempt from antibullying legislation. Furthermore, a law is flawed if it "lacks exceptions for religious, political, or philosophical student speech that is protected by the First Amendment" (p. 2). Drawing on a free speech argument for the right to speak or act negatively toward any gender diverse student merges with long-standing liberal political theory that defends absolute free speech. Critical multiculturalism, instead, considers a free speech defense in this case a shorthand method to allow harassment and bullying, especially when conservative national public relations campaigns cause fearful school personnel to cancel programs that promote equal treatment of students (Severson, 2012).

Safe Schools Programs

Liberal multiculturalists point to empirical data that counter the lifestyle argument and have responded to the recognition of diverse identities of LGBT youth by instituting "safe school" programs to be more inclusive of diverse sexualities and to counter bullying, an approach intolerable from a perspective of social conservatism. These programs, however, are too often limited by their focus on individual behaviors of perpetrators and victims rather than a systemic public institutional problem that school officials need to address (Loutzenheiser & Moore, 2009). Research on behalf of GLSEN supports a critical multicultural approach to systemic and structural solutions.

For example, an individualist strategy based in liberalism overlooks patterns of *group discrimination* documented in school athletics and physical education classes, where reports of harassment or bullying of LGBT students range from nearly 30% while playing sports to over 50% when in a physical education class (Kosciw et al., 2012). Hence, a need exists for across-the-board safe school policies with enforcement provisions. Kosciw et al. (2012) explain, "A 'comprehensive' policy is one that explicitly enumerates protections based on personal characteristics, including both sexual orientation and gender identity/ expression" (p. 53). This necessitates a proactive diversity training program for teachers and staff (Robinson & Espelage, 2012). Only through a schoolwide approach that identifies sources of discrimination and puts in place a comprehensive strategy can students with diverse gender identities and sexual orientations begin to find relief from the oppression they experience in their schools.

Despite significant gains for children, well-placed financial opposition remains to a safe school curriculum reflective of critical multiculturalism. Decades of political attacks on public schools led in the United States largely by radical Christian fundamentalists accentuated a general unease with issues of sexuality and gender differences by educators. Pulitzer Prize–winning reporter Chris Hedges (2006) identifies these Christian groups as "American fascists" for their "wealthy, right-wing sponsors" and tactics of intimidation (p. 14), strategies that in turn contributed to an anti-Muslim, anti-Arab zeitgeist.

PATRIARCHY, PATRIOTISM, AND THE DEMONIZATION OF ISLAM

In the Cold War atmosphere of the 1950s, Congress added the phrase "under God" to the U.S. Pledge of Allegiance and Dwight Eisenhower was the first president to publicly declare that the United States was a Judeo-Christian nation (A. Preston, 2012). Sixty years later, seeing an erosion of a dominant common culture of Christian patriarchy, a member of Congress representative of social conservatism declared that "America needs to be returned to its roots, its Judeo-Christian roots" (Akin, as cited in Eligion, 2012, p. A16). A liberal Episcopal priest observed how social conservatism "conjoin[s] the flag and cross" in many mainstream Christian churches (Shipman, 2012, p. A20). Social conservatism further conflates sexuality with patriotism and U.S. foreign policy. In the late 1960s the John Birch Society framed sex education as a "filthy Communist plot" (Associated Press, 1969). In the 2010s, a socially conservative narrative of declining birth rates created a backlash against increasing female access to birth control in a nationalistic context about a "decline of America" and an anxiety "about America's imperial future" (Carmon, 2013, paras. 3, 9).

The ideology of patriotism has its origins in patriarchy and signals to male citizens to unite for the patria, or fatherland, and the state. With roots that connect "property, authority, and status" (Vincent, 2005, p. 1722), patriotism in the 2010s serves as an unacknowledged manifestation of patriarchy and male dominance over expressions of diverse religious identities. The ideology of patriotism serves as a "just war" defense of family and territorial states. For more than 800 years Christian doctrine proclaimed "the religious duty of citizens to render themselves vulnerable to death for their patria" (Vincent, 2005, p. 1722). Hence, a certain kind of reactive patriotism springs from a long history of ideological patriarchy and Christian male control of home and society.

Patriotic Fear-Based Schooling

Since the events of September 11, 2001 (9/11), Christian patriarchy created dire consequences for adherents of the Islamic faith. A criminal attack by a small group of suicide terrorists who were Muslims destroyed the World Trade Center, a global symbol of capitalism located in New York City. This attack, which killed over 3,000 people, provided a patriotic drumbeat for war against Afghanistan, a nation that did not attack the United States. This led to demonizing and harassing Muslims as well as any other diverse people and groups mixed in the reactive American psyche as Muslim. Reflecting shortly after

9/11, critical educator Michael Apple (2002) observed how "the tropes of patriotism and vengeance all work together to create a mighty call not for justice but for vengeance" (p. 301). Apple summarized the racial and religious profiling atmosphere that led a liberal democracy to act illiberally: "Almost immediately, there were a multitude of instances throughout the nation of people who 'looked Arabic' being threatened and harassed on the street, in schools, and in their places of business" (p. 302). Christian patriarchy successfully conflated ethnicity and diverse religions in a narrative about enemies of the state. The discrimination unleashed on Muslims reflects political scientist Corey Robin's (2004) observations on how liberal democracies permit nongovernmental, civil groups to carry out "repressive fear" (p. 1062). Robin explains, "Because the Constitution makes it difficult for the state to wield weapons of fear with abandon, elites often rely upon these weapons of civil society, which are not subject to much constitutional restraint" (p. 1063). Major civil institutions that created fear after 9/11 were churches (Matthes, 2008) and schools.

After 9/11 a wave of patriotism descended on public schools. With no critical analysis of foreign policy causes behind those events (Apple, 2002; Chomsky, 2001/2011), the public school curriculum eliminated critical thinking and dissent and promoted loyalty to the U.S. invasion of Afghanistan. A September 2001 *New York Times* article under the headline "School Colors Become Red, White and Blue" reported, "As a surge of patriotism has washed over the country in the wake of the terrorist attacks, nowhere has the revival been more omnipresent than in schools" (Sack, para. 4). Representative of this moment 10 years after 9/11, one woman recalled that as a 15-year-old at the time of 9/11, she "had no concept of what it meant except that suddenly we were saying the Pledge of Allegiance again every day and having assemblies about patriotism, and everyone was flying their flags again out of nowhere" (Bright, as cited in Zernike, 2011, para. 2). Forgotten was a 1943 U.S. Supreme Court ruling against school officials who required their students to pledge allegiance to the United States. The court cited adverse effects on dissent and how "compulsory unification of opinion achieves only the unanimity of the graveyard" (*West Virginia State Board of Education v. Barnett*, 1943, p. 7). Further lost in these recollections is the backlash against Muslim Americans that continues to this day.

Ambiguity Toward Islam

Innocent American Muslims became the immediate victims of the aftermath of 9/11. That event gave rise to a socially conservative Christian narrative that rose in intensity with claims that Islam was a false religion, satanic and the righteous subject of annihilation (Hedges, 2006). The Federal Bureau of Investigation reported nearly 500 hate crimes committed against Muslims in the 3 months immediately after 9/11 (Doyle, 2010). People publicly taunted and harassed Muslim girls and women who wore traditional ethnic clothing. Although some schools took steps to incorporate Muslim and Arabic history and cultures, educators "cautioned and advised [students] to be wary of Arabs and Muslims" (E. W. King, 2012, p. 1283). This was in an atmosphere in which a political administration was "aggressively pursuing sinister nonwhites, yet while using religion and geography rather than race to identify those supposedly menacing the public" (López, 2014, p. 120).

While simultaneously respecting a diversity of religious freedom, people remain ambivalent about Muslims. Ten years after 9/11, 88% of the public agreed that a founding principle of the United States was religious freedom that included unpopular religious groups. Nevertheless, people were divided in their comfort level with Muslims. The level of uneasiness ranged from 41% over the idea of "Muslim elementary school teachers" and 46% over the possibility of a mosque built near their home to 47% contending "Islam and American values are incompatible" compared to 48% disagreeing (D. Cox, Dionne, Galston, & Jones, 2011, para. 3). Such public doubts help support legal authorizations "to broad, *undifferentiated racial and religious profiling* " (Center for Constitutional Rights, as cited in Ax, 2014, para. 8, emphasis added).

Effectiveness of Christian Patriarchy

Using the events of 9/11, hypermasculine Christian patriarchal ideology created a dominant social and political environment for discrimination against Arab Americans and American Muslims where it was possible to declare a "total war" against Islam (Bayoumi, 2012, p. 12). When asked at a private fundraiser event in 2007, the eventual 2012 Republican candidate for U.S. president stated that if he were elected, he could not foresee a justification to include a Muslim in his cabinet (Ijaz, 2007). Although Muslims represent less than 2% of the U.S. population, they represent 20% of the cases of job discrimination on the basis of religious affiliation. Despite the numerous unwelcoming signs by mainstream Americans, the number of mosques increased by 74% over the decade since 9/11 (Bayoumi, 2012). Curricular resources exist for schools to teach about Islam and Arab cultures, but the actual acceptance and implementation of these materials remains uncertain to overcome Islamphobia (E. W. King, 2012).

NAMING AND TEACHING ABOUT PATRIARCHY

A purpose throughout this chapter was to illustrate the corrosive effects of a socially conservative Christian patriarchal ideology on diverse sexualities and gender identities and on religious minorities such as Muslims. Patriarchy is connected to

political attitudes that support militarism, school prayer, and patriotism and oppose same-sex marriage and women's reproductive rights. Hegemonic Christian
patriarchy permits, for example, judges to issue sentences that require school-age
offenders to attend church because, as one judge explained, "I think Jesus can
help anyone" (Norman, as cited in Eckholm, 2012, p. A22).

Liberal multiculturalism's approach to solving discrimination at the individual level is ineffective because it avoids deeper structural ideological analyses
of religious and secular patriarchy. Liberal multiculturalism is also too easily
swayed toward social conservatism as observed in the aftermath of 9/11. Critical
multiculturalism names the system of patriarchy as a major source of discrimination and oppression and supports a curriculum through which teaching about
patriarchy can help clear patriarchy's smog. Such a critical approach would be a
major multicultural step to increase the knowledge base of young people about
the corrosive effects of patriarchy on the full expression of freedom and liberty
and make schools a safer and healthier place for all our children.

The challenges for teachers, administrators, teacher educators, and national accrediting organizations for educator preparation to attend to diversity
issues to better serve the myriad needs of marginalized children and youth is
the topic of the concluding chapter.

CHAPTER 8

Contested Diversity and Teacher Education

So ends
The story of a journey
You have heard and you have seen
You have seen what is common, what continually occurs
But we ask you:
Even if it's not very strange, find it estranging
Even if it is usual, find it hard to explain
What here is common should astonish you
What here's the rule, recognize as an abuse
And where you have recognized an abuse
Provide redress!

—Bertolt Brecht, *The Exception and the Rule*

Bertolt Brecht witnessed the rise of Nazi fascism and wrote the above verse for his play *The Exception and the Rule* 3 years before he became a German exile. More than three-quarters of a century later, he still calls out to us. Finding congruence with Brecht's 1930 words in our current moment in diversity debates, the standpoint of critical multiculturalism asks that we avoid seeing disparities and inequities as natural and justifiable in the adverse treatment of diverse populations. Instead, we need to acknowledge the estranging or alienating features of inequitable treatment of groups that do not have equal access to mainstream opportunities. Brecht would ask that we recognize the abuses of normalized discriminatory rules of law and practices and then provide remedies to an unfairness imposed on diverse groups. As demonstrated throughout these pages, not all ideological orientations consider the historical and contemporary treatment of diverse groups as strange, alienating, and abusive nor in need of transformative compensatory action.

Teachers, administrators, and teacher educators are the objects of public scrutiny as to how schools should respond to diversity. These same educator groups are also subjects who daily enact ideologically informed approaches to diversity. In practice, actions range from marginalization of diversity to a broad incorporation of multicultural education. Nevertheless, for more than 40 years, teacher education successfully managed multicultural expressions and commitments so that individualistic psychological and technical orientations remain a central curricular focus of these programs. In a comprehensive review of higher education programs, Cochran-Smith, Davis, and Fries (2004) poignantly observe,

> Although a "new multicultural teacher education" may indeed be envisioned as the way to meet the needs of students and families in the real world, it is far removed from the demands and traditions of another real world: the institutional reality of colleges and universities, which supports and maintains the status quo. (p. 954)

Isolated praiseworthy programmatic and individual faculty efforts aside, the tendency in teacher education is to exclude social, economic, and political factors that affect student learning: "Many of the fundamental assumptions about the purposes of schooling and the meritocratic nature of American society that have long been implicit in teacher education remain unchallenged and undermined by the other aspects of preparation" (p. 964). Faculty and programs that make multicultural commitments to address diversity debates face a double bind in that a status quo orientation spills over even more dramatically from higher education to primary and secondary schools, the public spaces in which teacher education graduates work directly with children.

Because critical multiculturalism works to counter hegemonic positions both inside and outside school districts and higher education, this orientation faces opposition. Therefore, one aim of this chapter is to look closely at examples of sources of opposition and resistance to diversity and multiculturalism that can negatively affect the schooling experience for thousands of children. Throughout this discussion, the next sections make parenthetical comparative references to previous chapters in this book that help to illuminate ideologically contested diversity. In order to understand the implications for diverse students and multicultural education, this chapter provides a critical multicultural assessment of higher education accreditation standards, both existing ones from the National Council for Accreditation of Teacher Education (NCATE) along with newer standards from the Council for Accreditation of Educator Preparation (CAEP). The chapter provides an overview of critical multicultural perspectives and practices and concludes with the importance of solidarity for critical social change.

HIGHER EDUCATION ACCREDITATION STANDARDS

In the United States, higher education state and national accreditation standards set diversity expectations and parameters for the education of teachers. The following sections critically examine the 21st-century accreditation standards of the influential organization NCATE that determine "which schools, colleges, and departments of education meet rigorous national standards in preparing teachers and other school specialists for the classroom" (NCATE, 2008c). As of 2014, NCATE accredited 670 institutions with another 70 colleges and universities in the process of seeking approval (NCATE, 2014). As NCATE merges into a new organization in the mid-2010s, the section then turns to the content of new documents and standards that programs seeking national accreditation will follow into the 2020s.

NCATE's Historically Vague Multicultural Advocacy

By using the term *diversity* in the absence of any mention of *multicultural*, turn-of-the-century NCATE (2001) standards in effect imposed an assimilationist assessment ideology upon state-level accrediting requirements that drive higher education teacher education practices. An analysis revealed that both NCATE standards and assessment rubrics were missing expectations that teacher candidates should demonstrate knowledge about the effects of color blindness and White supremacy on students of color (Vavrus, 2002; cf. Chapters 3–4). Seven years later NCATE (2008b) tinkered with diversity expectations that remain in effect until 2015.

Just one use of the term "multicultural" is found in the primary text of NCATE higher education accreditation standards (2008b), namely, in a mention of the importance of "educators who can reflect *multicultural* and *global perspectives* that draw on the histories, experiences, and representations of students and families from diverse populations" (p. 36, emphasis added). NCATE's glossary defines a "multicultural perspective" as "an understanding of the social, political, economic, academic, and historical constructs of ethnicity, race, socioeconomic status, gender, exceptionalities, language, religion, sexual orientation, and geographical area" (p. 87). The glossary definition is the one place where educators could hold higher education to a critical perspective. Yet, given the master narrative that surrounds these named historical constructs, the indeterminate language of this NCATE definition does not find its way into rubric assessments that determine acceptable higher education institutional practices. Unacknowledged in this NCATE goal is how the political economy of White supremacy, patriarchy, and class disparities directly impacts students and families from diverse populations.

Compounding this lack of political-economy acknowledgment is NCATE's (2008b) definition of "global perspective" as "an understanding of the interdependency of nations and peoples and the political, economic, ecological, and social concepts and values that affect lives within and across national boundaries" (p. 87). Liberal multiculturalism with an NCATE human relations global perspective, however, can choose to overlook interlocking elements of discrimination against marginalized populations, profit accruement on the backs of such groups, the prioritizing of military expenditures, and the decline of public funds for schools and other fundamental human needs as witnessed under neoliberal policies.

A critical multicultural alternative of *global solidarity for emancipation* of oppressed populations offers preparation programs a pragmatic insight into what it means to meet NCATE's (2008b) expectation that teachers "demonstrate classroom behaviors that create caring and supportive learning environments" by being able to "communicate with students and families in ways that demonstrate sensitivity to cultural and gender differences [and] develop a classroom and school climate that values diversity" (pp. 20, 34). An emphasis on global solidarity for emancipation helps teacher education make important connections between globally oppressed peoples and domestically disenfranchised populations that include immigrant and indigenous children and their families.

"Linguistic diversity." NCATE (2008a) announced the addition of "linguistic diversity to the rubrics" (para. 7). NCATE's ahistorical approach to "linguistic diversity," however, fails to help higher education institutions (1) to incorporate a critique of the neocolonial determination of a nation's acceptable languages and (2) to examine the origins of contemporary "English-only" movements by nativist monocultural, anti-immigration groups (cf. Chapter 6 in this book). Critical multicultural education, in contrast, posits the importance of educators' enacting instruction in ways that rupture naturalized and privileged exclusionary practices of schooling. Knowledgeable teachers actively participate in making a political climate that best serves second-language learners.

"Potential impact of discrimination." NCATE (2008a) inserted into its diversity standard the following statement: "Candidates are helped to understand the potential impact of discrimination based on race, class, gender, disability, sexual orientation, and language on students and their learning" (para. 7). In a settler nation such as the United States that defined itself on a patriarchal political economy of White male supremacy (cf. Chapters 3–7), historically subordinated groups experience discriminatory effects—not just as a "potential impact," as NCATE phrases it. NCATE's naming of commonly recognized categories of oppression is an important step. Nevertheless, NCATE did not guide higher education to explicitly incorporate into their practices historical legacies regarding how and why those in economically and politically privileged positions have developed exclusionary practices and policies, targeted specifically identified populations, and permitted manifestations of this legacy of discrimination in contemporary school settings. Teachers knowledgeable of how these historical patterns play out in their classrooms can develop instructional strategies that better meet the needs of diverse student populations.

Social Justice Dispositions. Prior to the publication of its new standards, NCATE (2007) issued a "Call for Action" with a subsection titled "NCATE and Social Justice." The statement asserts, "NCATE's standards require educators to demonstrate the knowledge, skills, and professional dispositions to work successfully with children of all races, ethnicities, disabilities/exceptionalities and socioeconomic groups" (para. 5). This obviously is an important goal, but NCATE rubric scoring remains indeterminate on how to meet these standards.

NCATE's efforts to clarify its social justice stance raises additional concerns for critical multiculturalism. NCATE (2007) explained that explicit acknowledgment of social justice was new for this higher education accrediting organization. That social justice was "well understood by NCATE's institutions" (para. 11) is merely asserted and lacks definition and any documented validity. Granted that *individual* critical multicultural educators are located in some of these institutions, this cannot simply be equated with *institutional* programmatic incorporation of social justice discourse except for a few noteworthy exceptions. Problematic for diverse children is a social justice assertion that exists as a floating signifier without a grounded context (cf. the Introduction).

Culture Abstracted from Social Justice. Under NCATE (2008b) standards, colleges and universities defaulted to the 50-state leadership of the Council of Chief State School Officers (1992) in the Interstate New Teacher Assessment and Support Consortium (INTASC) standards to articulate teacher dispositions. In these standards, INTASC employed liberal multiculturalism through abstracted references to "cultural sensitivity," "cultural norms," "cultural differences," and "human diversity" (Council of Chief State School Officers, 1992, pp. 14–15, 21–22). Framing diversity in these ways results in a teacher education program superficially celebrating diversity while embracing a culture-of-poverty ideology (cf. Chapter 5).

Disconnected from social justice, INTASC standards "represent a shared view among the states and within the profession of what constitutes competent beginning teaching" (Council of Chief State School Officers, n.d., para. 2). An analysis of INTASC and NCATE 2001 standards, taken together, concluded:

> Rather than a voice of multicultural authenticity, NCATE and INTASC multicultural indeterminacy is most likely a compromise among those nationally involved with managing professional teacher education. This condition reflects various political interpretations and positions on the actual existence, importance, and appropriateness in contesting potential racist exclusionary practices. (Vavrus, 2002, p. 55)

This conclusion about compromise holds with NCATE's 2008 standards and the emergence of a new national accrediting organization.

Looking to the 2020s

In 2012 NCATE began a process of consolidation into a new national accrediting body, the Council for Accreditation of Educator Preparation (CAEP). A stated purpose was to develop uniform data collection available for more rapid program feedback and adjustments and to increase communication between higher education preparation programs and school districts. The new organization is a response to external political pressures that are fueled by a belief that higher education requirements should be more demanding and accountable for the preparation of future public school teachers (Basu, 2012). Arthur Levine, former president of Teachers College at Columbia University, ominously observed, "Self-policing is critical; this might be the last chance for teacher education in this country" (as cited in Basu, 2012, para. 11).

CAEP issued new standards that accept "in their entirety" (2013a, p. 22) revamped INTASC teacher standards (Council of Chief State School Officers, 2011). Diversity is highlighted in both the CAEP and INTASC standards. For the well-being of diverse student populations, this potentially provides a welcomed step. By the early 2020s, a representative sample from institutional self-studies may provide data on how well these new standards are working in practice.

Increased Commitment to Diverse Students. Most encouraging from a critical multicultural standpoint is CAEP's (2013a) clear insistence that "diversity must be a pervasive characteristic of any quality preparation program" (p. 21). Furthermore, programs must make certain "that candidates develop proficiencies in specific aspects of diversity" in accordance with CAEP's standards by "embed[ding] diversity issues throughout all aspects of preparation programs" (p. 21). Examples provided of expected proficiencies include the following:

- Incorporation of multiple perspectives to the discussion of content, including attention to learners' personal, family, and community experiences and cultural norms.
- A commitment to deepening awareness and understanding the strengths and needs of diverse learners when planning and adjusting instruction that incorporates the histories, experiences and representations of students and families from diverse populations. . . .
- An understanding of [educators'] own frames of reference (e.g., culture, gender, language, abilities, ways of knowing), the potential biases in these frames, the relationship of privilege and power in schools, and the impact of these frames on educators' expectations for and relationships with learners and their families. (p. 21)

Representative of a promising change to accreditation expectations, these proficiencies are among the positions critical multiculturalism has promoted for the past 3 decades (cf. the Introduction).

A noteworthy change in the 2011 INTASC standards is a recognition of culturally relevant or responsive teaching. When culturally responsive teaching reduces learner differences to the ambiguities of culture, however, we recall Irvine and York's (1995) insight that

> research on learning styles using culturally diverse students fails to support the premise that members of a given group exhibit a distinctive style. . . . Clearly, learning-styles research is a useful beginning in designing appropriate instruction for culturally diverse students, and not an end in itself. (p. 494)

Yet, when learning styles are embedded in the context of culturally congruent instruction, learning gains can accrue to marginalized students of color. The theoretical tension here is to recognize that individual students of diverse backgrounds have preferred approaches to learning that may not connect to their cultural backgrounds.

Muddled Diversity. The new INTASC standards focus more clearly on diversity and use as examples for "group differences . . . race, ethnicity, ability, gender identity, gender expression, sexual orientation, nationality, language, religion, political affiliation, and socio-economic background" (Council of Chief State School Officers, 2011, p. 21). CAEP uses a similar definition for diverse students. INTASC'S "essential knowledge" for planning instruction references diversity only with the descriptor "cultural" (p. 16). It remains unclear if both documents assume that diversity falls under an umbrella of culture, because nowhere in either document are specific expectations spelled out for knowledge, skills, and dispositions related to race, ethnicity, sexuality, gender, and religion. This is reminiscent of NCATE's (2008b) glossary terms as discussed above that did not appear in rubric evaluations.

Without explicit guidance for those responsible for preservice and inservice teacher education, attention to contested diversity features of race, ethnicity, sexuality, gender, and religion are likely to remain problematic for the best interests of diverse groups of students. As is evident from the previous chapters of this book, any of these contested differences portend volatile ideology clashes. Critically, nevertheless, CAEP (2013a) does acknowledge how, as listed above, various "frames" of diversity categories impact "educators' expectations for and relationships with learners and their families" in the context of a "relationship of privilege and power in schools" (p. 21). What are labeled *frames* are *ideologies* that help teachers understand why diversity is a contested concept (cf. the Introduction and Chapters 1 and 2). For educators to realize how their own ideological orientations affect curriculum and instruction, assessment criteria must explicitly include attention to frames or ideologies.

Neoliberal Globalization Commitment. INTASC standards that CAEP incorporates state that teachers must know how to design curriculum "to engage learners in critical thinking, creativity, and collaborative problem solving related to *authentic local and global issues* " (Council of Chief State School Officers, 2011, p. 8, emphasis added). Missing is the requirement of the necessary background knowledge–INTASC's category of "essential knowledge"–to authentically address local and global issues. *Global* as used in these documents remains indeterminate except for CAEP's (2013b) draft recommendation that the ultimate goal is for teachers to prepare their students "to compete in today's global economy" (p. 5). Once again, the trope that education is responsible for making U.S. citizens economically competitive ignores the most recent capitalist debacle of the Great Recession of 2007–2009 and the disparities of income and wealth created under neoliberalism that have continued (cf. the Introduction and Chapter 5). From a critical multicultural standpoint, such a promise by CAEP in the development of its standards is disingenuous and a mere repetition of the same neoliberal phrasing from the 1992 INTASC standards. A critical multicultural orientation "renounces a finalizing narrative that projects a global economy in its current form as inevitable and necessary . . . [and] favors such local–global concepts as difference, plurality, and solidarity against oppression" (Vavrus, 2002, p. 104; cf. Cochran-Smith & Fries, 2011).

Absent Multicultural Perspectives. A critical multicultural orientation questions the absence of any reference to the word *multicultural* in either of the new CAEP or INTASC documents. Teachers, administrators, and teacher education programs do not suffer from a lack of information on how to incorporate diversity issues into the operations of schools and preparation programs through multicultural education. Despite an abundance of resources based in theory, research, and practice, the relevancy and legitimacy of multicultural education varies in accordance with ideological orientations. Substantial resistance apparently remains to inclusion of multicultural perspectives, a phrase that NCATE had at least defined but that was eliminated in the creation of CAEP. Research and practice are clear that multicultural education with a critical orientation improves the educational experiences of children with diverse identities.

Because schools are key historical sites for nation-states to socialize young people into a common dominant culture, the multicultural preparation of teachers for diversity remains contested. Hence, the disjunctive standoff between critical multicultural advocacy and mainstream accreditation agencies should not be entirely surprising to the reader. Within an ideology of critical multiculturalism is the development of a critical consciousness cognizant of unjust social systems that leads to a sense of agency to transform dominant institutional practices (Freire, 1970, 1998). Therefore, one explanation is the perception that multicultural education is too ideologically contentious for 50 state superintendents and a broad spectrum of educators to find agreement in consensus documents (cf. Cochran-Smith & Fries, 2011).

Moreover, normative teacher education and accreditation standards take an unexamined neoliberal ideological approach when they abstract diversity issues from social justice, avoid issues of socioeconomic class disparities, operate in a patriarchal smog, and use color blindness to silence practices of racial stratification built on the basis of skin color. In tacit support of a unified image of a common culture with assimilated diverse perspectives, public school officials suppress or cautiously manage diversity and multiculturalism. Nevertheless, contested diversity issues surface in public schools with critical diversity advocates challenging a status quo that is detrimental to the interests of diverse groups of children.

CRITICAL MULTICULTURAL PERSPECTIVES AND PRACTICES

Along with finding theoretical connections among critical pedagogy, critical race theory, and antiracist education, Sleeter and Bernal (2004) note that critical multicultural education "tends to emphasize, more than the other fields, individual agency and institutional practices by highlighting what teachers can do" (p. 253). Sleeter and Bernal, however, confront the nexus of this theory–practice dilemma: "Since practice is often uninformed by complex understanding of oppression, culture, and power, one might ask if it is truly possible to use oppositional discourses in mainstream schools" (p. 254). In the context of the above-outlined liberal multicultural accreditation-driven discourse of NCATE, INTASC, and CAEP, Sleeter and Bernal identify a significant challenge for critical multiculturalism to transform the education of teachers.

Nevertheless, research on teacher inservice education in New Zealand on the provision of equitable treatment of indigenous Maori students can be validly generalized to other settings. A collaborative, relationship-based model can "quickly move teachers past the defensiveness and resistance that is common in professional development for emancipatory pedagogies as they see themselves and their students in these narratives" (Sleeter, Bishop, & Meyer, 2011, p. 166). Such a learning environment for teachers holds significant promise for the enactment of critical curriculum and instruction designed to overcome discrimination against historically marginalized children. The question of who will actually provide a critically informed teacher education is important to consider. Based on research of college faculty identified as multicultural teachers,

Gorski, Davis, and Reiter (2012) found an unevenness in the knowledge and ideological orientations among their sample of 75 teacher educators. The findings from this study suggest that all multicultural educators need to incorporate in their critical pedagogy issues of racism, classism, linguistic discrimination, sexism, gender-identity discrimination, and systems of patriarchy that include the conservatism of hegemonic Christianity.

Conceptualizing Where To Start

As a starting point, teacher education programs should explicitly and legitimately incorporate studies on race, racism, and antiracism (cf. Chapters 3–6; Vavrus, 2002). Critical race theory, which provides a theoretical foundation for these concepts, is a perspective sorely missing in most education programs. Because critical race theory begins with the premise that "racism is normal, not aberrant" (Delgado, 1995, p. xiv), critical multiculturalism incorporates this perspective into pedagogical and institutional approaches. Critical pedagogy (cf. the Introduction) serves to link historical studies of White privilege and property rights with critical race theory to highlight legal and extralegal foundations of exclusionary practices.

For example, in recognition of the importance of incorporating critical multiculturalism into foreign or second language teaching, Kubota (2010) emphasizes "explicit engagement in antiracist pedagogies" to help teachers and their students contextualize racism experienced both inside and outside of schools (p. 106). In contrast to an orientation in liberal multiculturalism that frames language learners as individual units of analysis for instructional treatment, Bartolomé (2010) prioritizes an overt unveiling of ideologies for her English education students in their preparation for teaching children whose first language is not English (cf. Chapter 6). With this end in mind, Bartolomé's syllabi for her three applied linguistic courses are interdisciplinary. Moreover, to help her education students attend to "unequal social student hierarchies in the classroom" (p. 53), she uses Elizabeth Cohen's (1994) pragmatic and seminal work *Designing Groupwork*, which attends in detail to instructional procedures that can derail status groupings of K–12 students, a pedagogical strategy appropriate for all curricular subjects.

Hanley (2010) reminds us of the importance of imagination in a social justice curriculum: "How can we build a new world without imagining it? What good is curriculum of critique without the hope, empathy, and support that creativity evokes" (p. 199)? As discussed throughout this book, both conservative and liberal versions of 21st-century neoliberalism discourse prefer that we see no alternative to exploitive capitalism's desire to privatize that which is public and common and to have *public* schools serve private hierarchical and patriarchal interests. Despite this ideological onslaught, critical multicultural educators work with preservice and inservice educators to help them critically reflect on their own lives and positionality. For example, McShay (2010) takes an interdisciplinary approach to infuse critical multiculturalism into technology education by helping educators and young marginalized people create digital stories to develop "a social consciousness that would lead to political action" (p. 142). McShay's goal corresponds with Banks's (1993) highest level in his typology of multicultural curricular approaches, *social action*. The aim of social action is to empower young people with diverse identities and orientations to participate along with their allies in decisions about important social issues that can transform presumed predetermined life choices and opportunities. To arrive at a transformative juncture of social action for the benefit of diverse populations, teacher educators must provide safe but courageous learning opportunities for educators to reflect critically on their orientations and socially constructed identities.

Teacher Identity, History, and Agency

An educator's sense of agency and subjective identity are not transcendent of dominant power relations. Indeed, existing social structures and dominant ideologies can effectively domesticate a teacher's professional "voice" to resist transformative goals of critical multiculturalism. Individual educators exposed to critical histories often perceive themselves as neutral subjects living outside of history. Teachers and teacher candidates who encounter critical histories of White supremacy and patriarchy, for example, often deflect this information away from their identities in a manner that does not threaten stable status quo notions of themselves. Instead, what is needed is "the ability to historicize, at every moment, the present people and events we encounter individually and collectively" (Bracher, 2006, p. 121). This suggests a focus on the constructed identities educators form and the agency required to enact critically informed identities.

Each teacher's identity is fluid, situation specific, and historically contingent on power relations that constitute society's cultural, political, and economic practices (cf. Gee, 2001). Yet, too many education programs take a cookie-cutter approach to stamping out teachers whose identities conform to a constricted notion of professionalism. When student-teacher interns in public school classrooms lack critical multicultural support from their cooperating teachers, a reinscription of an intergenerational status quo ensues (Castro, 2010; Vavrus, 1994). A challenge for critical multiculturalism is how to help both preservice and inservice teachers develop dispositions based in a critical consciousness so that they can see the possibilities for transformative agency for the benefit of diverse populations of students. Such an approach acts on Kincheloe's (2005) observation that "teacher education provides little insight into the forces that shape identity and consciousness" (p. 155).

Teacher Identity and Critical Autoethnographies

The use of autobiographies in teacher education is not a new pedagogy. In multicultural education the primary purpose is to deepen individual understandings of positionality. The outcome is not always what critical multiculturalists anticipate. An unfocused autobiographical assignment on diversity can result, for example, in color blindness along with racial inequalities being "rearticulated to maintain [White] privilege rather than disrupt it" (Chubbuck, 2004, p. 329).

Autoethnographies offer a more focused alternative to the autobiography. With an ethnographic approach, identity formation links to social phenomena rather than imagined as historically autonomous from political forces. The autoethnography as "the personal text [serves] as critical intervention in social, political, and cultural life" (S. Jones, 2005, p. 763) and "reveals concretely realized patterns in one's own actions rather than the actions of others" (Roth, 2005, p. 4). When applied to a teacher's pedagogy, the process of excavating personal history in order to articulate a teacher's identity becomes "a way to put that identity on the line and risk needing to reform and recreate the self while also attempting to transform curricula" (Samaras, Hicks, & Garvey Berger, 2004, p. 915). For young teachers and teacher candidates born in the 1990s, and who came of age in the 2010s, such an exploration connects past and present diversity debates with their own dispositions and practices in a critically reflective manner (Rodriguez & Hallman, 2013).

To create an accessible and *deep* critical pedagogy that supports critical multiculturalism necessitates "the purposeful incorporation into critical pedagogy of social-psychological forces that interact with individual subjectivities in the formation of identities and subsequent behaviors" (Vavrus, 2006b, p. 92). This curricular strategy combines autoethnographic narratives with critical texts that preservice and inservice teachers interrogate through dialogue and related background lectures and workshops. Preservice and inservice teachers receive specific writing prompts that tie multicultural content to individual lived experiences. This can be done for a variety of multicultural topics that affect teachers' identities, such as issues of race/ethnicity, gender/sexuality, and globalization/alienation (Vavrus, 2006a, 2006b, 2009). A final writing prompt, regardless of the diversity issue, importantly asks educators to consider how this autoethnographic knowledge they have revealed to themselves now affects formation of their respective teacher identities. This is predictably the most difficult prompt for educators to consider because they now realize that (1) they are no longer outside a history that unfolds in front of them each day and (2) their identities shape the learning environments and curricular experiences that they create in their primary and secondary public school classrooms for diverse student populations. Through autoethnographies written within a critical pedagogy, teachers at all levels of their education understand that they hold the agency to make critical multicultural commitments that transform classroom practices and the life opportunities of their students.

IMPORTANCE OF SOLIDARITY

Public school teachers and their unions experienced the negative effects of neoliberalism during the 2010s through mainstream attempts to undermine the integrity of teaching, diminish the bargaining power of teachers, and create a political environment to privatize public education. The prioritizing of the private over the public in social conservatism regularly finds political support in charter school individualism of liberal multiculturalism that results in reinforcing and accelerating inequities for diverse student populations (Fabricant & Fine, 2012; Haimson & Ravitch, 2013; Ravitch, 2011). These are among the same ideological forces that outsource preservice teacher assessments, privatize testing costs to already debt-ridden college students, and significantly diminish the recommending authority of higher education educator preparation programs for teacher licensure ("Fees and Payment Schedule," 2014; Karlin, 2013; "Praxis Performance Assessments," 2014; Rios as cited in Cody, 2014). In regard to this profit-making trend for such private corporations as Pearson Education, the National Association for Multicultural Education (NAME) (2014) opposes the imposition of "a common and pre-determined curriculum on teacher education that severely limits faculty ability to enact their commitment to preparing teachers to promote critical multicultural education, social justice, and democratic citizenship" (p. 2).

To resist the rising neoliberal privatization of teaching and learning, NAME's critique calls on K–12 teachers, teacher educators, school administrators, parents, and communities members to join together in solidarity. When these groups collaborate and envision themselves as a social movement, broad public support is possible (Givan, 2014). A unified voice can speak to the merits of critical multiculturalism and against the dismantling of localized democracy and public education.

The task of contributing to beneficial social change for diverse young people is daunting from the standpoint of critical multiculturalism if immediate results are the goal. The history of racial, ethnic, economic, sexual, gender, and religious oppression is a major thread throughout U.S. history and remains in various contemporary forms today. By focusing on the long run with an eye on the horizon of equity and social justice and maintaining an awareness of the ideological roots of debated diversity, educators with a critical multicultural perspective and their allies lay a foundation of hope and possibility for all our children.

References

Aboud, F. E. (2009). Modifying children's racial attitudes. In J. A. Banks (Ed.), *The Routledge international companion to multicultural education* (pp. 199–209). New York, NY: Routledge.

Adams, D. W. (1995). *Education for extinction: American Indians and the boarding school experience, 1875–1928.* Lawrence: University Press of Kansas.

Addy, S., Engelhardt, W., & Skinner, C. (2013, January). *Basic facts about low-income children.* Retrieved from the National Center for Children in Poverty website: www.nccp.org /publications/pub_1074.html

Adelman, L. (Producer). (2003). *Race, the power of an illusion.* San Francisco, CA: California Newsreel.

Aez, P. A., Casado, A., & Wade, J. C. (2009). Factors influencing masculinity ideology among Latino men. *Journal of Men's Studies, 17*(2), 116–128. doi:10.3149 /jms.1702.116

Albert, M. (2013). *Parecon: Life after capitalism.* Brooklyn, NY: Verso.

Albo, G. (2002). Neoliberalism, the state, and the left: A Canadian perspective. *Monthly Review, 54*(1), 46–55.

Alexander, M. (2010). *The new Jim Crow: Mass incarceration in the age of colorblindness.* New York, NY: New Press.

Alliance Defending Freedom. (2012). Anti-bullying policy yardstick. Retrieved from www.huffingtonpost.com/2012/09/01/anti-bullying-policy-yardstick-released-by-fo-cus-on-family-controversial_n_1847964.html

Alvarez, L. (2013, December 3). Seeing the toll, schools revisit zero tolerance. *New York Times,* pp. A1, A19.

American Bar Association. (2012). *Criminal justice system improvements.* Retrieved from www. americanbar.org/content/dam/aba/migrated/poladv/transition/2008dec_crimjustice .authcheckdam.pdf

American Civil Liberties Union. (2008). What is the school-to-prison pipeline? Retrieved from www.aclu.org/racial-justice/what-school-prison-pipeline

Amir, S. (2014). Popular movements toward socialism. *Monthly Review, 66*(2), 1–32.

Amnesty International. (2004). *Threat and humiliation: Racial profiling, domestic security, and human rights in the United States.* Retrieved from www.amnestyusa .org/research/reports/threat-and-humiliation-racial-profiling-domestic-security -and-human-rights-in-the-united-states

Anyon, J. (2011). *Marx and education.* New York, NY: Routledge.

Anyon, Y. (2009). Sociological theories of learning disabilities: Understanding racial disproportionality in special education. *Journal of Human Behavior in the Social Environment, 19,* 44–57. doi:10.1080/10911350802631495

Apple, M. (2002). Pedagogy, patriotism, and democracy: On the educational meaning of 11 September 2001. *Discourse: Studies in the Cultural Politics of Education, 23*(3), 299–308. doi:10.1080/0159630022000029795

Archibold, R. C. (2013, October 24). Dominicans of Haitian descent cast into legal limbo by court. *New York Times,* pp. A1, A6.

Arizona Ethnic Studies Network. (n.d.). Banned book list. Retrieved from azethnicstudies .com/banned-books

Ash, T. G. (2012, November 22). Freedom & diversity: A liberal pentagram for living together. *New York Review of Books,* pp. 33–36.

Associated Press. (1969, March 27). Sex education called plot by communists. *Spokane Daily Chronicle.* Retrieved from news.google.com/newspapers?nid=1338&dat =19690327&id=JWxYAAAAIBAJ&sjid=FfgDAAAAIBAJ&pg=2972,3416651

Association of Qualitative Research. (2013). *Typology.* Retrieved from www.aqr.org.uk /glossary/?term=typology

Au, W. (2012). The long march toward revitalization: Developing standpoint in curriculum studies. *Teachers College Record, 114*(5), 1–30. Retrieved from www.tcrecord.org /content.asp?contentid=16421

Ax, J. (2014, February 20). New York police surveillance of Muslims constitutional: Judge. *Reuters.* Retrieved from www.reuters.com/article/2014/02/21/us-usa-muslims-newyork-idUSBREA1K01820140221

Baboulias, Y. (2013, September 18). A Golden Dawn member murdered an anti-fascist rapper in Athens last night. *Vice.* Retrieved from www.vice.com/en_uk/read/the -golden-dawn-murdered-an-antifascist-rapper-last-night

Bacon, D. (2008). *Illegal people: How globalization creates migration and criminalizes immigrants.* Boston, MA: Beacon Press.

Balibar, E. (1991). Racism and nationalism (C. Turner, Trans.). In E. Balibar & I. Wallerstein (Eds.), *Race, nation, class: Ambiguous identities* (pp. 37–67). London, England: Verso.

Balibar, E. (2002). *Politics and the other scene.* London, England: Verso.

Banks, J. A. (1993). Approaches to multicultural curriculum reform. In J. A. Banks & C. A. M. Banks (Eds.), *Multicultural education: Issues and perspectives* (pp. 195–214). Boston, MA: Allyn & Bacon.

Banks, J. A. (2008). Diversity, group identity, and citizenship education in a global age. *Educational Researcher, 37*(3), 129–139.

Banks, J. A. (2009a). Diversity and citizenship education in a global age. In J. A. Banks (Ed.), *The Routledge international companion to multicultural education* (pp. 303–322). New York, NY: Routledge.

Banks, J. A. (2009b). Multicultural education: Dimensions and paradigms. In J. A. Banks (Ed.), *The Routledge international companion to multicultural education* (pp. 9–32). New York, NY: Routledge.

Banks, J. A. (2013). Group identity and citizenship education in global times. *Kappa Delta Pi Record, 49,* 108–112. doi:10.1080/00228958.2013.759824

Baquedano-López, P., Alexander, R. A., & Hernandez, S. J. (2013). Equity issues in parental and community involvement in schools: What teacher educators need to know. In C. Faltis & J. Abedi (Eds.), *Review of Research in Education* (Vol. 37, pp. 149–182). Washington, DC: American Educational Research Association.

Barry, E. (2013, March 17). The Cossacks are back: May the hills tremble. *New York Times,* pp. A1, A12.

Bartels, L. (2014, April 8). Rich people rule! *Washington Post*. Retrieved from www .washingtonpost.com/blogs/monkey-cage/wp/2014/04/08/rich-people-rule/

Bartolomé, L. I. (2008). Introduction: Beyond the fog of ideology. In L. I. Bartolomé (Ed.), *Ideologies in education: Unmasking the trap of teacher neutrality* (pp. ix–xxix). New York, NY: Peter Lang.

Bartolomé, L. I. (2010). Daring to infuse ideology into language-teacher education. In S. May & C. E. Sleeter (Eds.), *Critical multiculturalism: Theory and praxis* (pp. 47–59). New York, NY: Routledge.

Basu, K. (2012, February 28). Raising the bar. *Inside Higher Ed*. Retrieved from www. insidehighered.com/news/2012/02/28/new-approach-gauging-quality-teacher -education-programs

Baum, B. (2006). *The rise and the fall of the Caucasian race: A political history of racial identity*. New York: New York University Press.

Bayoumi, M. (2012, July 2/9). Fear and loathing of Islam. *The Nation*, pp. 11–12, 14.

Behdad, A. (2005). *A forgetful nation: On immigration and cultural identity in the United States*. Durham, NC: Duke University Press.

Bell, D. (2002). Afterword: From class to culture. In D. Bell (Ed.), *The radical right* (3rd ed., pp. 447–503). New Brunswick, NJ: Transaction.

Bennett, K. P., & LeCompte, M. D. (1990). *How schools work: A sociological analysis of education*. New York, NY: Longman.

Berlin, I. (1969). Two concepts of liberty. In I. Berlin, *Four essays on liberty* (pp. 118–172). Oxford, England: Oxford University Press. (Original work published 1958)

Bezabler, L. (2013, October 7). Prisons over schools? *The Nation*, p. 8.

Biggers, J. (2011, September 28). AZ school chief compares Mexican–American studies to Hitler Jugend (as he endorses White supremacist-backed candidate). *Huffington Post*. Retrieved from www.huffingtonpost.com/jeff-biggers/az-school-chief-compares -_b_985390.html

Biggers, J. (2012). *State out of the union: Arizona and the final showdown over the American dream*. New York, NY: Nation Books.

Black, E. (2003). *War against the weak: Eugenics and America's campaign to create a master race*. New York, NY: Four Walls Eight Windows.

Black, J. (2003). *Oxford dictionary of economics* (2nd ed.). New York, NY: Oxford University Press.

Blackmon, D. (2008). *Slavery by another name: The re-enslavement of Black Americans from the Civil War to World War II*. New York, NY: Doubleday.

Blad, E. (2014, February 5). Report highlights weaknesses in tracking school sexual abuse. *Education Week*, p. 7.

Blake, J. (2013, January 19). Why conservatives call MLK their hero. *CNN U.S.* Retrieved from www.cnn.com/2013/01/19/us/mlk-conservative/index.html

Blow, C. (2013, December 21). "Duck dynasty" and quackery. *New York Times*, p. A19.

Bodine, D. (2012, April 20). 2012 National DNA day chatroom transcript. National Human Genome Research Institute. Retrieved from www.genome.gov/page.cfm?pageid =27548412&expert=David%20Bodine,%20Ph.D

Boroff, D., & Planas, R. (2012, January 24). Mitt Romney says he favors "self-deportation" when asked about immigration during GOP debate. *New York Daily News*. Retrieved from www.nydailynews.com/news/election-2012/mitt-romney-favors-self -deportation-asked-immigration-gop-debate-article-1.1010812

Bosman, J. (2007, February 18). With one word, children's book set off uproar. *New York Times,* pp. 1, 23.

Bowker, L. H. (1998). On the difficulty of eradicating masculine violence: Multisystem overdetermination. In L. H. Bowker (Ed.), *Masculinities and violence* (pp. 1–14). Thousand Oaks, CA: Sage.

Bracher, M. (2006). *Radical pedagogy: Identity, generativity, and social transformation.* New York, NY: Palgrave Macmillan.

Branigan, T. (2010, August 2). Mongolian neo-Nazis: Anti-Chinese sentiment fuels rise of ultra-nationalism. *guardian.co.uk.* Retrieved from www.guardian.co.uk/world/2010 /aug/02/mongolia-far-right

Brecht, B. (1954). *The exception and the rule: A play in nine scenes.* Boston, MA: Chrysalis series (Vol. 7, no. 11–12, Eric Bentley, Trans.). (Original work published 1930)

Britton, M. L., & Goldsmith, P. R. (2013). Keeping people in their place? Young-adult mobility and persistence of residential segregation in US metropolitan areas. *Urban Studies, 50*(14), 2886–2903. doi:10.1177/0042098013482506

Bronner, E. (2013, June 5). Complaint accuses U.S. judge in Texas of racial bias. *New York Times,* p. A17.

Brooks, D. (2013, July 4). Defending the coup. *New York Times.* Retrieved from www. nytimes.com/2013/07/05/opinion/brooks-defending-the-coup.html

Brown v. Board of Education, 347 U.S. 488 (1954). Retrieved from WestlawNext database.

Brown v. Board of Education, 349 U.S. 294 (1955). Retrieved from WestlawNext database.

Buckley, W. F., Jr. (2003). National Review: Credenda and statement of principles. In G. L. Schneider (Ed.), *Conservatism in America since 1930: A reader* (pp. 201–205). New York: New York University Press. (Original work published 1955)

Buhain, V. (2007, February 25). Lawmakers debate the content of sex education. *The Olympian,* p. C3.

Burton-Rose, D., Pens, D., & Wright, P. (1998). *The celling of America: An inside look at the U.S. prison industry.* Monroe, ME: Common Courage Press.

Cabrera, N. L., Milem, J. F., & Marx, R. W. (2012, June 20). *An empirical analysis of the effects of Mexican American studies participation on student achievement within Tucson Unified School District.* University of Arizona, College of Education. Retrieved from www.tucsonweekly.com/TheRange/archives/2012/11/12/want-more-evidence-that -mexican-american-studies-works

Calmes, J. (2014, March). Democrats try wooing ones who got away: White men. New York Times. Retrieved from www.nytimes.com/2014/03/03/us/politics/democrats -try-wooing-ones-who-got-away-white-men.html

Cambian Learning & National Academic Educational Partners. (2011, May 2). *Curriculum audit of the Mexican American Studies Department, Tucson Unified School District, Tucson, Arizona.* Miami Lakes, FL: Authors. Retrieved from www.tucsonweekly.com/TheRange /archives/2012/11/12/want-more-evidence-that-mexican-american-studies-works

Came, D., & Ireland, L. (2012, March). *Graduation and dropout statistics annual report 2010–11.* Olympia, WA: Office of Superintendent of Public Instruction. Retrieved from www.k12.wa.us/dataadmin/pubdocs/GradDropout/10-11/GradDropoutStats _2010-11.pdf

Cameron, D., & Kulick, D. (2006). General introduction. In D. Cameron & D. Kulick (Eds.), *The language and sexuality reader* (pp. 1–12). New York, NY: Routledge.

Canada, Government of. (2010). The labour market progression of LSIC immigrants—A perspective from the second wave of the longitudinal survey of immigrants to Canada (LSIC)—Two years after landing. Citizenship and Immigration Canada. Retrieved from www.cic.gc.ca/english/resources/research/lsic/section3.asp

Canada, Government of. (2012). Archived—Annual report of the operation of the Canadian Multicultural Act 2010–2011. Retrieved from www.cic.gc.ca/english/resources/publications/multi-report2011/part1.asp

Canadian Multicultural Act, R.S.C., 1985, c. 24 (4th Supp.). (1988). Retrieved from laws-lois.justice.gc.ca/eng/acts/C-18.7/20021231/P1TT3xt3.html

Canadians endorse multiculturalism, but pick melting pot over mosaic. (2010, November 8). *Angus Reid Public Opinion*. Retrieved from www.angus-reid.com/wp-content/uploads/2010/11/2010.11.08_Melting_CAN.pdf

Carbado, D. W., & Harris, C. I. (2008). The new racial preferences. *California Law Review, 96* (UCLA School of Law Research Paper No. 08-32). Retrieved from papers.ssrn.com/sol3/papers.cfm?abstract_id=1282268##

Carmon, I. (2013, February 21). Pregnancy is patriotic! *Salon*. Retrieved from www.salon.com/2013/02/21/decoding_the_fertility_panic/

Carnegie, A. (1889). *The gospel of wealth*. Retrieved from carnegie.org/fileadmin/Media/Publications/PDF/THE_GOSPEL_OF_WEALTH_01.pdf

Carnevale, A. P., Strohl, J., & Melton, M. (2011). *What's it worth? The economic value of college majors*. Washington, DC: Georgetown University, Center on Education and the Workforce. Retrieved from cew.georgetown.edu/whatsitworth

Castle, S. (2010, September 20). Anti-immigration party wins first seats in Swedish parliament. *New York Times*, p. A5.

Castles, S. (2009). World population movements, diversity, and education. In J. Banks (Ed.), *The Routledge international companion to multicultural education* (pp. 49–61). New York, NY: Routledge.

Castro, A. J. (2010). Challenges in teaching for critical multicultural citizenship: Student teaching in an accountability-driven context. *Action in Teacher Education, 32*(2), 97–109. doi:10.1080/01626620.2010.10463553

Center for Women and Politics. (2014). *Women in elective offices*. Retrieved from www.cawp.rutgers.edu/

Cha, J., & Kennedy, L. (2014, February 18). Millions to the polls: The right to vote for formerly incarcerated persons. *Demos*. Retrieved from www.demos.org/publication/millions-polls-right-vote-formerly-incarcerated-persons

Chicago Cultural Studies Group. (1992, Spring). Critical multiculturalism. *Critical Inquiry, 18*(3), 530–555.

Chomsky, N. (1996). *Class warfare: Interviewed by David Barsamian*. Vancouver, Canada: New Star Books.

Chomsky, N. (2011). *9/11: Was there an alternative?* (Rev. ed.). New York, NY: Seven Stories Press. (Original work published 2001)

Chubbuck, S. M. (2004). Whiteness enacted, Whiteness disrupted: The complexity of personal congruence. *American Educational Research Journal, 41*(2), 301–333.

Churchland, P. S. (2013a, May 14). Brain scans and brain scams. *Psychology Today*. Retrieved from www.psychologytoday.com/blog/neurophilosophy/201305/brain-scans-and-brain-scams#_edn2

Churchland, P. S. (2013b, May 7). Criminal genes and criminal brains: Are we there yet? *Psychology Today*. Retrieved from www.psychologytoday.com/blog/neurophilosophy/201305/criminal-genes-and-criminal-brains

Citizens United. (2012). Fulfilling our mission. Retrieved from www.citizensunited.org/fulfilling-our-mission.aspx

City of Richmond v. Corson, 488 U.S. 469 (1989). Retrieved from WestlawNext database.

Civil Rights Act of 1964. (1964). Public Law 88-352. Retrieved from www.gpo.gov/fdsys/granule/STATUTE-78/STATUTE-78-Pf241/content-detail.html

Clark, M. (2013, November 4). 49 states now have anti-bullying laws. How's that working out? *Governing the State and Localities*. Retrieved from www.governing.com/news/headlines/49-States-Now-Have-Anti-Bullying-Laws-Hows-that-Working-Out.html

Coates, R. D. (2008). Multiculturalism. In W. A. Darity, Jr. (Ed.), *International encyclopedia of the social sciences* (2nd ed., Vol. 5, pp. 316–318). Detroit, MI: Macmillan Reference USA.

Cochran-Smith, M., Davis D., & Fries, K. (2004). Multicultural teacher education: Research, practice, and policy. In J. A. Banks & C. A. M. Banks (Eds.), *Handbook of research on multicultural education* (2nd ed., pp. 931–975). San Francisco, CA: Jossey-Bass.

Cochran-Smith, M., & Fries, K. (2011). Teacher education for diversity: Policy and politics. In A. F. Ball & C. A. Tyson (Eds.), *Studying diversity in teacher education* (pp. 339–361). Lanham, MD: Rowman & Littlefield.

Cody, A. (2014, May 26). Teacher education leader Francisco Rios: edTPA leads schools to teach to the test. *Education Week*. Retrieved from blogs.edweek.org/teachers/living-in-dialogue/2014/05/teacher_education_leader_franc.html?qs=rios

Cohen, E. (2013, July 28). North Carolina lawmakers OK payments for victims of forced sterilization. *CNN U.S.* Retrieved from www.cnn.com/2013/07/26/us/north-carolina-sterilization-payments/index.html

Cohen, E. G. (1994). *Designing groupwork: Strategies for the heterogeneous classroom* (2nd ed.). New York, NY: Teachers College Press.

Cohen, E. G., & Lotan, R. A. (2004). Equity in heterogeneous classrooms. In J. A. Banks & C. A. M. Banks (Eds.), *Handbook of research on multicultural education* (2nd ed., pp. 736–750). San Francisco, CA: Jossey-Bass.

Cohen, P. (2008, September 22). Conservatives try new tack on campuses. *New York Times*, pp. A1, A22.

Cohen, P. (2010, October 17). "Culture of poverty" makes a comeback. *New York Times*, pp. A1.

Cole, M., Cole, S. R., & Lightfoot, C. (2005). *The development of children* (5th ed.). New York, NY: Worth.

Conde, A. (2012, Spring). Child migrant farmers in the United States: A quest for a better life. *NACLA Report on the Americas, 45*(1), 86–87.

Connolly, K. (2010, October 17). Angela Merkel declares death of German multiculturalism. *guardian.co.uk*. Retrieved from www.guardian.co.uk/world/2010/oct/17/angela-merkel-germany-multiculturalism-failures

Cooper, D. (2004). *Challenging diversity: Rethinking equality and the value of difference*. Cambridge, England: Cambridge University Press.

Council for the Accreditation of Educator Preparation (CAEP). (2013a, August 23). *CAEP accreditation standards*. Retrieved from caepnet.org/accreditation/standards/

Council for the Accreditation of Educator Preparation. (2013b, June 11). *CAEP accreditation standards and evidence: Aspirations for educator preparation.* Retrieved from caepnet.org/caep-accreditation-standards/standards/

Council of Chief State School Officers. (1992, September). *Model standards for beginning teacher licensure and development: A resource for state dialogue.* Washington, DC: Author.

Council of Chief State School Officers. (2011, April). *INTASC model core teaching standards: A resource for state dialogue.* Washington, DC: Author.

Council of Chief State School Officers. (n.d.). INTASC standards development. Retrieved from programs.ccsso.org/projects/interstate_new_teacher_assessment_and_support_consortium/projects/standards_development/

Council of Europe. (2010). *White paper on intercultural dialogue: "Living together as equals in dignity."* Strasbourg, France: Author.

Counts, G. S. (1978). *Dare the school build a new social order?* Carbondale: Southern Illinois University Press. (Original work published 1932)

Cox, D., Dionne, E. J., Galston, W. A., & Jones, R. P. (2011, September 6). What it means to be an American: Attitudes in an increasingly diverse America ten years after 9/11. *Brookings.* Retrieved from www.brookings.edu/research/reports/2011/09/06-american-attitudes

Cox, S., Pazol, K., Warner, L., Romero, L., Spitz, A., Gavin, L., & Barfield, W. (2014). Vital signs: Births to teens aged 15–17–United States, 1991–2012. *Morbidity and Mortality Weekly Report, 63* (early release), 1–7. Retrieved from www.cdc.gov/mmwr/early_release.html

Crenshaw, K. W. (1997). Color-blind dreams and racial nightmares: Reconfiguring racism in the post–civil rights era. In T. Morrison & C. B. Lacour (Eds.), *Birth of a nation'hood: Gaze, script, and spectacle in the O. J. Simpson case* (pp. 97–168). New York, NY: Pantheon.

Crosby, A. E., Ortega, L., & Stevens, M. R. (2011, January 14). Suicides: United States, 1999–2007. *Morbidity and Mortality Weekly Report, 60*(Supplement), 56–59. Retrieved from www.cdc.gov/mmwr/pdf/other/su6001.pdf

Dabach, D. B., & Faltis, C. (2012). Bilingual education. In J. A. Banks (Ed.), *Encyclopedia of diversity in education* (Vol. 1, pp. 212–216). Los Angeles, CA: Sage Reference.

Davetian, B. (2009). *Civility: A cultural history.* Toronto, Canada: University of Toronto Press.

Davis, A., Magee, R., the Soledad Brothers, & Other Political Prisoners. (1971). *If they come in the morning: Voices of resistance.* New York, NY: Third Press.

Davis, R. (2010, Summer). Culture as a weapon. *Middle East Report, 255.* Retrieved from www.merip.org/mer/mer255/culture-weapon

Day, D. (1981). *The long loneliness: An autobiography.* New York, NY: HarperCollins.(Original work published 1952)

DeJong-Lambert, W. (2007–2008, Winter). Rethinking Little Rock: The Cold War politics of school integration in the United States. *European Education, 38*(4), 65–81.

Delgado, R. (1995). Introduction. In R. Delgado (Ed.), *Critical race theory: The cutting edge* (pp. xiii–xvi). Philadelphia, PA: Temple University Press.

De Lissouvoy, N. (2008). *Power, crisis, and education for liberation: Rethinking critical pedagogy.* New York, NY: Palgrave Macmillian.

Dewan, S. (2013, July 6). Has "Caucasian" lost its meaning? *New York Times,* p. 4SR.

Dews, F. (2013, October 3). What percentage of U.S. population is foreign born? *Brookings.* Retrieved from www.brookings.edu/blogs/brookings-now/posts/2013/09 /what-percentage-us-population-foreign-born

de Vise, D. (2007, February 9). School picked to pilot sex-ed lessons. *Washington Post.* Retrieved from www.washingtonpost.com/wp-dyn/content/article/2007/02/08/ AR2007020801047_pf.html

DiLeonardo, R. (2012, June 25). Supreme Court rules mandatory life sentences for juveniles unconstitutional. *Jurist.* Retrieved from jurist.org/paperchase/2012/06/supreme -court-rules-mandatory-life-sentences-for-juveniles-unconstitutional.php

DiLulio, J. J., Jr. (1995, November 27). The coming of the super-predators. *Weekly Standard.* Retrieved from www.weeklystandard.com/print/Content/Protected/Articles /000/000/007/011vsbrv.asp

Dimond, A. (2005, December 20). Brooks, Matthews on illegal immigrants' "culture of criminality"; Parker: "[T]hey are not assimilating, they're not learning English. *MediaMatters for America.* Retrieved from mediamatters.org/video/2005/12/20 /brooks-matthews-on-illegal-immigrants-culture-o/134486

Diverse. (2001). *Webster's encyclopedic unabridged dictionary of the English language* (p. 574). New York, NY: Random House.

Dixon, T. (1905). *The clansman: An historical romance of the Ku Klux Klan.* New York, NY: Grosset & Dunlap.

Donadio, R. (2010, September 16). As Italy's government totters, a new power broker rises. *New York Times,* p. A6.

Donadio, R. (2013, October 21). Opera fights Hungary's rising anti-Semitism. *New York Times,* pp. A1, A6.

Dorgan, B. L. (2010). The tragedy of Native American youth suicide. *Psychological Services,* 7(3), 213–218. doi:10.1037/a0020461

Doyle, M. (2010, August 27). Hate crimes against Muslims rare, FBI data shows. *McClatchy Newspapers.* Retrieved from www.mcclatchydc.com/2010/08/27/99767/hate-crimes -against-muslims-rare.html

Dred Scott v. Sandford, 60 U.S. 393 (1857). Retrieved from WestlawNext database.

Ecenbarger, W. (2012). *Kids for cash: Two judges, thousands of children, a $2.8 million kickback scheme.* New York, NY: New Press.

Eckholm, E. (2012, November 22). Constitutional experts denounce Oklahoma judge's sentencing youth to church. *New York Times,* p. A22.

Eckholm, E. (2013, April 12). With police in schools, more children in court. *New York Times,* pp. A1, A13.

Eddy, M., & Cottrell, C. (2013, January 30). German politician's remark stirs outcry over sexism. *New York Times,* p. A9.

Einstein, A. (2002). Why socialism? *Monthly Review, 54*(1), 56–62. (Original work published 1949)

Eligion, J. (2012, August 22). A politician whose faith is central to his persistence. *New York Times,* p. A16.

Engel de Abreu, P. M. J., Cruz-Santos, A., Tourinho, C. J., Martin, R., & Bialystok, E. (2012). Bilingualism enriches the poor: Enhanced cognitive control in low-income minority children. *Psychological Science, 23*(11), 1364–1371. doi:10.1177/0956797612443836

Engen, T. O. (2009). Socialization, literacy, and empowerment. In J. A. Banks (Ed.), *The Routledge international companion to multicultural education* (pp. 252–262). New York, NY: Routledge.

Environic Institute. (2012). *Focus Canada 2012.* Toronto, Canada: Author. Retrieved from www.environicsinstitute.org/institute-projects/current-projects/focus-canada

Epstein, D., O'Flynn, S., & Telford, D. (2001). "Othering" education: Sexualities, silences, and schooling. In W. G. Secada (Ed.), *Review of research 25: 2000–2001* (pp. 127–179). Washington, DC: American Educational Research Association.

Erickson, F. D. (2012). Culture and education. In J. A. Banks (Ed.), *Encyclopedia of diversity in education* (Vol. 1, pp. 559–568). Los Angeles, CA: Sage Reference.

Erlanger, S. (2014, February 10). Swiss vote seen as challenge to Europe integration. *New York Times.* Retrieved from www.nytimes.com/2014/02/11/world/europe/swiss-immigration-vote-raises-alarm-across-europe.html

Ewing, J. (2012, September 9). Some religious leaders see a threat as Europe grows more secular. *New York Times,* pp. A5, A8.

Fabricant, M., & Fine, M. (2012). *Charter schools and the corporate makeover of public education: What's at stake?* New York, NY: Teachers College Press.

Fairclough, A. (1984). Martin Luther King, Jr. and the war in Vietnam. *Phylon, 45*(1), 19–39. Retrieved from www.jstor.org/stable/274976

Faludi, S. (1991). *Backlash: The undeclared war against American women.* New York, NY: Crown.

Faulkner, W. (1951). *Requiem for a nun.* New York, NY: Random House.

Feagin, J. R. (2012). *White party, White government: Race, class, and U.S. politics.* Hoboken, NJ: Taylor & Francis.

Fees and payment schedule, edTPA. (2014). Pearson Testing. Retrieved from www.edtpa.com/PageView.aspx?f=GEN_OperationalFees.html

Finlayson, A. (2012). Rhetoric and the political theory of ideologies. *Political Studies, 60*(4), 751–761. doi:10.1111/j.1467-9248.2012.00948.x

Fiske, S. T. (2011). *Envy up, scorn down: How status divides us.* New York, NY: Russell Sage.

Folbre, N. (2009). *Greed, lust, and gender: A history of economic ideas.* Oxford, England: Oxford University Press.

Foner, E. (2010, March 18). Twisting history in Texas. *The Nation.* Retrieved from www.thenation.com/article/twisting-history-texas

Ford, Z. (2012, December 3). APA revises manual: Being transgender no longer a mental disorder. *ThinkProgress.* Retrieved from thinkprogress.org/lgbt/2012/12/03/1271431/apa-revises-manual-being-transgender-is-no-longer-a-mental-disorder/

Frankenberg, E. (2013). The role of residential segregation in contemporary school segregation. *Education and Urban Society, 45*(5), 548–570. doi:10.1177/0013124513486288

Franklin, B. A. (1974, October 16). Textbook controversy: Are the books just a symbol? *St. Petersburg Times.* Retrieved from news.google.com/newspapers?nid=888&dat=19741016&id=SAswAAAAIBAJ&sjid=PnkDAAAAIBAJ&pg=4844,129273

Freedmen's Bureau Online. (n.d.). Retrieved from freedmensbureau.com/georgia/contracts/georgiacontract.htm

Freire, P. (1970). *Pedagogy of the oppressed* (M. B. Ramos, Trans.). New York, NY: Seabury Press.

Freire, P. (1998). *Teachers as cultural workers: Letters to those who dare teach* (D. Macedo, D. Koike, & A. Oliveira, Trans.). Boulder, CO: Westview Press.

Friedman, M. (2003). Defining principles: Capitalism and freedom. In G. L. Schneider (Ed.), *Conservatism in America since 1930: A reader* (pp. 68–90). New York: New York University Press. (Original work published 1962)

Frisch, K. (2010, May 19). *Washington Times* echoes anti-Muslim commentator in attack on Miss USA. *Media Matters for America*. Retrieved from mediamatters.org /blog/2010/05/19/washington-times-echoes-anti-muslim-commentator/164976

Gallagher, B. D., & Lore, John C., III. (2008, Summer). Shackling children in juvenile court: The growing debate, recent trends and the way to protect everyone's interest. *UC Davis Journal of Juvenile Law & Policy, 12*(2), 453–480. Retrieved from jjlp.law .ucdavis.edu/archives/vol-12-no-2/09_Article-Gallagher-Lore.pdf

Gallup Muslim–West perceptions index: Inaugural findings. (2011). *Gallup.* Retrieved from www.gallup.com/strategicconsulting/154289/REPORT-BILINGUAL-Gallup -Muslim-West-Perceptions-Index-Inaugural-Findings.aspx

Garcia, A., & Fitz, M. (2012, December 10). Progressive immigration policies will strengthen the American economy. Center for American Progress. Retrieved from www.americanprogress.org/issues/immigration/news/2012/12/10/47406/progressive -immigration-policies-will-strengthen-the-american-economy/

Gay, G. (2010). *Culturally responsive teaching: Theory, research, and practice* (2nd ed.). New York, NY: Teachers College Press.

Gay, Lesbian and Straight Education Network (GLSEN). (2005, October 11). *From teasing to torment: School climate in America—A national report on school bullying.* Retrieved from www.glsen.org/cgi-bin/iowa/all/news/record/1859.html

Gee, J. P. (2001). Identity as an analytic lens for research in education. In W. G. Secada (Ed.), *Review of research 25: 2000–2001* (pp. 99–125). Washington, DC: American Educational Research Association.

Genia, E. M. (2012, Summer). The landscape and language of indigenous cultural rights. *Arizona State Law Journal, 44*(2), 653–679.

Germic, S. (2008). Nativism. In W. A. Darity, Jr. (Ed.), *International encyclopedia of the social sciences* (2nd ed., Vol. 5, pp. 430–431). Detroit, MI: Macmillan Reference USA.

Gibson, C., & Jung, K. (2002). *Historical census statistics on population totals by race, 1790 to 1990, and by Hispanic origin, 1970 to 1990, for the United States, regions, divisions, and states.* U.S. Census Bureau. Retrieved from www.census.gov/population/www/documentation /twps0056/twps0056.html

Givan, R. K. (2014, Winter). Why teacher unions make such useful scapegoats. *New Labor Forum, 23*(1), 68–75.

Glaze, L. E., & Herberman, E. J. (2013). Correctional population in the United States, 2012. U.S. Department of Justice. Retrieved from www.bjs.gov/index.cfm

Global reach of neo-Nazis. (2010, August 2). *Guardian.* Retrieved from www.guardian .co.uk/world/2010/aug/02/global-reach-neo-nazis

Global views on immigration. (2011, August). *Ipsos.* Retrieved from www.ipsos-na.com /download/pr.aspx?id=10883

Goldstone, L. (2011). *Inherently unequal: The betrayal of equal rights by the Supreme Court, 1865–1903.* New York, NY: Walker & Company.

Gonzales, J. (2011, January 14). Charters schools' windfall is public kids' loss as state has city on hook for $32 million. *New York Daily News.* Retrieved from www.nydailynews. com/new-york/education/charters-schools-windfall-public-kids-loss-state-city-hook -32-million-article-1.148968

Goode, E. (2013, July 26). U.S. prison populations decline, reflecting new approach to crime. *New York Times,* pp. A10–A11.

Goodell, W. (1853). *The American slave code in theory and practice: Its distinctive features shown by the statutes, judicial decisions, and illustrative facts* (3rd ed.). New York, NY: American and Foreign Anti-Slavery Society.

Goodman, A. (2014, January 8). The FBI, the NSA and a long-held secret revealed. *Truthdig.* Retrieved from www.truthdig.com/report/item/the_fbi_the_nsa_and_a_long-held_secret_revealed_20140108

Goodman, A., & Moynihan, D. (2012). *The silenced majority: Stories of uprisings, occupations, resistance, and hope.* Chicago, IL: Haymarket Books.

Goodman, H. A. (2014, April 23). Illegal immigrants benefit the U.S. economy. *The Hill.* Retrieved from thehill.com/blogs/congress-blog/foreign-policy/203984-illegal-immigrants-benefit-the-us-economy

Gorman, J. (2014, May 27). All circuits are busy. *New York Times,* pp. D1–2.

Gorski, P. (2006, July 19). Responding to Payne's response. *Teachers College Record* (ID Number: 12605). Retrieved from www.tcrecord.org/Content.asp?ContentId =12605

Gorski, P. (2011). Unlearning deficit ideology and the scornful gaze: Thoughts on authenticating the class discourse in education. In R. Ahlguist, P. Gorski, & T. Montaño (Eds.), *Assault on kids: How hyper-accountability, corporatization, deficit ideology, and Ruby Payne are destroying our schools* (pp. 152–173). New York, NY: Peter Lang.

Gorski, P. (2013). *Reaching and teaching students in poverty: Strategies for erasing the opportunity gap.* New York, NY: Teachers College Press.

Gorski, P., Davis, S. N., & Reiter, A. (2012). Self-efficacy and multicultural teacher education in the United States: The factors that influence who feels qualified to be a multicultural teacher educator. *Multicultural Perspectives, 14*(4), 220–228.

Gottesdiener, L. (2013, August 6). A dream foreclosed: As Obama touts recovery, new book reveals racist roots of housing crisis. *Democracy Now.* Retrieved from www.democracynow.org/2013/8/6/a_dream_foreclosed_as_obama_touts

Gould, S. J. (1996). *The mismeasure of man* (Rev. ed.). New York, NY: W.W. Norton.

Greenwald, A. G., & Krieger, H. (2006). Implicit bias: Scientific foundations. *California Law Review, 94*(4), 945–967.

Greenwald, G. (2014). *No place to hide: Edward Snowden, the NSA, and the U.S. surveillance state.* New York, NY: Metropolitan Books.

Gregory, A., Cornell, D., & Fan, X. (2011). The relationship of school structure and support to suspension rates for Black and White high school students. *American Educational Research Journal, 48*(4), 904–934.

Griffith, D.W. (2002). *The birth of a nation* [Motion picture]. United States: Kino on Video. (Original work produced 1915)

Guerino, P., Harrison, P. M., & Sabol, W. J. (2012, February 9). *Prisoners in 2010* (Rev. ed.). Washington, DC: U.S. Department of Justice, Bureau of Justice Statistics. Retrieved from www.bjs.gov/content/pub/pdf/p10.pdf

Gutmann, A., & Thompson, D. (2012). *The spirit of compromise: Why governing demands it and campaigning undermines it.* Princeton, NJ: Princeton University Press.

Haberman, C. (2014, April 6). When youth violence spurred "superpredator" fear. *New York Times.* Retrieved from www.nytimes.com/2014/04/07/us/politics/killing-on-bus-recalls-superpredator-threat-of-90s.html

Hahnel, R. (2012). *Of the people, by the people: The case for a participatory economy.* Oakland, CA: AK Press.

Haidt, J., & Kesebir, S. (2010). Morality. In S. Fiske, D. Gilbert, & G. Lindzey (Eds.), *Handbook of social psychology* (5th ed., pp. 797–832). Hoboken, NJ: Wiley.

Haimson, L., & Ravitch, D. (2013, May 6). Unequal schools. *The Nation,* 41–43.

Hall, R. E. (Ed.). (2008). *Racism in the 21st century: An empirical analysis of skin color.* New York, NY: Springer.

Hall, S. (2000). Conclusion: The multi-cultural question. In B. Hesse (Ed.), *Un/Settled multiculturalism: Diasporas, entanglements, "transruptions"* (pp. 209–241). London, England: Verso.

Hammond, E. M. (2006, June 7). Straw men and their followers: The return of biological race. *Is race real? A web forum organized by the Social Science Research Council.* Retrieved from raceandgenomics.ssrc.org/Hammonds/

Hanna, M. (2013, July 17). Groups seek to end solitary confinement of juveniles in N.J. *Philly.com.* Retrieved from articles.philly.com/2013-07-17/news/40614825_1_solitary-confinement-juvenile-detention-juvenile-justice-commission

Hanley, M. S. (2010). The arts and social justice in a critical multicultural education classroom. In A. F. Ball & C. A. Tyson (Eds.), *Studying diversity in teacher education* (pp. 191–201). Lanham, MD: Rowman & Littlefield.

Harmon, D., & Loh, J. (2010). The index of linguistic diversity: A new quantitative measure of trends in the status of world languages. *Language Documentation & Conservation, 4,* 97–151. Retrieved from scholarspace.manoa.hawaii.edu/bitstream/handle/10125/4474/harmonloh.pdf

Harper, D. (2013). Diversity. *Online etymology dictionary.* Retrieved from www.etymonline.com/index.php?term=diversity

Harrington, M. (1969). *The other America: Poverty in the United States* (New introduction ed.). New York, NY: Macmillian. (Original work published 1962)

Harrington, M. (1976). *The twilight of capitalism.* New York, NY: Simon & Schuster.

Harris, C. (1993). Whiteness as property. *Harvard Law Review, 106*(8), 1707–1791.

Hart, C. L. (2013, November 18). Pot reform's race problem. *The Nation,* 17–18.

Harvey, D. (2014). *Seventeen contradictions and the end of capitalism.* New York, NY: Oxford University Press.

Harwood, J. (2013, March 2). Deep philosophical divide underlies impasse. *New York Times,* p. A10.

Hatemi, P. K., Gillespie, N. A., Eaves, L. J., Maher, B. S., Webb, B. T., Heath, A. C., . . . Martin, N. G. (2011). A genome-wide analysis of liberal and conservative political attitudes. *Journal of Politics, 73*(1), 1–15. doi:10.1017/S0022381610001015

Hedges, C. (2006). *American fascists: The Christian right and the war on America.* New York, NY: Free Press.

Hennes, E. P., Nam, H. H., Stern, C., & Jost, J. T. (2012). Not all ideologies are created equal: Epistemic, existential, and relational needs predict system-justifying attitudes. *Social Cognition, 30,* 669–688. doi:10.1521/soco.2012.30.6.669

Henrich, J., & Boyd, R. (2002). On modeling cognition and culture. *Journal of Cognition & Culture, 2*(2), 87–112. doi 10.1163/156853702320281836

Heyes, C. (2012). Identity politics. *Stanford encyclopedia of philosophy.* Retrieved from plato.stanford.edu/entries/identity-politics/

Hidden Barriers. (2014). *Workplace fairness.* Retrieved from www.workplacefairness.org/sc/discrimination.php

Hirsch, E. D. (2009–2010, Winter). Creating a curriculum for the American people: Our democracy depends on shared knowledge. *American Educator, 33*(4), 6–13, 38.

Hockenos, P. (2010, May 24). Central Europe's right-wing populism. *The Nation,* 18–19.

Homelessness and the Reagan legacy. (2013, February 1). *Liberation.* Retrieved from www.pslweb.org/liberationnews/newspaper/vol-7-no-2/homelessness-and-the-reagan-legacy.html

Hooghe, M. (2008). Ethnocentrism. In W. A. Darity, Jr. (Ed.), *International encyclopedia of the social sciences* (2nd ed., Vol. 3, pp. 11–12). Detroit, MI: Macmillan Reference USA.

Horn, C. L., & Kurlaender, M. (2006). *The end of Keyes: Resegregation trends and achievement in Denver Public Schools.* Cambridge, MA: The Civil Rights Project. Retrieved from civilrightsproject.ucla.edu/research/k-12-education/testing-and-assessment/the-end-of-keyes2014resegregation-trends-and-achievement-in-denver-public-schools/

Horsmanden, D. (2013). Fear of slave revolts. Retrieved from the Digital History website: www.digitalhistory.uh.edu/disp_textbook.cfm?smtID=3&psid=83

Huggins, N. I. (1991). The deforming mirror of truth: Slavery and the master narrative of American history. *Radical History Review, 49,* 25–48.

Hugo Chávez departs. (2002, April 13). *New York Times.* Retrieved from www.nytimes.com/2002/04/13/opinion/hugo-chavez-departs.html

Human Rights Watch. (2012a). *Growing up locked down: Youth in solitary confinement in jails and prisons across the United States.* Retrieved from www.hrw.org/sites/default/files/reports/us1012ForUpload.pdf

Human Rights Watch. (2012b). *U.S.: End life without parole for juvenile offenders, Amicus Curiae brief filed with the Supreme Court.* Retrieved from www.hrw.org/news/2012/01/26/us-end-life-without-parole-juvenile-offenders

Hunt, E. K. (2003). *Property and prophets: The evolution of economic institutions and ideologies* (Updated 7th ed.). Armonk, NY: M. E. Sharpe.

Huntington, S. P. (1997). The erosion of American national interests. *Foreign Policy, 76*(5), 28–49.

Huntington, S. P. (2004). *Who are we? The challenges to America's national identity.* New York, NY: Simon & Schuster.

Hynds, A. (2012). Challenges to the development of solidarity: Working across intersections of power and privilege in New Zealand. In C. E. Sleeter & E. Soriano (Eds.), *Creating solidarity across diverse communities* (pp. 163–179). New York, NY: Teachers College Press.

Ijaz, M. (2007, November 27). A Muslim belongs in the cabinet. *Christian Science Monitor.* Retrieved from www.csmonitor.com/2007/1127/p09s01-coop.html

Institute for Children, Poverty, and Homelessness. (2013). *The American almanac of family homelessness.* New York, NY: Author. Retrieved from www.icphusa.org/Publications/AmericanAlmanac/

International Conference on Population and Development. (2014). *Sexual and reproductive health and rights for all.* Retrieved from www.icpdtaskforce.org/beyond-2014/policy-recommendations.html

International Organization for Migration. (2010a). *International dialogue on migration 2010: Migration and social change.* Geneva, Switzerland: Author. Retrieved from www.iom.int/jahia/webdav/shared/shared/mainsite/about_iom/en/council/99/MC_INF_303.pdf

International Organization for Migration. (2010b). *World migration report 2010*. Geneva, Switzerland: Author. Retrieved from publications.iom.int/bookstore/free/WMR_2010_ENGLISH.pdf

Irons, P. (2002). *Jim Crow's children: The broken promise of the Brown decision*. New York, NY: Viking.

Irvine, J. J., & York, D. E. (1995). Learning styles and culturally diverse students: A literature review. In J. A. Banks & C. A. M. Banks (Eds.), *Handbook of research on multicultural education* (pp. 486–497). New York, NY: Macmillian.

Isin, E. F., Neyers, P., & Turner, B. S. (2009). Editorial: The thinking citizenship series. *Citizenship Studies, 13*(1), 1–2.

Isserman, M. (2009). Michael Harrington: Warrior on poverty. *New York Times*. Retrieved from www.nytimes.com/2009/06/21/books/review/Isserman-t.html

Jacques, M. (2012, October 26). A point of view: How China sees a multicultural world. *BBC News Magazine*. Retrieved from www.bbc.co.uk/news/magazine-20083309

Jarecki, E. (2012, December 3). Voting out the drug war. *The Nation*, 5–6.

Jayson, S. (2007, April 16). Sex-education clash churns over grants. *USA Today*. Retrieved from www.usatoday.com/printedition/life/20070416/d_abstinence16.art.htm

Johnson, L. B. (1964, January 8). *President Lyndon B. Johnson's annual message to the Congress on the State of the Union*. LBJ Presidential Library. Retrieved from www.lbjlib.utexas.edu/johnson/archives.hom/speeches.hom/640108.asp

Jones, R. (2012, Fall). Why build a border wall? *NACLA Report on the Americas, 45*(3), 70–72.

Jones, S. (2005). Autoethnography: Making the personal political. In N. K. Denzin & Y. S. Lincoln (Eds.), *The Sage handbook of qualitative research* (3rd ed.) (pp. 763–791). Thousand Oaks, CA: Sage.

Joshee, R. (2009). Multicultural education in Canada: Competing ideologies, interconnected discourses. In J. A. Banks (Ed.), *The Routledge international companion to multicultural education* (pp. 96–108). New York, NY: Routledge.

Jost, J. T., & Amodio, D. M. (2012). Political ideology as motivated social cognition: Behavioral and neuroscientific evidence. *Motivation and Emotion, 36*, 55–64. doi:10.1007/s11031-011-9260-7

Juteau, D. (2008). Multicultural citizenship beyond recognition. In E. Isin (Ed.), *Recasting the social in citizenship* (pp. 69–99). Toronto, Canada: University of Toronto Press.

Kanai, R., Feilden, T., Firth, C., & Rees, G. (2011, April 26). Political orientations are correlated with brain structure in young adults. *Current Biology, 21*, 1–4. doi:10.1016/j.cub.2011.03.017

Kanter, J. (2012, November 15). Britain opposes quotas for women on boards. *New York Times*, p. B9.

Karlin, R. (2014, July 31). Teacher hopefuls hit hard by costs. *Times Union*. Retrieved from www.timesunion.com/local/article/Teacher-hopefuls-hit-hard-by-costs-5661373.php

Karp, D. (2010, Winter). Unlocking men, unmasking masculinities: Doing men's work in prison. *Journal of Men's Studies, 18*(1), 63–83. doi:10.3149/jms.1801.63

Keller, H. (2002). How I became a socialist. *Monthly Review, 54*(4), 45–50. (Original work published 1912)

Kelly, K. (2005, October 17). Just don't do it: Are we teaching our kids too much about sex? Or not nearly enough? *US News and World Report*. Retrieved from www.usnews.com/usnews/health/articles/051017/17sex.htm

Kessler-Harris, A. (2001). *In pursuit of equity: Women, men, and the quest for economic citizenship in 20th century America.* New York, NY: Oxford University Press.

Keyes v. Denver School District, 413 U.S. 189 (1973). Retrieved from WestlawNext database.

Kim, E. K. (2013, September 16). New Miss America's Indian heritage sparks racist comments. *Today.* Retrieved from www.today.com/style/new-miss-americas-heritage-evokes-racist-comments-twitter-8C11167234

Kincheloe, J. (1983). *Understanding the new right and its impact on education.* Bloomington, IN: Phi Delta Kappa.

Kincheloe, J. (2005). Critical ontology and auto/biography: Being a teacher, developing a reflective teacher persona. In W. Roth (Ed.), *Auto/biography and auto/ethnography: Praxis of research method* (pp. 155–174). Rotterdam, the Netherlands: Sense.

King, E. W. (2012). Islamophobia in U.S. society and schools, recognizing and countering. In J. A. Banks (Ed.), *Encyclopedia of diversity in education* (Vol. 2, pp. 1281–1284). Los Angeles, CA: Sage Reference.

King, M. L., Jr. (1991a). I have a dream. In J. M. Washington (Ed.), *A testament of hope: The essential writings and speeches of Martin Luther King, Jr.* (pp. 217–220). San Francisco, CA: HarperSanFrancisco. (Originally delivered 1963)

King, M. L., Jr. (1991b). Letter from Birmingham city jail. In J. M. Washington (Ed.), *A testament of hope: The essential writings and speeches of Martin Luther King, Jr.* (pp. 289–302). San Francisco, CA: HarperSanFrancisco. (Original work published 1963)

King, M. L., Jr. (1991c). A time to break silence. In J. M. Washington (Ed.), *A testament of hope: The essential writings and speeches of Martin Luther King, Jr.* (pp. 231–244). San Francisco, CA: HarperSanFrancisco. (Originally delivered 1967)

Kirchick, J. (2013, May 6). Missing the point: Hungarian leader whitewashes anti-Semitism. *Spiegel Online International.* Retrieved from www.spiegel.de/international /europe/prime-minister-viktor-orban-downplays-rising-anti-semitism-in-hungary-a -898319.html

Kirk, R. (2003). The conservative mind. In G. L. Schneider (Ed.), *Conservatism in America since 1930: A reader* (pp. 107–121). New York: New York University Press. (Original work published 1960)

Kocieniewski, D. (2013, December 28). Academics who defend Wall St. reap reward. *New York Times,* pp. A1, B7.

Koon, D. S. (2013, April). *Exclusionary school discipline: An issue brief and review of the literature.* Chief Justice Earl Warren Institute on Law and Social Policy, University of California, Berkeley School of Law. Retrieved from www.boysandmenofcolor.org /wp-content/uploads/2013/04/Exclusionary-School-Discipline-Warren -Institute.pdf

Kosciw, J. G., Greytak, E. A., Bartkiewicz, M. J., Boesen, M. J., & Palmer, N. A. (2012). *The 2011 national school climate survey: The experiences of lesbian, gay, bisexual and transgender youth in our nation's schools.* Gay, Lesbian & Straight Education Network. Retrieved from glsen.org/nscs

Kubota, R. (2010). Critical multicultural education and second/foreign language teaching. In S. May & C. Sleeter (Eds.), *Critical multiculturalism: Theory and praxis* (pp. 99–111). New York, NY: Routledge.

Kymlicka, W. (2007). *Multicultural odysseys: Navigating the new international politics of diversity.* Oxford, England: Oxford University Press.

Kymlicka, W. (2010). *The current state of multiculturalism in Canada and research themes on Canadian multiculturalism: 2008–2010.* Citizenship and Immigration in Canada, Government of Canada. Retrieved from www.cic.gc.ca/english/resources/publications/multi-state/index.asp

Lacey, M. (2011, January 8). Citing "brainwashing," Arizona declares a Latina class illegal. *New York Times,* pp. A1, A12.

Ladson-Billings, G. (2004). New directions in multicultural education. In J. A. Banks & C. A. M. Banks (Eds.), *Handbook of research on multicultural education* (pp. 50–64). San Francisco, CA: Jossey-Bass.

Lambie, I., & Randell, I. (2013). The impact of incarceration on juvenile offenders. *Clinical Psychology Review, 33,* 448–459.

Lancaster, R. N. (2006, June 7). Sex and race in the long shadow of the Human Genome Project. *Is race real? A web forum organized by the Social Science Research Council.* Retrieved from raceandgenomics.ssrc.org/Lancaster/

Lassiter, M. D., & Crespino, J. (2010). Introduction: The end of southern history. In M. D. Lassiter & J. Crespino (Eds.), *The myth of southern exceptionalism* (pp. 3–22). New York, NY: Oxford University Press.

Lauderdale, P. (2008). Justice, social. In W. A. Darity, Jr. (Ed.), *International encyclopedia of the social sciences* (2nd ed., Vol. 4, pp. 241–243). Detroit, MI: Macmillan Reference USA.

Le Blanc, P., & Yates, M. (2013). *A freedom budget for all Americans: Recapturing the promise of the civil rights movement in the struggle for economic justice today.* New York, NY: Monthly Review Press.

Ledgerwood, A., Mandisodza, A. N., Jost, J. T., & Pohl, M. J. (2011). Working for the system: Motivated defense of meritocratic beliefs. *Social Cognition, 29*(2), 322–340. doi:10.1521/soco.2011.29.3.322

Leonardo, Z. (2009). Afterword. In W. Au, *Unequal by design: High-stakes testing and the standardization of inequality* (pp. 147–153). New York, NY: Routledge.

Leroi, A. M. (2005, March 14). A family tree in every gene. *New York Times,* p. A23.

Let states decide on marijuana. (2014, July 27). *New York Times,* p. 10SR.

Levine, H. (2013, November 18). The scandal of racist marijuana arrests. *The Nation,* 18–20, 22.

Levy, C. J. (2010, August 6). Soviet legacy lingers as Estonia defines its people. *New York Times,* p. A7.

Liptak, A. (2014, April 23). Justices back ban on race as factor in college entry. *New York Times,* pp. A1, A12.

Lobel, J. (2008). Prolonged solitary confinement and the Constitution. *Journal of Constitutional Law, 11*(1), 115–138. Retrieved from https://www.law.upenn.edu/journals/conlaw/articles/volume11/issue1/Lobel11U.Pa.J.Const.L.115%282009%29.pdf

Locke, J. (2003). *Two treatises of government and a letter concerning toleration* (I. Shapiro, Ed.). New Haven, CT: Yale University Press. (Original work published 1690)

Loewen, J. W. (2005). *Sundown towns: A hidden dimension of American racism.* New York, NY: New Press.

López, I. H. (2006). *White by law: The legal construction of race* (Rev. and updated). New York: New York University Press.

López, I. H. (2014). *Dog whistle politics: How coded racial appeals have reinvented racism and wrecked the middle class.* New York, NY: Oxford University Press.

Loutzenheiser, L. W., & Moore, S. D. M. (2009). Safe schools, sexuality, and critical education. In M. W. Apple, W. Au, & L. A. Gandin (Eds.), *The Routledge international handbook of critical education* (pp. 150–162). New York, NY: Routledge.

Lowrey, A. (2013, September 11). Top 10% took home half of U.S. income in 2012. *New York Times,* pp. B1, B3.

Lowrey, A. (2014, January 5). 50 years later, War on Poverty is a mixed bag. *New York Times,* pp. A1, A4.

Maccoby, E. E. (2005). Gender and group process: A developmental perspective. In M. Gauvain, & M. Cole (Eds.), *Readings on the development of children* (4th ed., pp. 187–191) New York, NY: Worth.

MacEwan, A., & Miller, J. A. (2011). *Economic collapse, economic change: Getting to the roots of the crisis.* Armonk, NY: M.E. Sharpe.

Marcuse, H. (1970). *Essay on liberation.* Boston, MA: Beacon Press.

Married women's property laws. (n.d.). Law Library of Congress. Retrieved from lcweb2 .loc.gov/ammem/awhhtml/awlaw3/property_law.html#top

Marsh, J. (2011). *Class dismissed: Why we cannot teach or learn our way out of inequality.* New York, NY: Monthly Review Press.

Marshall, E., & Sensoy, O. (2011). Introduction. In E. Marshall & O. Sensoy (Eds.), *Rethinking popular culture and media* (pp. 1–11). Milwaukee, WI: Rethinking Schools.

Marszalek, J. (2013, January 24). Galaxy poll shows most Australians think multiculturalism works well. *news.com.au.* Retrieved from www.news.com.au/lifestyle /galaxy-poll-shows-most-australians-think-multiculturalism-works-well /story-fneszs56-1226560409721

Martinez, M. (2011, January 5). Arizona education chief moves to ban ethnic studies in Tucson school. *CNN U.S.* Retrieved from www.cnn.com/2011/US/01/04/arizona .ethnic.studies.ban/

Martinez, M. (2012, January 12). Tucson school board suspends Mexican-American studies program. *CNN U.S.* Retrieved from www.cnn.com/2012/01/11/us/arizona -mexican-american-studies/

Matthes, M. (2008). *The making of American Christian patriotism in the sermons of 9/11.* Paper presented at the annual meeting of the American Political Science Association, Boston, MA.

Matthews, D. (2012, July 11). Poverty in the 50 years since "the other America," in five charts. *Washington Post.* Retrieved from www.washingtonpost.com/blogs/wonkblog /wp/2012/07/11/poverty-in-the-50-years-since-the-other-america-in-five-charts/

Mauer, M., & King, R. S. (2007). *Uneven justice: State rates of incarceration by race and ethnicity.* Washington, DC: The Sentencing Project. Retrieved from www.sentencingproject .org/doc/publications/rd_stateratesofincbyraceandethnicity.pdf

May, S. (1999). Critical multiculturalism and cultural difference: Avoiding essentialism. In S. May (Ed.), *Critical multiculturalism: Rethinking multicultural and antiracist education* (pp. 11–41). Philadelphia, PA: Falmer Press.

May, S. (2012). Critical multiculturalism and education. In J. A. Banks (Ed.), *Encyclopedia of diversity in education* (Vol. 1, pp. 472–478). Thousand Oaks, CA: Sage.

May, S., & Sleeter, C. (2010). Introduction. In S. May & C. Sleeter (Eds.), *Critical multiculturalism: Theory and praxis* (pp. 1–16). New York, NY: Routledge.

McCarthy, C. (1994). Multicultural discourse and curriculum reform: A critical perspective. *Educational Theory, 44*(1), 81–98.

McCormick, T. J. (1995). *America's half-century: United States foreign policy in the Cold War and after* (2nd ed.). Baltimore, MD: Johns Hopkins University Press.

McCurry, S. (2010). *Confederate reckoning: Power and politics in the Civil War south.* Cambridge, MA: Harvard University Press.

McDermott, R., & Hatemi, P. K. (2014). Political ecology: On the mutual formation of biology and culture. *Advances in Political Psychology, 35*(Suppl. 1), 111–127.

McGreal, C. (2010, May 16). Texas schools board rewrites US history with lesson promoting God and guns. *Guardian.* Retrieved from www.theguardian.com/world/2010/may/16/texas-schools-rewrites-us-history

McKernan, S., Ratcliffe, C., Steuerle, E., & Zhang, S. (2013). *Less than equal: Racial disparities in wealth accumulation.* Washington, DC: Urban Institute. Retrieved from www.urban.org/publications/412802.html

McLaren, P. (1994). White terror and oppositional agency: Towards a critical multiculturalism. In D. T. Goldberg (Ed.), *Multiculturalism: A critical reader* (pp. 45–74). Cambridge, MA: Blackwell.

McLaren, P., & Farahmandpur, R. (2005). *Teaching against global capitalism and the new imperialism: A critical pedagogy.* Lanham, MD: Rowman & Littlefield.

McShay, J. C. (2010). Digital stories for critical multiculturalism: A Freireian approach. In S. May & C. E. Sleeter (Eds.), *Critical multiculturalism: Theory and praxis* (pp. 139–150). New York, NY: Routledge for the American Educational Research Association.

Meem, D. T., Gibson, M. A., & Alexander, J. F. (2010). *Finding out: An introduction to LGBT studies.* Los Angeles, CA: Sage.

Meyer, E. J. (2009). *Gender, bullying and harassment: Strategies to end sexism and homophobia in schools.* New York, NY: Teachers College Press.

Millhiser, I. (2012, January 12). Rand Paul explains his family's opposition to Civil Rights Act. *ThinkProgress.* Retrieved from thinkprogress.org/justice/2012/01/09/400521/rand-paul-explains-his-familys-opposition-to-civil-rights-act-its-about-controlling-property/

Milliken v. Bradley, 418 U.S. 717 (1974). Retrieved from WestlawNext database.

Mills, C. W. (2009). Psychology and social science. *Monthly Review, 61*(7), 47–52. (Original work published 1958)

Minami, M., & Ovando, C. (2004). Language issues in multicultural contexts. In J. A. Banks & C. A. M. Banks (Eds.), *Handbook of research on multicultural education* (2nd ed., pp. 567–588). San Francisco, CA: Jossey-Bass.

Moriearty, P. (2012, September 24). Restoring rehabilitation to the American juvenile justice system. *Jurist.* Retrieved from jurist.org/forum/2012/09/perry-moriearty-juvenile-justice.php

Moriearty, P. L. (2010). Framing justice: Media, bias, and legal decisionmaking. *Maryland Law Review, 69*(4), 849–909. Retrieved from digitalcommons.law.umaryland.edu/mlr/vol69/iss4/4/

National Association for Multicultural Education. (2014). *NAME position statement on the edTPA.* Retrieved from nameorg.org/2014/01/position-edtpa/

National Association for the Advancement of Colored People (NAACP). (2005). *Dismantling the school-to-prison pipeline.* New York, NY: Author. Retrieved from www.naacpldf.org/files/publications/Dismantling_the_School_to_Prison_Pipeline.pdf

National Association for the Advancement of Colored People (NAACP). (2013). Criminal fact sheet. Retrieved from www.naacp.org/pages/criminal-justice-fact-sheet

National Center on Family Homelessness. (2010). Children. Retrieved from www.familyhomelessness.org/children.php?p=ts#

National Council for Accreditation of Teacher Education (NCATE). (2007). NCATE issues call for action. Retrieved from www.ncate.org/public/102407.asp?ch=148

National Council for Accreditation of Teacher Education (NCATE). (2008a). NCATE unit standards revision. Retrieved from www.ncate.org/documents/standards/SummaryMajorChangesUnitStd.pdf

National Council for Accreditation of Teacher Education (NCATE). (2008b). *Professional standards for the accreditation of teacher preparation institutions.* Washington, DC: Author. Retrieved from www.ncate.org/public/standards.asp

National Council for Accreditation of Teacher Education (NCATE). (2008c). What is NCATE? Retrieved from www.ncate.org/public/faqaboutNCATE.asp?ch=1

National Council for Accreditation of Teacher Education (NCATE). (2014). About NCATE. Retrieved from www.ncate.org/Public/AboutNCATE/tabid/179/Default.aspx

National Education Association. (1991). *The Kanawha County textbook controversy.* In R. L. Lewis & J.C. Hennen, Jr. (Eds.), West Virginia: Documents in the history of a rural-industrial state (pp. 308–319). Dubuque, IA: Kendall/Hunt Publishing. (Original work published 1975)

National Park Service. (2013). *Jim Crow laws.* Retrieved from www.nps.gov/malu/forteachers/jim_crow_laws.htm

Nelson, S. (Director/Writer). (2010). *Freedom riders* [Motion picture]. United States: Public Broadcasting Service.

Nevarez, G. (2013, February 8). Victory over Tucson school district could lead to Mexican American studies reinstatement. *Huffington Post.* Retrieved from www.huffingtonpost.com/2013/02/08/victory-over-tucson-school-district-case-mexican-american-studies_n_2647077.html

Newport, F. (2006). Canadians more positive about immigration than Americans or Britons. *Gallup.* Retrieved from www.gallup.com/poll/21592/canadians-more-positive-about-immigration-than-americans-britons.aspx

Nixon, R. (2014, January 21). Food banks anticipate impact of cuts to food stamps. *New York Times.* Retrieved from www.nytimes.com/2014/01/22/us/politics/food-banks-anticipate-impact-of-cuts-to-food-stamps.html

Norton, M. I., & Sommers, S. R. (2011). Whites see racism as a zero-sum game that they are now losing. *Perspectives on Psychological Science, 6*(3), 215–218. doi:10.1177/1745691611406922

Nussbaum, M. C. (2010). *Not for profit: Why democracy needs the humanities.* Princeton, NJ: Princeton University Press.

Obama, B. (2010a, September 14). *Back to school speech.* The White House. Retrieved from www.whitehouse.gov/the-press-office/2010/09/13/remarks-president-barack-obama-prepared-delivery-back-school-speech

Obama, B. (2010b, December 16). *Remarks by the president at the White House tribal nations conference.* The White House. Retrieved from www.whitehouse.gov/the-press-office/2010/12/16/remarks-president-white-house-tribal-nations-conference

Obama, B. (2013a, February 12). *Remarks by the president in the State of the Union address.* The White House. Retrieved from www.whitehouse.gov/the-press-office/2013/02/12/remarks-president-state-union-address

Obama, B. (2013b, May 20). Transcript: Obama's commencement speech at Morehouse College. *Wall Street Journal.* Retrieved from blogs.wsj.com/washwire/2013/05/20/transcript-obamas-commencement-speech-at-morehouse-college/

Office of Superintendent of Public Instruction. (2014, February 27). *Number of homeless students tops 30,000.* Retrieved from www.k12.wa.us/Communications/pressreleases2014/HomelessStudents.aspx

Olson, L. (2001). *Freedom's daughters: The unsung heroines of the civil rights movement from 1830 to 1970.* New York, NY: Scribner.

O'Reilly, B. (2012, November 6). Bill O'Reilly: The White establishment is now the minority. *Fox Nation.* Retrieved from nation.foxnews.com/bill-oreilly/2012/11/07/bill-o-reilly-white-establishment-now-minority

Orfield, G. (2013a, October 24). *A new civil rights agenda for American education: Creating opportunity in a stratified multiracial nation.* Presentation for the Tenth Annual Brown Lecture in Education Research, American Educational Association webcast. Retrieved from www.aera.net/EventsMeetings/AnnualBrownLectureinEducationResearch/tabid/10210/Default.aspx

Orfield, G. (2013b). Choice theories and the schools. In G. Orfield, E. Frankenberg, & Associates (Eds.), *Educational delusions? Why choice can deepen inequality and how to make schools fair* (pp. 37–66). Berkeley: University of California Press.

Orfield, G., & Frankenberg, E. (2013). Conclusion: A theory of choice with equity. In G. Orfield, E. Frankenberg, & Associates (Eds.), *Educational delusions? Why choice can deepen inequality and how to make schools fair* (pp. 255–270). Berkeley: University of California Press.

Orfield, G., Kucsera, J., & Siegel-Hawley, G. (2012). E pluribus . . . *separation: Deepening double segregation for more students.* The Civil Rights Project. Retrieved from civilrightsproject.ucla.edu/research/k-12-education/integration-and-diversity/mlk-national/e-pluribus...separation-deepening-double-segregation-for-more-students/

Overview. (n.d.). *Equal Rights Amendment.* Retrieved from www.equalrightsamendment.org/overview.htm

Pang, V. O., & Park, C. D. (2011). Creating interdisciplinary multicultural teacher education. In A. F. Ball & C. A. Tyson (Eds.), *Studying diversity in teacher education* (pp. 63–80). Lanham, MD: Rowman & Littlefield.

Parents Involved in Community Schools v. Seattle School District, 551 U.S. 701 (2007). Retrieved from WestlawNext database.

Parker, A., & Preston, J. (2013, May 8). Paper on immigrant I.Q. dogs critic of overhaul. *New York Times.* Retrieved from www.nytimes.com/2013/05/09/us/heritage-analysts-dissertation-on-immigrant-iq-causes-furor.html

Parker, W. C. (2012). Democracy, diversity, and schooling. In J. A. Banks (Ed.), *Encyclopedia of diversity* (Vol. 2, pp. 613–620). Los Angeles, CA: Sage Reference.

Pasek, J., Krosnick, J. A., & Tompson, T. (2012, October). *The impact of anti-Black racism on approval of Barack Obama's job performance and on voting in the 2012 presidential election*. Retrieved from www.stanford.edu/dept/communication/faculty/krosnick/docs/2012/2012%20Voting%20and%20Racism.pdf

Patel, L. (2013). *Youth held at the border: Immigration, education, and the politics of inclusion*. New York, NY: Teachers College Press.

Payne, R. (2005). *A framework for understanding poverty* (4th ed.). Highlands, TX: aha! Process.

Payne, R. K. (2009, May 17). Using the lens of economic class to help teachers understand and teach students from poverty: A response. *Teachers College Record* (ID Number: 15629). Retrieved from www.tcrecord.org/Content.asp?ContentId=15629

Pettigrew, T. F. (2004). Intergroup contact: Theory, research, and new perspective. In J. A. Banks & C. A. M. Banks (Eds.), *Handbook of research on multicultural education* (2nd ed., pp. 770–781). San Francisco, CA: Jossey-Bass.

Pew Charitable Trusts. (2010). *Collateral costs: Incarceration's effect on economic mobility*. Washington, DC: Author. Retrieved from http://www.pewtrusts.org/~/media/legacy/uploadedfiles/pcs_assets/2010/CollateralCosts1pdf.pdf

Pfaffenberger, B. (2008). Society. In W. A. Darity, Jr. (Ed.), *International encyclopedia of the social sciences* (2nd ed., Vol. 7, pp. 316–318). Detroit, MI: Macmillan Reference USA.

Pfeiffer, D. (2011, April 27). President Obama's long form birth certificate. *The White House Blog*. Retrieved from www.whitehouse.gov/blog/2011/04/27/president-obamas-long-form-birth-certificate

Phillips-Fein, K. (2011, Jan.). Right from the start: The roots of the conservative grievance industry. *Bookforum*. Retrieved from www.bookforum.com/inprint/017_04/6672

Piff, P. K., Kraus, M. W., Côté, S., Cheng, B. H., & Keltner, D. (2010). Having less, giving more: The influence of social class on prosocial behavior. *Journal of Personality and Social Psychology, 99*(5), 771–784. doi:10.1037/a0020092

Piff, P. K., Stancato, D. M., Côte, S., Mendoza-Denton, R., & Keltner, D. (2012). Higher social class predicts increased unethical behavior. *Proceedings of the National Academy of Sciences, 109*(11), 4086–4091. doi:10.1073/pnas.1118373109

Piketty, T. (2014). *Capital in the twenty-first century* (A. Goldhammer, Trans.). Cambridge, MA: Belknap Press of Harvard University Press.

Pincus, F. L. (2006). *Understanding diversity: An introduction to class, race, gender, and sexual orientation*. Boulder, CO: Lynne Rienner.

Planas, R. (2012, November 14). Mexican American studies: Tucson courses improved achievement, new report says. *Huffington Post*. Retrieved from www.huffingtonpost.com/2012/11/14/mexican-american-studies-students_n_2132443.html

Plessy v. Ferguson, 163 U.S. 537 (1896). Retrieved from WestlawNext database.

Plyler v. Doe, 47 U.S. 202. Retrieved from Westlaw Next database.

Pollock, M. (2008). *Because of race: How Americans debate harm and opportunity in our schools*. Princeton, NJ: Princeton University Press.

Pomy, M. (2013, January 31). Federal judge rules juvenile life sentences unconstitutional. *Jurist*. Retrieved from jurist.org/paperchase/2013/01/federal-judge-rules-juvenile-life-sentences-unconstitutional.php

Postiglione, G. A. (2009). The education of ethnic minority groups in China. In J. A. Banks (Ed.), *The Routledge international companion to multicultural education* (pp. 501–511). New York, NY: Routledge.

Powell, L. F. (1971, August 23). *Confidential memorandum: Attack on American free enterprise system*. Retrieved from law.wlu.edu/deptimages/Powell%20Archives/PowellMemorandumTypescript.pdf

Praxis performance assessments. (2014). Eductional Testing Service. Retrieved from www.ets.org/ppa/educator_programs/faq/

President: Full results. (2012, December 10). *CNN Politics*. Retrieved from www.cnn.com /election/2012/results/race/president#exit-polls

Preston, A. (2012, July 1). A very young Judeo-Christian tradition. *Boston Globe*. Retrieved from www.bostonglobe.com/ideas/2012/06/30/very-young-judeo-christian-tradition /smZoWrkrSLeMZpLou1ZGNL/story.html

Preston, J. (2013, October 7). Ailing cities extend hand to immigrants. *New York Times*, pp. A1, A17.

Price, D. H. (2004). *Threatening anthropology: McCarthyism and the FBI's surveillance of activist anthropologists*. Durham, NC: Duke University Press.

Price, D. H. (2011). *Weaponizing anthropology: Social science in service of the militarized state*. Oakland, CA: AK Press/Counterpunch.

Price, D. H. (2013, August). A social history of wiretaps. *CounterPunch*. Retrieved from www.counterpunch.org/2013/08/09/a-social-history-of-wiretaps-2/

Puente, S. (2012, October 3). 50 students, 1 teacher: Illinois' tough bilingual school reality. *Huffington Post*. Retrieved from www.huffingtonpost.com/sylvia-puente/chicago -preschool-problem_b_1929797.html

Quinn, A. (2013, October 25). Book news: Arizona lifts ban on 7 Mexican American studies books. National Public Radio. Retrieved from www.npr.org/blogs /thetwo-way/2013/10/25/240704193/book-news-arizona-lifts-ban-on-7-mexican -american-studies-books

Raine, A. (2013, April 26). The criminal mind. *Wall Street Journal*. Retrieved from online .wsj.com/article/SB10001424127887323335404578444682892520530.html

Rau, A. B. (2014, January 14). Controversial bill to expand religious practices advances. *azcentral.com*. Retrieved from www.azcentral.com/news/politics/articles /20140115religious-protections-bill-advances.html

Ravitch, D. (2011). *The death and life of the great American school system: How testing and choice are undermining education*. New York, NY: Basic Books.

Reagan, R. (2003). "The great communicator": Three speeches. In G. L. Schneider (Ed.), *Conservatism in America since 1930: A reader* (pp. 341–361). New York: New York University Press. (Original work published 1983)

Redeaux, M. (2011). A framework for maintaining White privilege: A critique of Ruby Payne. In R. Ahlguist, P. Gorski, & T. Montaño (Eds.), *Assault on kids: How hyper-accountability, corporatization, deficit ideology, and Ruby Payne are destroying our schools* (pp. 177–198). New York, NY: Peter Lang.

Reifowitz, I. (2012). *Obama's America: A transformative vision of our national identity*. Washington, DC: Potomac Books.

Reisman, D. (1993). *Abundance for what?* New Brunswick, NJ: Transaction. (Original work published 1964)

Republican Party of Texas. (2012). *Report of platform committee and rules committee*. Retrieved from www.tfn.org/site/DocServer/20...pdf?docID=3201

Rich, A. (1983). Compulsory heterosexuality and lesbian existence. In E. Abel & E. K. Abel (Eds.), *The signs reader: Women, gender, and scholarship* (pp. 139–168). Chicago, IL: University of Chicago Press.

Rickman, W. (2010). A study of self-censorship by school librarians. *School Library Research, 13*. Retrieved from www.ala.org/aasl/slr/vol13

Roberts, S. (2012, January 31). Study of census results finds that residential segregation is down sharply. *New York Times,* p. A13.

Roberts, S., & Baker, P. (2010, April 2). Asked to declare his race, Obama checks "Black." *New York Times.* Retrieved from www.nytimes.com/2010/04/03/us/politics/03census.html

Robertson, C. (2011, September 26). Alabama inmate sues to read southern history book. *New York Times.* Retrieved from www.nytimes.com/2011/09/27/us/alabama-inmate-sues-to-read-southern-history-book.html

Robin, C. (2004, Fall). Fragmented state, pluralist society: How liberal institutions promote fear. *Missouri Law Review, 69*, 1061–1093. Retrieved from www.webcitation.org/64TegBPZi

Robin, C. (2011). *The reactionary mind: Conservatism from Edmund Burke to Sarah Palin.* New York, NY: Oxford University Press.

Robinson, J. P., & Espelage, D. L. (2012). Bullying explains only part of LGBTQ-heterosexual risk disparities: Implications for policy and practice. *Educational Researcher, 41*(8), 309–319.

Robinson, K., & Ferfolja, T. (2007). Playing it up, playing down, playing it safe: Queering teacher education. *Teaching and Teacher Education.* doi:10.1016/j.tate.2007.11.004

Rodriquez, T. L, & Hallman, H. L. (2013). Millennial teacher: A storied landscape of diversity in "new time." *Multicultural Perspectives, 15*(2), 65–72.

Rogoff, B. (2003). *The cultural nature of human development.* New York, NY: Oxford University Press.

Rohter, L. (1994, May 15). Battle over patriotism curriculum. *New York Times,* p. A22.

Rollert, J. P. (2012, October 21). Sleight of the "invisible hand." *New York Times.* Retrieved from opinionator.blogs.nytimes.com/2012/10/21/sleight-of-the-invisible-hand/

Romaine, S. (2009). Language, culture, and identity across nations. In J. A. Banks (Ed.), *The Routledge international companion to multicultural education* (pp. 373–384). New York, NY: Routledge.

Romaine, S. (2011). Identity and multilingualism. In K. Potowski & J. Rothman (Eds.), *Bilingual youth: Spanish in English-speaking societies* (pp. 7–30). Amsterdam, the Netherlands: John Benjamins.

Romero, S., & Austen, I. (2013, October 8). Brazil leader asks Canada to explain its spying. *New York Times,* p. A10.

Ross, R. K., & Zimmerman, K. H. (2014, February 16). Real discipline in school. *New York Times,* p. A17.

Ross, S., & Agiesta, J. (2012, October 27). AP poll: Majority harbor prejudice against Blacks. *AP: The big story.* Retrieved from bigstory.ap.org/article/ap-poll-majority-harbor-prejudice-against-blacks

Roth, W. (2005). Auto/biography and auto/ethnography: Finding the generalized other in the self. In W. Roth (Ed.), *Auto/biography and auto/ethnography: Praxis of research method* (pp. 3–16). Rotterdam, the Netherlands: Sense.

Rury, J., & Mirel, J. (1997). The political economy of urban education. In M. W. Apple (Ed.), *Review of research in education* (Vol. 22, pp. 49–110). Washington, DC: American Educational Research Association.

Russia: Protest over gay rights. (2010, September 22). *New York Times,* p. A8.

Saad, L. (2012, December 14). Most in U.S. say Americans are divided on important values. Retrieved from www.gallup.com/poll/159257/say-americans-divided-important-values.aspx

Sacco, D. T., Silbaugh, K., Corredor, F., Casey, J., & Doherty, D. (2012, February). *An overview of state anti-bullying legislation and other related laws.* Barkman Center for Internet and Society at Harvard University. Retrieved from cyber.law.harvard.edu/publications/2012/state_anti_bullying_legislation_overview

Sack, K. (2001, September 28). School colors become red, white and blue. *New York Times.* Retrieved from www.nytimes.com/2001/09/28/us/a-nation-challenged-the-students-school-colors-become-red-white-and-blue.html

Sakal, L. (2014, May 28). *Breaking down mass incarceration in the 2010 census: State-by-state incarceration rates by race/ethnicity.* Retrieved from the Prison Policy Initiative website: www.prisonpolicy.org/reports/rates.html

Samaras, A. P., Hicks, M. A., & Garvey Berger, J. (2004). Self-study through personal history. In J. J. Loughran, M. L. Hamilton, V. K. LaBoskey, & T. Russell (Eds.), *International handbook of self-study of teaching and teacher education practices: Part II* (pp. 905–942). Dordrecht, the Netherlands: Kluwer Academic.

Samuels, L. (2010). Improvising on reality: The roots of prison abolition. In D. Berger (Ed.), *The hidden 1970s: Histories of radicalism* (pp. 21–38). New Brunswick, NJ: Rutgers University Press.

Sang-Hun, C. (2012, December 7). In changing South Korea, who counts as "Korean"? *New York Times,* p. A10.

Schmitt, J., Warner, K., & Gupta, S. (2010, June). *The high budgetary cost of incarceration.* Center for Economic and Policy Research. Retrieved from www.cepr.net/index.php/publications/reports/the-high-budgetary-cost-of-incarceration/

Schools and censorship: Banned books. (n.d.). People for the American Way. Retrieved from www.pfaw.org/issues/freedom-of-speech/schools-and-censorship-banned-books

Severson, K. (2012, October 15). Seeing a gay agenda, a Christian group protests an anti-bullying program. *New York Times,* p. A15.

Shaefer, H. L., & Edin, K. (2012, February). *Extreme poverty in the United States, 1966 to 2011.* National Poverty Center. Retrieved from npc.umich.edu/publications/policy_briefs/brief28/

Shipman, B. M. (2012, July 19). Are liberal Christians becoming rare? *New York Times,* p. A20.

Sleeter, C. E. (2001). An analysis of critiques of multicultural education. In J. A. Banks & C. A. M. Banks (Eds.), *Handbook of research on multicultural education* (pp. 81–94). San Francisco, CA: Jossey-Bass.

Sleeter, C. E. (2011). *The academic and social value of ethnic studies: A research review.* Washington, DC: National Education Association. Retrieved from www.nea.org/assets/docs/NBI-2010-3-value-of-ethnic-studies.pdf

Sleeter, C. E. (2012a). Building solidarity for education in complex societies: What we have learned. In C. E. Sleeter & E. Soriano (Eds.), *Creating solidarity across diverse communities* (pp. 198–208). New York, NY: Teachers College Press.

Sleeter, C. E. (2012b). Ethnic studies, research on. In J. A. Banks (Ed.), *Encyclopedia of diversity in education* (Vol. 2, pp. 842–843). Los Angeles, CA: Sage Reference.

Sleeter, C. E., & Bernal, D. D. (2004). Critical pedagogy, critical race theory, and antiracist education. In J. A. Banks & C. A. M. Banks (Eds.), *Handbook of research on multicultural education* (2nd ed., pp. 240–258). San Francisco, CA: Jossey-Bass.

Sleeter, C. E., Bishop, R., & Meyer, L. (2011). Professional development for culturally responsive and relationship-based pedagogy. In C. E. Sleeter (Ed.), *Professional development for culturally responsive and relationship-based pedagogy* (pp. 163–177). New York, NY: Peter Lang.

Sleeter, C. E., & Grant, C. A. (1999). *Making choices for multicultural education: Five approaches to race, class, and gender* (3rd ed.). New York, NY: Macmillan.

Small, M. L., Harding, D. J., & Lamont, M. (2010). Reconsidering culture and poverty. *Annals of the American Academy of Political and Social Science, 629*(1), 6–27. doi:10.1177/0002716210362077

Smith, A. (2001). *The wealth of nations.* London, England: Electronic Book. (Original work published 1776)

Smith, M. L. (2002, Summer). Race, nationality, and reality: INS administration of racial provisions in U.S. immigration and nationality law since 1898. *Prologue Magazine, 34*(2). Retrieved from www.archives.gov/publications/prologue/2002/summer/immigration-law-1.html#f11

Smith, R. J., Becker, J., & Goldstein, A. (2005, July 27). Documents show Roberts influence in Reagan era. *Washington Post.* Retrieved from www.washingtonpost.com/wp-dyn/content/article/2005/07/26/AR2005072602070.html

Solitary Watch. (2012). *Solitary confinement: FAQ.* Retrieved from solitarywatch.com/faq

Song, S. (2009). Democracy and noncitizen voting rights. *Citizenship Studies, 13*(6), 607–620. doi:10.1080/13621020903309607

Song, S. (2010). Multiculturalism. *Stanford encyclopedia of philosophy.* Retrieved from plato.stanford.edu/entries/multiculturalism/

Specter, M. (2014, January 6). The gene factory. *New Yorker,* pp. 34–43.

Spring, J. (2010). *The American school, a global context: From the Puritans to the Obama administration* (8th ed.). New York, NY: McGraw-Hill.

Staples, B. (2014, January 13). A flashback to the reign of J. Edgar Hoover. *New York Times,* p. A18.

Stearns, P. N. (1998). Why study history? Retrieved from the American Historical Society website: www.historians.org/about-aha-and-membership/aha-history-and-archives/archives/why-study-history-(1998)

Stephan, W. G., & Stephan, C. W. (2004). Intergroup relations in multicultural education groups. In J. A. Banks & C. A. M. Banks (Eds.), *Handbook of research on multicultural education* (2nd ed., pp. 782–798). San Francisco, CA: Jossey-Bass.

Stokes, M. (2007). *D. W. Griffith's The Birth of a Nation: A history of "the most controversial motion picture of all time."* New York, NY: Oxford University Press.

Stotsky, S. (1999). *Losing our language: How multicultural classroom instruction is undermining our children's ability to read, write, and reason.* New York, NY: Free Press.

Stritikus, T., & Lucero, A. (2012). Immigration and education. In J. A. Banks (Ed.), *Encyclopedia of diversity in education* (Vol. 2, pp. 1138–1141). Los Angeles, CA: Sage.

Suárez-Orozco, M., & Suárez-Orozco, C. (2013, April 23). Immigrant kids, adrift. *New York Times,* p. A21.

Sugrue, T. J. (2010). *Not even the past: Barack Obama and the burden of race.* Princeton, NJ: Princeton University Press.

Sumner, W. (1952). *What social classes owe to each other.* Caldwell, ID: Caxton. (Original work published 1883)

Swann v. Charlotte-Mecklenburg Board of Education, 402 U.S. 1 (1971). Retrieved from WestlawNext database.

Taber, C. S., & Lodge, M. (2006). Motivated skepticism in the evaluation of political beliefs. *American Journal of Political Science, 50*(3), 755–769.

Takao Ozawa v. United States, 260 U.S. 178 (1922). Retrieved from WestlawNext database.

Tan, L. (2012, October 1). Embracing ethnic diversity: Melting-pot reality okay with New Zealanders. *New Zealand Herald.* Retrieved from www.nzherald.co.nz/nz/news/article.cfm?c_id=1&objectid=10837572

Texas Administrative Code. (2011). *Chapter 113. Texas essential knowledge and skills for social studies.* Retrieved from ritter.tea.state.tx.us/rules/tac/chapter113/ch113c.pdf

Thatcher, M. (2013). Interview for *Women's Own.* Margaret Thatcher Foundation. (Original work published September 23, 1987). Retrieved from www.margaretthatcher.org/speeches/displaydocument.asp?docid=106689

Thórisdóttir, H., & Jost, J. T. (2011). Motivated closed-mindedness mediates the effect of threat on political conservatism. *Political Psychology, 32*(5), 785–811. doi:10.1111/j.1467-9221.2011.00840.x

Tienda, M. (2013). Diversity ≠ inclusion: Promoting integration in higher education. *Educational Researcher, 42*(9), 467–475.

Travis, J., McBride, E. C., & Solomon, A. L. (2005, June). *Families left behind: The hidden costs of incarceration and reentry.* Urban Institute, Justice Policy Center. Retrieved from www.urban.org/UploadedPDF/310882_families_left_behind.pdf

United Nations. (1990, December 14). Resolution 45/113: Rules for the protection of juveniles deprived of their liberty. General Assembly. Retrieved from www.un.org/documents/ga/res/45/a45r113.htm

United Nations. (2008, March). *United Nations declaration on the rights of indigenous peoples.* Retrieved from undesadspd.org/IndigenousPeoples/DeclarationontheRightsofIndigenousPeoples.aspx

United Nations. (2009, April 28). *Racism, racial discrimination, xenophobia and related forms of intolerance, follow-up to and implementation of the Durban Declaration and programme of action: Report of the special rapporteur on contemporary forms of racial discrimination, xenophobia and related intolerance.* Retrieved from www2.ohchr.org/english/bodies/hrcouncil/docs/11session/A.HRC.11.36.Add.3.pdf

United Nations. (2010). *The world's women 2010: Trends and statistics.* New York, NY: Author. Retrieved from unstats.un.org/unsd/demographic/products/Worldswomen/WW2010pub.htm#

United Nations Children's Fund (UNICEF). (2012, May). International migrant children and adolescents facts and figures. Retrieved from www.unicef.org/socialpolicy/files/UNICEF_Factsheet_Children_and_Adolescent_Migrants_May_2012.docx

United Nations Economic and Social Council. (2013, March 12). *Indigenous youth: Identity, challenges and hope.* Retrieved from imuna.org/indigenous-youth-identity-challenges-and-hope

United Nations Educational, Scientific, and Cultural Organization (UNESCO). (1950). *The race question.* Retrieved from unesdoc.unesco.org/images/0012/001282/128291eo.pdf

United Nations Human Development Programme. (2004). *Human development report 2004: Cultural liberty in today's diverse world.* Retrieved from hdr.undp.org/en/content/human-development-report-2004

UN News Centre. (2013, September 11). Number of international migrants rises above 232 million, UN reports. Retrieved from www.un.org/apps/news/story.asp?NewsID=45819&Cr=migrants&Cr1=#.UkMUubx54qa

United States v. Bhagat Singh Thind, 261 U.S. 204 (1923). Retrieved from WestlawNext database.

University of Illinois at Chicago. (2008). Race guides neighborhood evaluation, study says. *ScienceDaily.* Retrieved from www.sciencedaily.com/releases/2008/11/081120144238.htm

University of South Carolina. (2012, November 1). This is your brain on politics: Neuroscience reveals brain differences between Republicans and Democrats. *ScienceDaily.* Retrieved from www.sciencedaily.com/releases/2012/11/121101105003.htm#UJOuWSl85CI.facebook

Urbina, I. (2013, June 4). Blacks are singled out for marijuana arrests, federal data suggests. *New York Times,* p. A11.

U.S. Department of Education. (2013). *For each and every child: A strategy for education equity and excellence.* Retrieved from www.foreachandeverychild.org/The_Report.html

U.S. Department of Energy. (2013). Minorities, race, and genomics. Human Genome Project Information Archive 1990–2003. Retrieved from web.ornl.gov/sci/techresources/Human_Genome/elsi/minorities.shtml

U.S. Department of Labor. (1965). *The Negro family: The case for national action.* Ann Arbor: University of Michigan Library.

U.S. Department of Labor. (2011). Women in the labor force: A data book. Retrieved from www.bls.gov/cps/wlf-databook2011.htm

U.S. Department of Labor. (2014). Labor force statistics from the current population survey (1964–2013). Retrieved from data.bls.gov/pdq/SurveyOutputServlet

U.S. Department of State. (2007, April 23). *Periodic report of the United States of America to the U.N. Committee on the Elimination of Racial Discrimination concerning the International Convention on the Elimination of All Forms of Racial Discrimination.* Retrieved from www.state.gov/documents/organization/83517.pdf

U.S. Department of State. (n.d.). The Immigration Act of 1924 (the Johnson–Reed Act). Office of the Historian. Retrieved from history.state.gov/milestones/1921-1936/ImmigrationAct

Valenti, J. (2013, April 15). Rape—Still not a joke. *The Nation, 2,* 4.

Vass, J. S., & Gold, S. R. (1995). Effects of feedback on emotion in hypermasculine males. *Violence & Victims, 10*(3), 217–226.

Vavrus, M. (1994). A critical analysis of multicultural education infusion during student teaching. *Action in Teacher Education, 16*(3), 47–58.

Vavrus, M. (2002). *Transforming the multicultural education of teachers: Theory, research, and practice.* New York, NY: Teachers College Press.

Vavrus, M. (2006a, March). *Resisting the effects of teacher alienation in an era of globalization.* Paper presented at the International Globalization, Diversity, and Education Conference, Washington State University, Pullman.

Vavrus, M. (2006b). Teacher identity formation in a multicultural world: Intersections of autobiographical research and critical pedagogy. In D. Tidwell & L. Fitzgerald (Eds.), *Self-study and diversity* (pp. 89–113). Rotterdam, the Netherlands: Sense.

Vavrus, M. (2008). Culturally responsive teaching. In T. L. Good (Ed.), *21st century education: A reference handbook* (Vol. 2, pp. 49–57). Thousand Oaks, CA: Sage.

Vavrus, M. (2009). Sexuality, schooling, and teacher identity formation: A critical pedagogy for teacher education. *Teaching and Teacher Education: An International Journal of Research and Studies, 25*(3), 383–390.

Vavrus, M. (2010). Critical multiculturalism and higher education: Resistance and possibilities within teacher education. In S. May & C. Sleeter (Eds.), *Critical multiculturalism: Theory and praxis* (pp. 19–31). New York, NY: Routledge.

Vavrus, M. (2012). Diversity: A contested concept. In J. Banks (Ed.), *Encyclopedia of diversity in education* (Vol. 2, pp. 667–676). Thousand Oaks, CA: Sage.

Verkuten, M. (2010). Multiculturalism and tolerance: An intergroup perspective. In R. J. Crisp (Ed.), *The psychology of social and cultural diversity* (pp. 147–170). Chichester, England: Wiley-Blackwell.

Vincent, A. (2005). Patriotism. In M. C. Horowitz (Ed.), *New dictionary of the history of ideas.* (Vol. 4, pp. 1721–1724). Detroit, MI: Charles Scribner's Sons.

Virginia General Assembly. (1705). *An act concerning servants and slaves* (excerpts). Retrieved from www.encyclopediavirginia.org/_An_act_concerning_Servants_and _Slaves_1705

Virginia slave laws. (2012). Retrieved from the Digital History website: www.digitalhistory .uh.edu/disp_textbook_print.cfm?smtid=3&psid=71

Voting rights act of 1965. (1965). Public Law 89-110. Retrieved from www.gpo.gov/fdsys /granule/STATUE-79/STATUTE-79-Pg437/content-detail.html

Wakslak, C. J., Jost, J. T., & Bauer, P. (2011). Spreading rationalization: Increased support for large-scale and small-scale social systems following system threat. *Social Cognition, 29*(2), 288–302. doi:10.1521/soco.2011.29.3.288

Wallach, B. (2005). *Understanding the cultural landscape.* New York, NY: Guilford Press.

Wallerstein, I. (2011). *The modern world system IV: Centrist liberalism triumphant, 1789–1914.* Berkeley: University of California Press.

Waterfield, B., & Samuel, H. (2010, September 15). Europe compares France Roma expulsion to Nazi deportations. *Telegraph.co.uk.* Retrieved from www.telegraph.co.uk /news/worldnews/europe/france/8002518/Europe-compares-France-Roma -expulsion-to-Nazi-deportations.html

Watkins, W. H. (2001). *The White architects of Black education: Ideology and power in America, 1865–1954.* New York, NY: Teachers College Press.

Watkins, W. H. (2012). Introduction. In W. H. Watkins (Ed.), *The assault on public education: Confronting the politics of corporate school reform* (pp. 1–6). New York, NY: Teachers College Press.

Werz, M. (2004). The fate of emancipated subjectivity. In J. Abromeit & W. M. Cobb (Eds.), *Herbert Marcuse: A critical reader* (pp. 209–223). New York, NY: Routledge.

Wessler, S. F. (2012, October 4). Near silence on poverty in presidential debate. *Colorlines.* Retrieved from colorlines.com/archives/2012/10/near_silence_on_poverty_in_the _presidential_debate.html

West Virginia State Board of Education v. Barnett, 319 U.S. 624 (1943). Retrieved from WestlawNext database.

Wheeler, W. (2012, November 18). Europe's new fascists. *New York Times,* pp. 4SR, 7SR.

Whisnant, R. (2013, Fall). Feminist perspectives on rape. In Edward N. Zalta (Ed.), *Stanford encyclopedia of philosophy.* Retrieved from plato.stanford.edu/archives/fall2013/entries/feminism-rape

White House. (2011, March 29). Statement of administrative policy. Retrieved from www.whitehouse.gov/sites/default/files/omb/legislative/sap/112/saphr471h_20110329.pdf

Wicker, T. (1982, May 18). In the nation, Reagan turns radical. *New York Times.* Retrieved from www.nytimes.com/1982/05/18/opinion/in-the-nation-reagan-turns-radical.html

Will, G. F. (2013, April 3). Schools push a curriculum of propaganda. *Washington Post.* Retrieved from www.washingtonpost.com/opinions/george-f-will-schools-push-a-curriculum-of-propaganda/2013/04/03/6d25550e-9bc1-11e2-a941-a19bce7af755_story.html

Wilpert, G. (2007). *Changing Venezuela by taking power: The history and policies of the Chávez government.* New York, NY: Verso.

Wilson, W. (1902). *A history of the American people* (Vol. 5). New York, NY: Harper and Brothers.

Wineburg, S. (2001). *Historical thinking and other unnatural acts: Charting the future of teaching the past.* Philadelphia, PA: Temple University Press.

Wise, T. J. (2005). *Affirmative action: Racial preference in Black and White.* New York, NY: Routledge.

Wormser, R. (2002). D. W. Griffith's *The Birth of a Nation* (1915). *Rise and fall of Jim Crow.* Retrieved from www.pbs.org/wnet/jimcrow/stories_events_birth.html

Zakaria, F. (2012, April 2). Incarceration nation. *Time Magazine.* Retrieved from content.time.com/time/magazine/article/0,9171,2109777,00.html

Zernike, K. (2011, May 3). 9/11 inspires student patriotism and celebration. *New York Times.* Retrieved from www.nytimes.com/2011/05/04/us/04youth.html

Zeskind, L. (2009). *Blood and politics: The history of White nationalist movement from the margins to the mainstream.* New York, NY: Farrar, Straus Giroux.

Zinn, H. (1997). *The Zinn reader: Writings on disobedience and democracy.* New York, NY: Seven Stories Press.

Zinn, H. (2002). *You can't be neutral on a moving train: A personal history of our times* (New preface). Boston, MA: Beacon Press.

Zinn, H. (2003). *A people's history of the United States: 1492 to present.* Boston, MA: Beacon Press.

Index

175

About the Author

Michael Vavrus is author of *Transforming the Multicultural Education of Teachers: Theory, Research, and Practice* (2002, Teachers College Press) as well as articles and chapters on diversity and multiculturalism. He is a past president of the Association of Independent Liberal Arts Colleges for Teacher Education and past president of the Washington chapter of the American Association of Colleges for Teacher Education. Dr. Vavrus is a professor at The Evergreen State College in Olympia, Washington.